The Existence Puzzles

The Existence Puzzles

An Introduction to Population Ethics

M. A. ROBERTS

OXFORD
UNIVERSITY PRESS

OXFORD
UNIVERSITY PRESS

Oxford University Press is a department of the University of Oxford. It furthers the University's objective of excellence in research, scholarship, and education by publishing worldwide. Oxford is a registered trade mark of Oxford University Press in the UK and certain other countries.

Published in the United States of America by Oxford University Press
198 Madison Avenue, New York, NY 10016, United States of America.

Library of Congress Cataloging-in-Publication Data
Names: Roberts, Melinda A., 1954– author.
Title: The existence puzzles : an introduction to population ethics / M. A. Roberts.
Description: New York, NY : Oxford University Press, [2024] |
Includes bibliographical references and index.
Identifiers: LCCN 2023032479 (print) | LCCN 2023032480 (ebook) |
ISBN 9780197544143 (hardback) | ISBN 9780197544167 (epub)
Subjects: LCSH: Population—Moral and ethical aspects.
Classification: LCC HB849.42.R635 2024 (print) |
LCC HB849.42 (ebook) | DDC 179.7—dc23/eng/20230912
LC record available at https://lccn.loc.gov/2023032479
LC ebook record available at https://lccn.loc.gov/2023032480

DOI: 10.1093/oso/9780197544143.001.0001

Printed by Integrated Books International, United States of America

MIX
Paper
FSC FSC® C183721

This book is dedicated with my deepest appreciation to Annabel and Thomas Roberts-McMichael, Alan McMichael and Wlodek Rabinowicz.

Also in memoriam to John A. Robertson, Professor of Law, University of Texas at Austin.

Contents

Principles

Accepted principles (together, *person-based consequentialism*):

Accessibility axiom
Anti-symmetry of moral betterness relation between futures
Existence condition (EC)
Existence condition with induction (EC+I)
Existence condition for choice with probable value (ECC+PV)
Existence-sensitive addition principle
Nonexistence comparability
Pareto reduction principle
Restricted anonymity principle
Same people Pareto principle
Transitivity (of moral value relations across futures)
Trichotomy (of moral value relations across futures)
Also: Other substantive person based moral principles not yet identified (e.g., a priority principle)
Also: Other conceptually necessary principles (principles we have no choice but to accept; e.g., where *x* and *y* are possible futures, if *x* is better than *y* for a person *p*, then *y* is worse than *x* for *p*; if *x* is better than *y*, *y* is worse than *x*)

Rejected principles:

Existence condition for choice with expected value (ECC+EV)
Mere addition principle
Pareto plus principle
Raw addition principle (axiom of traditional total view; i.e., totalism)
Unrestricted anonymity principle

Cases and Figures

Preface

Population ethics starts with an inquiry into how distinctions regarding *how many* people will exist and just *who* will exist bear on moral law. How does population variability bear on questions of whether one outcome, or possible world, or possible future is morally better than another and what we morally ought to do?

In the past, population ethics did not seem particularly central to the rest of ethics. For the most part, moral philosophers ignored the question whether cases in which the coming into existence of additional people or of one person rather than another required any special analysis. They disregarded the phenomenon of population variability in their moral theorizing.[1]

[1] Sidgwick was an exception. He paid at least some attention to questions raised by population variability around the turn of the past century as he considered precisely what form of utilitarianism to adopt and, specifically, whether the correct theory would factor in the size of the relevant population (Sidgwick 2006, 410-413 (first published 1874)). For discussion, see Section 1.2 (on the total view or *totalism*) and Chap. 1 note 13 on the average view or *averagism*).

Another exception was Salt. He explicitly focused on the moral significance of the *existential status* of non-human animals when he argued that moral law favors the non-human animal already in existence over the non-human animal whose existence was yet to be decided (Salt 1892). In making that distinction—as Singer explains (Singer 2011, 105–108)—Salt aimed to refute the troubling claim by Stephen that the "pig has a stronger interest than anyone in the demand for bacon. If all the world were Jewish, there would be no pigs at all" (Singer 2011, 105; quoting Stephen 1896).

I'll just note now that the argument of this book will be that Salt was closer to understanding moral law than Stephen but that both erred. Salt erred by at least suggesting that an individual's *existential* status determines that individual's *moral* status—that it's only *existing* non-human animals who have any moral claim not to be slaughtered for their meat. We return to that issue in Section 2.3 (why moral status isn't plausibly grounded in existential status). And Stephen erred by promoting the horrendous fallacy that the pig who *now* exists and *now* faces slaughter in any way benefits from (has an "interest" in) we humans leaving in place the plan that, once upon a time, had consigned the pig to the slaughterhouse. There's no reason in the world that *that very pig* could not have *both* existed *and* enjoyed a long and happy life. It's obvious, in other words, that the plan hatched before the pig existed isn't one that needs to be left in place after the pig exists *in*

By the late 1960s or so, however, population ethics began to inch its way in from the cold.

It's not clear to me *why* that happened just when it did.[2] After all, human beings everywhere, always, at different times in their lives, have been alternately deliriously happy or thoroughly dismayed by the prospect of bringing new people into existence.

It may have been the fact that, by the late 1960s or so, a handful of moral philosophers, perhaps most immediately inspired by G. E. Moore,[3] had started to pay closer attention to the utilitarian theories produced by their more distant intellectual forebears Bentham, Mill, and Sidgwick.[4] The idea utilitarianism aimed to capture was that the moral evaluation of the *choices* that we make is rooted in what sorts of *consequences* those choices bring about for people—in the *utility* of those choices—and not in anything more esoteric or mystical than that. The *morally obligatory* choice is the choice that produces the best consequences—the greatest amount of the good, the most *wellbeing*[5]—for people that agents *can* produce. Which is

order for the pig to exist. And perhaps more important: it's a fallacy to think that the plan hatched before the pig is conceived—the *actual* plan, the plan that ends in the pig's being slaughtered—improves the pig's chances of coming into existence against *each and every available alternate plan.* See Section 6.4.1 (the nonidentity problem).

[2] The route may have been an indirect one, through the discussion of vegetarianism, meat-eating, and the moral status of non-human animals. (Singer's *Animal Liberation* was first published in 1975; an earlier paper, "All Animals Are Equal," appeared in 1974, and his "Animal Liberation" in 1973.) See note 1. Singer suggested to me that the new-found interest in population variability may also have reflected philosophers' own renewed interest in applied ethics in the 1960s. Or it may have been triggered, as Singer also suggested, by concerns regarding overpopulation arising out of the environmental movement that itself commenced in the late 1960s (see Ehrlich 1968).

[3] Moore 1912.

[4] Parfit excluded, philosophers working at Oxford in the late 1960s and 1970s seemed not to find the utilitarian approach as credible as did philosophers working elsewhere. Oxford-trained Australian philosophers Peter Singer (Singer 1972a, 1972b) and J. C. C. Smart (Smart 1956; Smart and Williams 1973) by then had strong interests in utilitarianism, as did Fred Feldman (1975, 1986) in the United States and John Harsanyi (1977) in Australia and the United States. Narveson's own work in 1967 and 1976 aimed less at refuting utilitarianism and more at correcting what he then seemed to consider an oversight in its formulation.

[5] *Wellbeing* is mainly left undefined for purposes of this book but can be understood to involve whatever it is that makes life so precious for the one who lives. For more on wellbeing, see Chapter 1 note 3.

just to say that the *morally wrong* choice is the choice that produces consequences that are less than the best: the choice that makes things worse for people when agents had the option of making things better for people instead.

Most consequentialists working today share that simple but compelling idea. Not surprisingly, the theories meant to spell out that idea differ in their details. Thus consequentialists continue to debate whether wellbeing is a positive, felt emotion (like happiness) or, alternatively, something we may not have any immediate conscious awareness of at all (like the capabilities we have; the things we immediately can do if we happen to want to do those things).

Even so, there's a good amount of consensus. Thus most consequentialists today, thanks to Peter Singer, agree that moral law extends not just to human beings but to many non-human animals as well.[6] Fully accepting that point, I'll understand the term *person* in what follows to include many (but not all) human beings and many (but not all) non-human animals alike.[7]

It's just as likely, however, that the increased attention moral philosophers in the late 1960s or so were starting to give utilitarianism was just the backdrop for the emergence of population ethics. The actual catalyst may have been Jan Narveson's clever juxtaposition of two deeply held intuitions against each other. The one is the simple idea that we've just described—the idea that has fueled utilitarianism from the beginning and that in hindsight we may well have accepted more or less forever—and the other an idea that Narveson himself had more recently excavated from the depths of our moral consciousness. Thus, according to Narveson, we are "in

[6] Singer 1975.

[7] For purposes of this book, a *person* (whether human or non-human) is understood to be a *conscious being* whose thoughts and experiences are connected (e.g., by memory or possibly by anticipation) from one moment to another. For more on what counts as a person, see Chapter 1 note 5.

favor of *making people happy*" but entirely "neutral about *making happy people*."[8]

Let's call that first idea the *basic maximizing intuition*. And we—let's just say—wholeheartedly accept that idea.[9] What the second idea—let's call it the *basic existential intuition*—then adds is this: Wait a minute, we need to be clear that the "making things better for people" that morality requires *doesn't* include bringing them into existence to begin with, however worth having that existence may happen to be. Curing a child of a terrible disease, other things equal, clearly makes the world a morally better place. Creating another child to begin with *just creates another child*. It doesn't, on its own and independent of its consequences for still other people, make the world a morally better place.

To say anything else is to say that failing to cure the one child of a terrible disease can be perfectly morally counterbalanced by leaving the one child to suffer and simply bringing another child—say, a

[8] Narveson 1976, 73 (emphasis added). Narveson's succinct way of putting the distinction may have drawn the attention of moral philosophers to the question of how population variability—that is, how existential status—bears on moral law. Parfit's work (Parfit 1976, 1987) then propelled the inquiry forward, perhaps by way of opposition to Narveson. Still another major figure whose work no doubt drew attention around the same time as Narveson's was David Heyd. Heyd, whose most complete account of his approach is found in Heyd 1992, clearly shared Narveson's sense that what we ought to do for a person is, in some way or another, related to whether that person exists or not. See also Heyd 2009.

Interestingly to me, Parfit was a lecturer at Princeton around the time Kripke's semantics for modal logic—that is, his possible world theory—was beginning to capture the attention of both the local and the global philosophical communities. This is not to say that Parfit owed any of his pathbreaking arguments or ideas to Kripke. It's just to say that the imagining we can do and the hypotheticals that are now a mark of population ethics have all been greatly facilitated by possible world theory. For my own part, I can't see how to make any clear progress in population ethics without keeping the basics of modal logic and Kripke's work firmly in mind (Kripke 1959a, 1959b; Lewis 1986; Feldman 1986, 1997).

[9] An important clarification: to accept the basic maximizing intuition—and I do—is *not* necessarily to commit oneself to the *traditional total view* (or *totalism*)—that is, the form of utilitarianism that simply sums up—or *aggregates*—raw, unadjusted wellbeing levels across a given future to determine how that future compares against others in respect of moral betterness. As we shall see in Section 1.4, one can just as easily understand the basic maximizing intuition not to *aggregate* wellbeing but rather to *granulate* and *disentangle* distinct persons' distinct wellbeing levels.

happier, healthier child—into existence to begin with. And that—intuitively—*can't* be right.

Thus the basic existential intuition acts as a critical constraint on the basic maximizing intuition. In cautioning us not to take the basic maximizing intuition too far, the basic existential intuition in effect lends a credibility to the basic maximizing intuition, a sentiment that otherwise seems implausibly extreme: imposing on us the procreative obligation to bring ever more people into existence at least in cases in which the existence of additional people matters to no one else and (with nothing to stop it) very possibly in cases in which it matters very much to still other people who do or will exist.

And ditto the basic maximizing intuition: it acts as a critical constraint on the basic existential intuition. By cautioning us not to read too much into the basic existential intuition, the basic maximizing intuition lends support to the basic existential intuition. Other things equal, our producing ten children rather than two, or two children rather than none, doesn't make things morally better. However, producing *any* additional child and then creating *less* wellbeing for that child when, at no cost to anyone else, we *could have created more* does make things morally worse.

It might be helpful (though not necessary) to put the distinction Narveson meant to draw in terms of a widely comparative, *modal*, account of *loss*. When we make things better for an *existing* or *future* child by way of curing that child's terrible disease, we are rescuing a child from what we can call an *ordinary* loss. When we make things better for another child, a *possible* child, by way of *bringing that child into existence* to begin with, we are rescuing a child from—at least, we are avoiding on behalf of a child—what we can call an *existential* loss. Other things equal, we morally must do our best to prevent the one sort of loss. But with respect to the other sort of loss, moral law itself just doesn't kick in. The rules of aesthetics or religion or politics or misogyny or evolutionary instinct might apply. But moral law itself stays silent.

Avoiding a loss on behalf of a child who, without our intervention, will continue to suffer a terrible disease and avoiding a loss on behalf of a child who, without our intervention, will never exist at all thus occupy *two very distinct moral planes*. We intuitively think we are often obligated to avoid the one sort of loss. But to think we are also often obligated to avoid the other is—well—somewhat terrifying.

Now, to agree that bringing a child into a worth-having existence is to *avoid a loss* on behalf of that child presupposes a thesis that some theorists have considered controversial: that bringing an additional child into a worth-having existence and thus delivering that child from what has been called the "abyss"[10] of nonexistence makes things better for—creates more of the good for, more wellbeing for—*that child*. One might at first pass think that the acceptance of that thesis—and I do accept it, and for purposes of this book assume it; we can call it *nonexistence comparability*—would mean the immediate collapse of the basic existential intuition itself.[11] One might at first pass think that the basic existential intuition would then simply evaporate into thin air. But it doesn't seem that it does. Rather, the basic existential intuition seems rooted in something having to do with the one child's *existing and suffering*—and not in the idea that bringing a child into a worth-having existence can't, as a matter of metaphysics or perhaps logic, make things better for the child. The hold that the basic existential intuition has on us remains undiminished *despite* nonexistence comparability. Even if we accept nonexistence comparability, we *still think* that we

[10] Salt 1892.

[11] I think that it's hard to show that nonexistence comparability isn't both plausible and cogent. The thesis is certainly one that we seem easily to deploy. I think, for example, that it's *better* for me that I exist and have the existence I in fact have than that I never have existed at all, and I hope the same is true for you. Moreover, we can all imagine scenarios in which a particular sort of existence makes things *worse* for us than never having existed at all. For more on nonexistence comparability and, specifically, its cogency, see Appendix A.

make things morally better by "making people happy" and *not* by "making happy people."

And now a puzzle—generic in form for the moment, and more concretely and repeatedly instantiated in the chapters that follow—begins to take shape.

More precisely: it begins to take shape in the minds of anyone who finds *both* of the two aforementioned basic intuitions within their moral consciousnesses.[12] For anyone else, there is a built-in off ramp. For anyone else, there really is no puzzle. There is just the one intuition or the other or perhaps no intuition at all.

But for those of us who do have both intuitions, tensions begin to emerge. Why, after all, doesn't more of the good—more wellbeing—*always* make things morally better, whether it comes in the form of curing a child's terrible disease or comes in the form of bringing another child, a healthier child, into existence to begin with? The wellbeing levels—the potential *losses* that the two children face—may be *exactly the same* in all dimensions. And, as we shall soon see, the one child—the child who exists and suffers—cannot credibly be argued to have anything but *exactly the same* moral status as the child who never exists at all.[13] So why doesn't bringing the additional child into a worth-having existence make things morally better?

And yet we think it doesn't. We clearly understand that failing to cure the one child of a terrible disease just isn't the moral equivalent of—and *can't* be morally counterbalanced by—leaving the one child to suffer and bringing another child, a healthier child, into existence to begin with.

[12] Thus to say that the two basic intuitions are deeply held and widely shared is *not* to say that they are *universally* held. Moreover, it's not the purpose of this book to install intuitions in anyone's moral consciousness—or to convince them that they do have intuitions that they don't in fact have. For those who *don't* happen to have both intuitions, whether the puzzle can be solved may be of some intellectual interest but likely doesn't have the real urgency that it has, for example, for me.

[13] Thus in Section 2.3 the argument is made that any attempt to ground a person's *moral* status in that person's *existential* status is doomed to fail.

And thus the puzzle: two intuitions that each have a strong hold on us and that seem on a collision course with each other. To actually solve the puzzle—in its generic form—is to figure out how to avoid the collision.

Now, we can always avoid the collision—the apparent inconsistency—on paper by simply *deeming* one intuition or the other false. But as long as both intuitions continue to have a strong hold on us, simply *deeming* the one intuition or the other false doesn't even begin to solve the puzzle. We can't just toss out the puzzle pieces. To actually solve the puzzle is instead to show how the *one intuition can be reconciled against the other*. It's instead to show how the *pieces of the puzzle fit together*.

But let's back up. Is a solution to the puzzle really that hard to come by? (Do we need a whole book?) Can't the inquiry into how population variability bears on moral law just conclude with the itemization of the two basic intuitions? Why can't moral philosophers—and lawyers, economists, climate scientists, and all the rest of us—*just agree* that both intuitions are critical to our understanding of moral law?

It's fascinating to me that things aren't that simple. After Narveson made his indelible remark, many consequentialist-minded theorists very quickly worked to convince themselves that the two basic intuitions can't be reconciled with each other: that we are instead *compelled* to reject the one intuition or the other.[14] Which is just another way of saying that the puzzle can't be solved.

Thus, as we shall see in the chapters that follow, a series of nicely put together arguments, each grounded in one or more vivid, concrete, variable population cases, demonstrate that it just won't work

[14] It seems that lawyers and economists, for the most part, either just didn't foresee the collision—the potential for inconsistency—or understood at some level that it is one that (as this book argues) we can figure out a way to avoid. Philosophers have had more doubts.

to think of the basic existential intuition as a caveat, an exception, a cautionary afterthought on the basic maximizing intuition.[15]

Those same consequentialist-minded theorists, upon the further determination that, as between the two basic intuitions, the basic maximizing intuition surely was correct, quickly came to consider the basic existential intuition a veritable well-spring of inconsistency. *It had to go*, puzzle or no puzzle.

And—given that the basic existential intuition was "just an intuition" to begin with—the fact that it still seemed alive and well within our own moral consciousnesses could be safely ignored. Not to be stopped by puzzles and parlor games, those theorists could then freely proceed to describe with confidence what they took to be a significant fragment of moral reality.

And that has been the dominant narrative ever since. But it makes for a poor story.

For one thing—as we shall see in each of the chapters that follow—on closer scrutiny the nicely put together arguments, while raising incredibly important questions, don't actually force the conclusion they claim. More bluntly: they aren't valid arguments, and they don't actually force the conclusion that Narveson made a mistake—or that we are, after all, obligated to "make happy people."

And for another, stopping there—resting easy with that conclusion; declaring the inquiry into population variability complete—*ignores the only data that we have.* When it comes to understanding moral law, all we have are our deeply held, widely shared intuitions—including, for example, the intuition that curing the one child of a terrible disease and bringing another child, a happier,

[15] Among the first of that series is the argument that Jeff McMahan put forward to show the difficulty in reconciling the two halves of "the asymmetry" against each other (McMahan 1981; see Chapter 2). Though the specific aims (and the vocabulary) vary from McMahan's, many other arguments as well—as we shall see going forward—would, if correct, seem (given the demands of consistency, cogency, and conceptual necessity) to foreclose any reconciliation between what I am here calling the basic maximizing intuition and the basic existential intuition. Pessimism in respect of reconciliation was perhaps most pointedly articulated in Arrhenius 2000, 263–264.

healthier child, into existence to begin with are two very different things; the intuition that moral law just doesn't allow the one child's loss to be written off against the other child's gain.

Of course we can always on paper reject an intuition—we can always deem an intuition, a principle, false. But that's just not the same as *believing*—as understanding, as accepting—that it's false. If we do no more than deem one deeply held, widely shared intuition or the other false, then we are simply throwing out one of the puzzle pieces. We're not actually solving the puzzle; we're just setting it aside.

Now, setting puzzles aside isn't ordinarily such a terrible thing. (We need to get on with our lives.) When it comes to our moral theorizing, however, it can be a very terrible thing. In that context, to set the puzzle aside is to ignore a good chunk of the *only data that we have*. In which case we can all too easily find ourselves taking our own moral theorizing in a direction that we ourselves find utterly confounding.

Better, in other words, not to set the puzzle aside but to actually *solve* it.

Accordingly, the story I propose in this book takes a different turn. Yes, if we are compelled to reject one or the other of the two basic intuitions, it may well be that it's the basic existential intuition that must go. And consistency—it goes without saying—is critical. And so is cogency. And—just to be clear from the start on the formal constraints that I will hold in place throughout this book—so is compliance with each of the various conceptual principles that we seem to have no choice but to accept (that is, each *conceptually necessary principle*).[16]

But the idea that we are *compelled—forced*, by the demands of consistency, cogency, and conceptual necessity—to reject either the

[16] Other philosophers, including Temkin and Rabinowicz, are more open to rejecting some of those conceptual principles, including, respectively, the transitivity and trichotomy of the moral value relations between futures; see Sections 1.6, 3.3.2, and 3.3.3.

basic maximizing intuition or the basic existential intuition seems to me both a leap of logic and to create at least as many problems as it solves.

My goal thus is to actually solve the puzzle. It's to show that two basic intuitions can in fact be reconciled against each other—that they can, after all, thrive in a healthy, wholesome, organic tension.

And thus the argument of this book: that, in population ethics if not in life, we can have our cake and eat it, too.[17]

* * *

The method of this book? Rather than understanding the variable population cases as counterexamples that "prove" that one or the other of the two basic intuitions must be false, we should see those cases as giving rise to a collection of puzzles—the *existence puzzles*—that are there for us to solve. And, as we all know, good puzzles are never solved by throwing puzzle pieces into the fire. Instead, we solve the puzzle by coming to see how its various pieces—*all* of them; from our deeply held, widely shared intuitions all the way through to the conceptual principles we seem to have no choice but to accept—fit naturally together. Thus: the *puzzle method.*

To say that is *not* to say that every deeply held, widely shared moral intuition that we have ever had is written in concrete. When a *new platform* of deeply held, widely shared intuition has been established in place of an original intuition—one that enables us to understand clearly *just where* we originally went wrong—we may well find that the original intuition has lost its hold on us. We may well find that the original intuition has evaporated—that it's been

[17] We don't, in other words, want to abandon consequentialism—to become deontologists; to reject the basic *maximizing* intuition; to say that the goodness or badness of consequences *isn't* the central defining feature of whether a given choice is morally permissible or not. Nor, I think, do we want to accept the excesses of a moral regime that denounces the basic *existential* intuition: to say that the misery another person has avoidably been forced to endure can be balanced out by the worth-having existence of an additional person.

eliminated from our moral consciousness. And—for purposes of solving *our* puzzle—the original intuition is then not a piece of *our* puzzle at all. In which case it would actually be a mistake to try to force it to fit with the other puzzle pieces.

So that can happen. But to avoid hiding the ball, I don't see that happening with the basic maximizing intuition *or* the basic existential intuition *or* the formal constraints that come with consistency, cogency, and the conceptual principles we seem to have no choice but to accept.

* * *

I consider the reconciliation of the two basic intuitions against each other a matter of great urgency. That that is something we can achieve seems to be a minority view. Still, I am not the only optimist. Though many contemporary consequentialists have suggested that the two basic intuitions can't be reconciled against each other, a handful of consequentialist-minded philosophers—philosophers who at least consider a choice's consequences a *significant part* of whether the choice is permissible or not—have favored reconciliation.[18]

Where this book departs from those efforts at reconciliation is in the *constraints* I am retaining on how the work of reconciliation is itself to proceed: that is, that it will proceed not just within the confines of consistency and cogency—we all agree on those—but also within the confines of the various conceptual principles we seem to have no choice but to accept.

Why not allow ourselves more free rein than that? Why not shake ourselves free of at least some of those conceptual principles? Why not take a more inventive approach?

As I see things, those principles—and we'll identify them as we go along—are themselves pieces of the puzzle. They are conceptual *necessities*. Which means that we can't solve the puzzles by throwing any of those principles into the fire, either.

[18] I have in mind here Temkin and Rabinowicz; see Sections 1.6, 3.3.2, and 3.3.3.

***

Taking the inquiry into population variability seriously isn't important only for purposes of cleaning up our otherwise messy moral theorizing. The moral principles we fashion as we work our way through the variable population cases generate important practical implications as well.

At a local level, a very close-to-home level, they include implications for some of the most intimate and personally critical choices we will ever make over the course of our entire lives.

Consider, for example, issues of *procreative privacy*: whether you ought to produce a child, or another child, or a child at the expense of the child you already have, or one child rather than another child.

Is there any basis in *moral* principle for understanding the otherwise indeterminate due process clause of the Fourteenth Amendment of the U.S. Constitution to protect our interest in choosing *for ourselves* whether we produce a child or not? Does *moral* principle instruct that, other things equal, our producing ten children rather than two, or two children rather than none, makes things *morally better*? Or is the truth instead that, other things equal, whether we conceive and bear the additional child is *morally neutral*? That, other things equal, it's not wrong not to conceive and bear a child? That, in that arena, we may do just as we please?

Is the abortion that doesn't end the life of a person already in existence but instead prevents an additional person from coming into existence to begin with—the earlier abortion, the abortion that takes place within about the first five months or so of pregnancy—morally wrong?[19] The sharp right turn on abortion and, by implication, contraception that the U.S. Supreme Court has recently taken

[19] I have argued elsewhere that the early or middle-term abortion, other things equal, doesn't make the world morally worse and is perfectly permissible. The late abortion, the abortion that ends the life of a *person*—a conscious being whose thoughts and experiences are connected from one moment to another—and thus makes things worse for—results, that is, in a reduction of wellbeing (i.e., a loss) for—that person within the context of a future in which that person *exists* is another matter (Roberts 2010).

in *Dobbs v. Jackson Women's Health* (2022) makes that question more urgent than ever.

Issues of constitutional privacy go beyond abortion and contraception. Does it make the world morally worse, and is it wrong, to conceive and give birth to one child—perhaps a child whose life will be burdened in certain ways due to a genetic abnormality—when the agent could have conceived and given birth to another child—a more "perfect" child—instead? Has the time come—as *Dobbs* suggests—to let states revert back to the rule of *Buck v. Bell* (1927) ("three generations of imbeciles [being] enough," the state has the authority to sterilize "mental defectives") from the rule of *Skinner v. Oklahoma* (1942) (establishing an equal protection right against forced sterilization and, more generally, a "right to have offspring," itself, at least prior to *Dobbs*, foundational to the right of privacy under the due process clause)? Or does moral law instead provide that, other things equal, we may produce the one child or the other as we please, though we are at the same time *obligated*—it hardly needs to be said—to do the best we can, taking into account the needs and interests of others, for whichever child we do produce?[20]

At a global level, the population theory we adopt will have profound implications for issues of overpopulation, climate change, environmental policy, resource allocation, and human extinction.

[20] Issues of population variability also arise in the law of negligence. Do *parents*, either on their own behalf or on behalf of their child, have a valid claim in negligence against a physician or other medical professional whose omissions—failures, e.g., to test for genetic abnormalities—have contributed to that child's coming into existence? Negligence claims require a demonstration of a relevant duty, the breach of that duty, and (most critically for purposes here) that that breach *harms* the plaintiff. But does bringing a genetically abnormal child into an existence that is itself worth having *harm* that child—impose, that is, a *loss* on that child; make that child *worse off*—even in the case where that child *could not have existed* but for the genetic abnormality?

The parents' action for damages is called *wrongful birth*. The action on behalf of the child is called *wrongful life*. I have argued elsewhere that it's not existence with the genetic abnormality that harms the child but rather the economic, physical, and emotional burden that (in some cases) comes with the parents' obligation to address that abnormality that burdens the whole family, including the child born with the genetic abnormality (Roberts 2009b).

Are policies that limit population growth morally acceptable means of addressing climate change? Of protecting the environment? Of conserving resources? Or must we instead tolerate climate change and other forms of environmental degradation so that the human population can grow ever larger—so that ever more people can come into existences that are worth having (even if not *well* worth having)? Must we, as Bostrom, MacAskill, and others argue, *put all our other projects* (malarial nets, feeding the hungry) *on hold* so that we can devote most of our resources into slightly increasing the (negligible) chance that the human species and its successors will endure indefinitely?[21] Must we do virtually *all that we can* to make sure that the so-called *existential risk*—the risk of the elimination of all of humanity—never eventuates? Is *that* the message from ethics we really mean to approve for injection into ever more

[21] Bostrom 2013 makes the argument that we should answer these questions in the affirmative (see also Ord 2020). If the work of this book is correct, however, Bostrom has made a critical mistake. He writes that "the expected value of reducing existential risk by a mere one millionth of one percentage point is at least a hundred times the value of a million human lives" (Bostrom 2013, 19). But in making that calculation—that a million lives ended is not too much to pay to create an additional miniscule chance that the ranks of future generations will be swelled by millions and millions of additional lives—he considers one person's losing that person's own worth-having existence (one person's *dying*, in other words) be the *exact moral equivalent* of another person's never coming into existence to begin with. Bostrom has arguments in favor of that construction of longtermism, arguments perhaps driven by the "hard mathematical logic" of expected value theory (Lewis-Kraus 2022, referencing, not Bostrom, but Bankman-Fried). But his arguments aren't, in fact, driven by the "hard mathematical logic" of expected value theory or of anything else. In considering how expected value—and more generally probability—bears on the evaluation of choice, we have options *beyond* what Bostrom suggests (see Chapter 6). His arguments are instead driven by the substantive *moral* position that one child's terrible disease being cured and another child's being brought into existence to begin with are moral equivalents. And that's, I think, a mistake. Moreover, it's a position we can avoid *without* making the *further* mistake of discounting of the moral status of future people or of merely possible people as against people who now actually exist—or the moral significance of the risks that future people or merely possible people face as against the moral significance of the risks that people now actually exist face (see Chapters 2 and, again, Chapter 6). The idea (as described by MacAskill 2022) that the "nonexistence of future generations [is] a *moral* loss" (36; emphasis added); that "[e]nsuring [humanity's] survival is there just as great a priority as improving our trajectory" (36), and that other things equal "having more happy people makes the world a better place" (169) are thus instances of taking the basic maximizing intuition *far* too far.

prolific AI systems by the tech industry? Or do we instead think that bringing ever more people into existence *isn't*, other things equal, a moral obligation—and that, when other things aren't equal, it's instead sometimes morally wrong? When people now and for generations to come must suffer so that human extinction can itself be delayed into the indefinite future?

If the lawyers and judges looking to moral principle for guidance in their efforts to understand and apply the law, and policymakers looking to moral principle to figure out whether they should advocate in favor of one forward-looking policy or another, *aren't* tearing their hair out along with the rest of us, it may only be because they think they already have all the answers or because they don't quite realize how difficult the questions are or because it just hasn't yet occurred to them that there *are* any questions.

It's clear that the collection of moral principles emerging out of the inquiry into population variability—that moral theory—will have much to say about how the law—constitutional law, the law of negligence—is to be interpreted and applied, and about public policy. *Any* area of moral philosophy that begins with questions of *how many* people and *just who* we are morally obligated to bring into existence should immediately be recognized as an area we must pay close attention to.

This book aims to solve five puzzles—the *existence puzzles*—that arise when we begin to think carefully about the moral significance of bringing an additional person, or one person rather than another person, into existence. Along the way, a number of principles will be formally proposed. Together, they form an off the beaten path form of maximizing consequentialism, one that we can call *person-based consequentialism*. Some of those principles are meant to capture, in precise terms, underlying intuitions. And some are conceptual principles that we seem to have no choice but to accept. But *all* the principles this book actually stands behind will be principles we can *test*: principles we can apply to concrete cases we think—we *think*, subject to further exploration—we already understand and thus can use to rule out (to counterexample) principles that misfire: principles that tell us one thing when we *know* that that one thing is clearly false.

The collection of principles we'll end up with won't constitute a *complete* moral theory. It won't instruct, for every pair of possible futures we want to compare in respect of their moral betterness, whether one future is better than another or, for every choice we want to evaluate, whether that choice is permissible. But it will be enough to answer the practical questions raised just above—including questions regarding the *Dobbs* decision—and at least provide a good start in understanding how population variability in general and existential status in particular bear on moral law.

Acknowledgments

For their valuable and detailed comments, I am deeply grateful to referees Wlodek Rabinowicz and Larry Temkin as well as two anonymous referees for this book. I am also deeply grateful to Peter Ohlin for identifying the perfect referees and for his work in keeping the book on track as both a substantive contribution to the existing literature and an introduction to population ethics.

I am forever grateful to Fred Feldman, Jeff McMahan, Peter Singer, and David Wasserman for their careful and insightful comments regarding the existential theses I've put forward over the years and—just as much—for their continuing expressions of interest in my work.

I'm deeply grateful as well each of the following individuals for their incisive comments on earlier drafts of this book and the portions of this book I have presented at conferences and also for their critical discussions of the issues this book takes up: Matthew Adler, Per Algander, Chrisoula Andreou, Gustaf Arrhenius, Ralf Bader, David Boonin, John Broome, Mark Budolfson, Krister Bykvist, Tim Campbell, Göran Duus-Otterström, Nir Eyal, Elizabeth Finneron-Burns, Tomi Francis, Johann Frick, Johan Gustafsson, Gary Hardegree, Elizabeth Harman, Anders Herlitz, Ori Herstein, David Heyd, Doug Husak, Frances Kamm, Pierre LeMorvan, Chris Meacham, Julia Mosquera, Doug Portmore, Gideon Rosen, Julian Savulescu, Dean Spears, Torbjörn Tännsjö, Peter Vallentyne, and (alphabetically last but far from least) Michael Zimmerman.

Special thanks are owed to Alex Pegher, a great student of population ethics whose frank yet sometimes quite witty comments on earlier drafts of this book both urged me on and made me laugh, and to Thomas Roberts-McMichael, whose double-major in English along with his logic courses served him well as he edited portions of this book with the aim of making things, if not morally better, then less annoying.

Finally, I am grateful to the Population Wellbeing Initiative (University of Texas at Austin), the Institute for Futures Studies (Stockholm), the University Center for Human Values (Princeton University), and the College of New Jersey for their support of my efforts in connection with this book. Without that support, this book would never have come into existence at all.

1

Recent history and current perplexed state of population ethics

1.1 Population variability and the inquiry into existential status

How a person's *existential status* bears on the moral theorizing that we do is, I think, the most urgent and most interesting challenge that moral philosophers today face. The tasks of figuring out, first, whether and when the fact that a person does or will exist in one outcome, or possible world or possible future, but not in another makes the one future *morally better* than the other and, second, whether and how that same fact bears on what we *morally ought to do* are absolutely critical to putting together a moral theory that we might actually want to defend.[1] Theories that go off track in how they complete those tasks will only cloud our understanding of moral law and—even as they purport to offer sound practical guidance regarding what we ought to do—lead us all dangerously

[1] Possible worlds, or *futures*, are finely detailed objects. A given future will contain the choice that brings about a particular array of consequences, the consequences themselves in all their specificity, and the causal mechanism (butterfly effect and all) by which that choice brings about those consequences.

We can think of possible futures as the many, many different ways in which *this* world may unfold going forward. Thus the future in which you put on your red t-shirt tomorrow morning is distinct from the future in which you put on your white t-shirt tomorrow morning. That tiny thing is enough to ensure that we are talking about *distinct* possible futures. We thus can't literally *change* a given possible future; futures have all their properties necessarily. All we can do, at a given time, is make choices that, together with other things going on (the past, the choices of other agents, the laws of physics), will move us forward from where we are now in the direction of one future rather than another. For more on this point and why it's critical, see Section 3.4.

The Existence Puzzles. M. A. Roberts, Oxford University Press. © Oxford University Press 2024.
DOI: 10.1093/oso/9780197544143.003.0001

astray. We want to understand how population variability bears on moral law. And we need that understanding for the guidance it will provide in the many contexts in which we—whether as individual moral agents or as participants in a collective of moral agents—find ourselves in a position to decide just how many people and just who shall exist.[2]

As noted in the Preface, a number of moral philosophers started to take those questions seriously in the late 1960s or so. Accepting—as I do—that some form or another of maximizing consequentialism is surely correct, those philosophers considered the moral value of a given choice to rest in the *consequences* of that choice, with the *morally obligatory* choice being the choice that produces the best consequences—the most good; the most wellbeing[3]—that moral agents can produce for people and the *morally wrong* choice being any choice that produces consequences that are less than the best for people.

[2] One might also ask what makes one future *aesthetically*, *prudentially*, *overall*, or *all things considered* better than another. I do none of that here. Nor can I see how talking about *betterness* but insisting that by "betterness" we don't mean moral betterness would be helpful if our goal is—as it is here—to say something about moral law and what it obligates us to do. Nor am I clear on what problem the project of understanding betterness but not moral betterness is aiming to solve. For purposes here, then, my focus will remain on what makes one future *morally* better than another, just as it is on what makes one choice *morally* permissible and another choice *morally* wrong.

[3] How wellbeing is to be defined—what it is to make things *better for* a person in a morally relevant sense—remains under debate. Mill wrote that a choice is "right"—we'll say *morally permissible*—to the extent that it "tend[s] to promote happiness, [morally] wrong as [it] tend[s] to produce the reverse of happiness." Mill 2002 (first published 1861), chapters I and II. Both Bentham 1996 (first published 1789) chapter 1, with his focus on pleasure, and Mill, with his focus on a more intricate concept of happiness, considered the highest good to consist in a *positive, felt emotion*. They adopted, that is, a *hedonic* form of utilitarianism.

If creating more wellbeing for people is not a matter of generating more of a positive, felt emotion for them, then what is it to create more wellbeing for people? Is it to provide them with additional *resources* of a particular sort? To satisfy their personal *preferences* to a greater degree? To imbue them with additional *capabilities*, giving them the talents and skills they need to do more of anything that they happen to want to do? (Sen 1995, 2005).

It seems plausible to me that wellbeing may itself comprise distinct values. Thus *gaining capabilities* might mean a higher wellbeing level and *taking joy in* those capabilities may well mean a still higher wellbeing level. See Feldman 2010 (on the concept of attitudinal hedonism).

Feldman put the underlying idea—the *basic maximizing intuition*—especially well: we ought to do the best we can, and we make things *morally* better by making things *better for* people.[4] Singer added that that idea—that intuition—holds not just for what we can do for human beings but also for what we can do for many non-human animals as well.[5] When other things are equal—when we hold constant how things go for *everyone else* in terms of both their existence and their wellbeing levels—and the option exists for us to make things better for a given person—to create more wellbeing for that person—it makes things *morally worse* and is *morally wrong* for us to make things worse for that person instead—to create less wellbeing for that person when we could have created more.

As noted in the Preface, the catalyst for the interest in population variability may well have been Narveson's juxtaposition of the two basic intuitions against each other. We are—so says the basic maximizing intuition—"in favor of making people happy." *But* we are also—so says the *basic existential intuition*—"neutral about making happy people."[6] Narveson seemed at that point to concede that the basic maximizing intuition was compelling: we really ought to create the most good that we can for people. But he insisted that it was a mistake to take that intuition too far. The basic maximizing

[4] Feldman 1986.

[5] See Preface. Mill had earlier proposed that we should instead be thinking about how to make things better for "*all* sentient creation" (Mill 1863). Torturing a cat for no reason whatsoever makes the future morally worse. Other things equal—and often when they're not—the future where the horse is left to graze in the pasture is morally better than the future in which the horse is first terrorized in the kill-pen and then destroyed.

We don't, though, want to extend the term "person" too far. For a thing to be a person for purposes of articulating moral law, that thing surely must have a *connected consciousness*. To be a person, a thing must have some form of recollection of things past or anticipation of things to come. (*Self*-consciousness, though, seems too high a standard; cf. Singer 2011, 74–75.) Thus it seems highly implausible that ticks, for example, or early human fetuses or live human bodies whose higher brain functions have permanently ceased should be counted as persons for purposes of determining what we can do, and need to do, to make things morally better.

[6] Narveson 1976, 73 (emphasis added). See also Narveson 1967.

intuition is best understood, in other words, to be constrained by the basic existential intuition.

Parfit aimed to capture the same idea—an idea, I should add, he ultimately rejected—when he wrote that "what is bad must be bad for someone."[7] What is morally worse or morally wrong must make things *worse for* someone who does or will exist.

Now, Narveson's and Parfit's own formulations of the underlying intuition generated considerable interest but were too imprecise to test or apply. Still other formulations they and other theorists offered at other points were quickly determined to be either similarly imprecise or—if precise enough to be tested—clearly problematic.

Accordingly, an early item of business in what follows will be to capture what seems compelling in Narveson's and Parfit's own initial formulations but leave the deficiencies in their formulations behind: that is, to fashion a handful of principles that capture the basic existential intuition *and* that we might actually *want* to defend *and* that we can test.[8]

[7] Parfit 1987, 363.

[8] Fashioning a principle that both captures the underlying intuition and is a principle we might actually want to defend is easier said than done. The fact is that most formulations of the basic existential intuition that have been put forward are fatally flawed. (It's often called the *person-affecting intuition*. I avoid that term here to avoid confusion between what this book proposes and those failed attempts.) Fatally flawed attempts include the following:

> Only people who *now* exist in a given future matter for purposes of comparing that future against others; only if that future is worse than another for at least one of *those* people can the one future be worse than the other (*moral presentism*).
>
> Only people who do or will exist in the uniquely *actual* future (only *actual* people) matter; only if one future is worse than another for one of *those* people can the one future be worse than the other (*moral actualism*).
>
> Only people who *do* or *will exist* in a given future matter for purposes of comparing that future against others; only if that future is worse than another for at least one of *those* people can the one future be worse than the other (*moral existencism*).
>
> Only people who *do* or *will* exist in *all* of the futures the case involves matter for purposes of comparing the one future against the other; only if the one future is worse than the other for at least one of *those* people can the one future be worse than the other (*moral necessitarianism*).

But for the moment the point is more basic: once the population variability bell had been rung, it could not be unrung. Since the late 1960s or so, the interest in the inquiry into how population variability bears on moral law has grown ever more intense, with virtually all the increasingly large community of population ethicists urgently working to answer at least some of the questions they now face.

1.2 The case of Jaime versus Harry

The case of *Jaime versus Harry* helps, I think, to clarify the issues at stake. Imagine that you, a doctor, are required to choose between curing one child's terrible disease, let's say Jaime's, and bringing another child, Harry, into a worth-having existence by way of intracytoplasmic sperm injection (ICSI).[9] You can't do both.

> One future is worse than another future *only if* the one future is worse *than the other* for a person who does or will exist in the one future.
>
> One future is *better* than another future *only if* the one future is better than the other for a person who does or will exist in the one future.

The first four principles are demonstrably false (see Section 2.3). The fifth leaves many of the existence puzzles fully intact and leads to inconsistency (see Section 3.4). The sixth disallows the result that the future in which a person *doesn't* exist—in a wrongful life case (see Preface note 20); a case in which the life is *less* than worth living—can be the *better* future. For examples of papers in which one or more of the above-listed principles has been (mistakenly, I think) proposed as capturing the underlying intuition, see Dasgupta 2018, Parfit 2017, Boonin 2014, Arrhenius 2009, C. Hare 2007, and Temkin 1993. Still other problematic formulations include the *neutrality intuition* (see Chapter 3) and an account that relies on an especially problematic counterfactual account of harm (see Chapter 6 note 20).

[9] ICSI involves the injection of a single sperm cell directly into an egg cell, followed by the transfer of the resulting embryo (embryo transfer, or ET) to the uterus of the genetic (or surrogate) mother. The stipulation that ICSI is your option for bringing Harry into existence sidesteps Persson's argument (2017, 78–79) that the already-existing child is to be favored over the possible future child on the grounds that the choice to procreate often gives any *particular* possible future child *only the barest chance* of ever coming into existence at all, and we should favor *certainly* improving things for one child over *only very improbably* improving things for another child. Thus the chances that it's Harry, rather than some other child, whose coming into existence is at stake are thus very high—just as high, let's say, as the chances that your intervention will cure Jaime of his terrible disease.

Without your intervention, Jaime will be left to suffer the terrible disease, a disease that means that the joys of his life will routinely be counterbalanced by pain and suffering. It's thus a stipulation of the case that, absent your intervention, Jaime will be left with an overall, lifetime wellbeing level of zero.

What about Harry? Without your intervention, Harry will never exist at all. Never existing at all—a state that would seem clearly to offer no pleasure or pain, no burdens or benefits—plausibly also comes with a zero wellbeing level.

You thus make things worse for Jaime by failing to cure him of his terrible disease, and, per nonexistence comparability, you make things worse for Harry by failing to bring him into existence to begin with.[10]

Figure 1.2 sums up the case.

Figure 1.2: Jaime versus Harry		
	c1: the choice to cure Jaime and leave Harry out of existence	c2: the choice not to cure Jaime and to bring Harry into existence
probability →	1	1
wellbeing ↓	f1	f2
+10	**Jaime**	**Harry**
+0	*Harry*	**Jaime**

Figure 1.2: Jaime versus Harry

In the case of Jaime versus Harry, it's stipulated that you, the moral agent, are a doctor whose abilities are wide-ranging. After all, you have the ability to cure the one child's disease *and* the ability to use ICSI to bring the other child into existence. In other cases, of course, the moral agents may well be the child's own parents. But procreative agents aren't limited to just doctors and parents. They include *everyone* who happens to be involved in one way or another, either by act or by omission, in the bringing into existence of additional people. The fertility specialists, the lawyers, the justices who have just recently eliminated the constitutional right of early abortion, the policymakers who may be concerned that overpopulation will exacerbate climate change or that underpopulation will adversely affect the social security "trust fund"—they are all *procreators*, all *childmakers*, in their own way. They are all moral agents making choices that will help to determine *how many* people, and just *who*, shall exist.

[10] As noted in the Preface, I take *nonexistence comparability* for granted for purposes here. Thus the future in which Harry has a worth-having existence is *better for Harry* than the future in which Harry never exists—and the future in which he doesn't have that existence is *worse for Harry* than the future in which he does exist. Arguments

We should take a moment here to establish some conventions that will apply here and throughout this book. (i) A person's name appears in **bold** in any future in which that person does or will exist; if a person never exists at all in a given future, the name appears in *italics*. (ii) While the listed futures—f1 and f2 in this case—may contain people beyond Jaime and Harry, no one else's wellbeing or existence is at stake. (Other things are equal, in other words, between f1 and f2.) (iii) The wellbeing levels for each of Jaime and Harry in each future are numerically indicated in the far left column.[11] (iv) A row toward the top of the figure shows the *probability* that a given future will arise out of a given choice. Thus, for the case at hand, c1 *with certainty* gives rise to f1, and c2 to f2.[12] (v) Finally, the choices displayed in the figure exhaust the agents' available choices, and the futures displayed in the figure exhaust the futures that (with some positive degree of probability) may arise out of those choices—that is, the *accessible* futures.

We'll say more about the *accessibility relation* in Section 1.8.1. For now, the important point is that, as we try to figure out what we want to say about the case in front of us, we needn't worry about any mysterious third accessible future in which things are either better or worse for either Harry or Jaime or anyone else at all.

challenging the cogency of that principle (Is there a subject term? How can the statement that nonexistence is worse for a thing that never exists be either true or false?) aren't, I think, compelling, and we seem easily to understand the comparison at issue. For more on nonexistence comparability, see Appendix A.

[11] The wellbeing levels specified in Figure 1.2 and elsewhere needn't be understood to come in defined units. Rather, they simply indicate when it is that one future is *better for* a person than another future is for that same person or for another person altogether. They, in other words, can be understood here to have their *ordinal* values only. There are two exceptions. First, it's plausible to think that zero has its *cardinal* value as well when used to describe how much wellbeing a person has in a future in which that person never exists. And, second, a proposal regarding how varying probabilities affect the evaluation of choice will require the stipulated wellbeing levels to have actual cardinal values (see Section 6.3, on the concept of probable value).

[12] Until we turn to Chapter 6, the probability at play in all of our cases—that is, the probability based on information available to the agent just prior to choice that that choice will give rise to a future having certain features—will remain a nice round 1.

Those conventions in place, we turn to the critical question: Can you, as the agent, morally *make up for* leaving Jaime to suffer his terrible disease by bringing Harry into existence? Can you *make up for* making things *worse* for Jaime by making things *better* for Harry?

Notably, a traditional form of consequentialism—what I'll call the *traditional total view*, or *totalism*; we might even call it *status quo consequentialism*—looks at things very differently. And, Narveson might say, very counterintuitively.

According to totalism—specifically, the traditional total view—one future is morally better than another if and only if the summation of the wellbeing levels of all the people who do or will exist in the one future is greater than that same summation for the other future.[13] On that way of determining when you've done the best you can for people, it *just doesn't matter* morally whether you cure Jaime of his terrible disease or instead leave Jaime to suffer and bring Harry into existence. f1 is *exactly* as good as f2, and both c1 and c2 are perfectly *permissible.*

But that's not, according to the basic existential intuition, how the moral calculus that underlies the basic maximizing intuition can plausibly be thought to work. To accept that fact is the first step

[13] In contrast to totalism, the *average view—averagism*—would determine whether one future is better than another by taking those same summations but then dividing each by the number of people who do or will exist in the particular future. (For both theories, we can just note that what is summed up are the *utilities*—the *numbers* assigned to each person's wellbeing level in each future—not the *features* of the particular future that bring it about that a person has one wellbeing level rather than another.)

Unlike totalism, averagism generates the intuitively correct result in the case of Jaime versus Harry. But it's safe to say that averagism clearly fails on still other grounds. For a case from population ethics that confirms that position, see Parfit's Hell Three (we don't make things better by adding to a population of people whose existences are less than worth having still other people whose existences are also less than worth having, even if that addition improves the average; Parfit 1987, 422). For purposes here, we'll set averagism aside.

Just to note: ruling out averagism doesn't mean we are stuck with totalism; see the discussion at the end of this section (on the option as a more granulated approach).

in figuring out how that moral calculus *does* work. Or so says the existentialist.[14]

Readers will work out their own intuitions regarding Jaime versus Harry. My sense, however, is that we'll all feel pretty strongly that the future in which Jaime is cured is *morally better* than the future in which Harry exists and Jaime is left to suffer. We'll all feel pretty strongly that c1 and c2 aren't both permissible—that this just isn't the sort of case where we as moral agents, stepping into the doctor's shoes, are permitted to do just as we please.[15] We'll all feel pretty strongly that the *moral obligation* is to rescue Jaime and abandon Harry to the "abyss" of nonexistence.

Surely, in other words, f1 is *morally better* than f2, and c2 is *wrong*.

Is what looks to be a collision between our two basic intuitions really unavoidable? As noted in the Preface, nonexistence comparability—which I assume for purposes here—instructs that f1 really does make things worse for Harry than f2. Moreover, it's just not plausible—as we shall see—to say that Jaime has some special moral status that Harry lacks—that is, that the deeply held, widely shared basic maximizing intuition protects Jaime but not Harry.

[14] Maximizing consequentialism is thus a very big umbrella, covering not just totalism but many other theories as well. Moreover, we can't just *assume* that totalism will answer all the questions that the basic existential intuition itself raises correctly. More plausibly, between maximizing consequentialism on the one hand and intuition on the other, we will find a two-way street. If we think that maximizing consequentialism has implications for population ethics—and I think we do—we should keep in mind that population ethics, by steering us away from some forms of maximizing consequentialism and in the direction of others, may have implications for consequentialism as well.

[15] Singer's *replaceability argument* at least suggests that Singer would dispute the intuition that the agent can't make up for leaving Jaime to suffer by bringing Harry into existence. Singer's argument, which seems to assume that the total view is correct, concludes that "if we [painlessly] kill one animal, we can replace it with another as long as that other will lead a life as pleasant as the one killed would have led" (Singer 2011, 106). At the same time, Singer himself, at times, has explored options for avoiding the conclusion of that argument (Singer 2011, 108).

It may then seem to follow that the basic maximizing intuition is *indifferent* to whether Jaime is rescued or Harry is brought into existence.

But it's a mistake, I think, to accept that inference. It's a mistake to think that we can pull out of the deep well of the basic maximizing intuition the idea that it *doesn't matter morally* whether Jaime is rescued or Harry is brought into existence—the idea, that is, that there's no distinction to be drawn between making things better for a child by way of curing that child's terrible disease and making things better for a child by way of bringing that child into existence to begin with.[16]

To think that there's no distinction to be drawn is to take the basic maximizing intuition beyond its natural boundaries. It seems there's *got* to be room in there somewhere, in other words, for the basic existential intuition to have a say in the matter as well.

1.3 A quick turn back to the traditional total view

While moral philosophers began to take the question of how population variability bears on moral law seriously in the late 1960s or so, most of them utterly failed to take that question seriously enough.

Instead, they quickly decided that the traditional form of consequentialism—the *traditional total view*, or *totalism*—was, notwithstanding Narveson, perfectly competent to address questions of population variability. Many of them indeed came to think that we are actually compelled by "weighty philosophical arguments" to say that population variability can't make a difference to our moral analysis.[17] Whatever our "gut" is telling us, it's

[16] Narveson called the inference a fallacy and said it had the "air of sophistry" (Narveson 1967, 62).

[17] Persson's critique of the edicts of common-sense morality and of our evolutionary inheritance is highly persuasive, and his argument that often such edicts should be abandoned in favor of "weighty philosophical arguments" is surely correct (Persson 2017).

our "brains"—that is, those weighty philosophical arguments that our little brains present us with—that we must listen to. Whatever our "gut" is telling us, we are compelled to abandon the basic existential intuition in favor of the basic maximizing intuition.[18]

The upshot? Curing one child's terrible disease and bringing another child, a happier, healthier child, into a worth-having existence are just two ways of making things better for people and thus of making things *morally better*. And thus the reversion to the traditional total view.

In my view, however, those weighty philosophical arguments don't, on their own, complete the inquiry into how population variability bears on moral law. For one thing, however weighty, those arguments—as we shall see—aren't as weighty as they may at first glance appear to be.[19] They don't in fact *compel* the conclusion that the basic existential intuition—or, more generally, that one or the other of the two basic intuitions—must be false.

But, more important at this juncture, they don't work to actually *solve* the puzzles. As long as the basic existential intuition itself remains alive and well in our moral consciousness—as long as it remains among the scant moral data that we have to work with at

I agree with Persson that common-sense morality and our evolutionary inheritance often fail us. I agree that our moral theory should derive less from our "gut" and more from our "brain." But in a way the point of this entire book is to remind us that not all weighty philosophical arguments are sound and that we can distinguish between (a) the edicts of common-sense morality and our evolutionary inheritance—gut—on the one hand and (b) deeply held, widely shared, closely scrutinized intuition—what lies between gut and brain; call it *heart*—on the other.

[18] The "gut" versus "brain" analogy is from Persson, who, along with many other moral philosophers, takes the position that we are compelled to reject what I am calling the basic existential intuition (Persson 2017).

[19] This is *not* to say that the weighty philosophical arguments can simply be set aside. As we shall see, those arguments—from Broome, Arrhenius, McMahan, Singer, Persson, and others—raise incredibly important questions and are critical to our getting things right. They don't, I think, show that the basic existential intuition is false—or that we are compelled to reject that intuition in favor of the traditional total view or, more generally, the notion that the additional person's worth-having existence, other things equal, makes things morally better. But they do help us appreciate the pitfalls we must avoid in formulating more credible versions of our basic intuitions—of the basic maximizing intuition *and* the basic existential intuition alike.

a given time—we complete the inquiry into population variability only when we've actually solved the puzzles. And we actually solve the puzzles only when we've reconciled two basic intuitions against each other. For it's only at that point that we can have some hope of coming up with a moral theory that we will actually want—at the level of gut, brain, *and* heart—to defend.[20]

Rejecting the basic existential intuition—at least, *trying* to reject it; simply *deeming* it false—may well help us avoid inconsistency at a superficial level. And avoiding inconsistency is, we all agree, a good thing. But if we've done no more than avoid inconsistency, then we've done no more than fit some of the puzzle pieces together while throwing the rest into the fire.

Of course, even deeply held, widely shared intuitions are sometimes properly rejected. They become intuitions—"intuitions"—that we don't, at the end of the day, just say we reject or try to reject or deem false but also in fact *come to accept* as false.[21] And we can't,

[20] Of course, as noted in the Preface, for anyone for whom one or the other or both of the two basic intuitions is just missing, there really is no puzzle.

[21] The method of this book thus includes the license to appeal to our strongly held, widely shared intuitions. But is it a mistake to give intuition any critical role to play in our moral theorizing at all? Broome writes that

> [o]ur moral intuitions are formed and polished in our homely interactions with the few people we have to deal with in ordinary life. . . . One thing we must not do is rely on our intuitions outside the domain where we have grounds for thinking they are reliable. . . . We have no grounds [e.g.] for thinking our intuitions about very large numbers are reliable (Broome 2004, 57–48).

That basis for questioning our own intuitions applies even when the intuitions at issue remain "steadfastly intact" (Broome 2004, 37). (Of course, as Jaime versus Harry demonstrates, not all the interesting cases in population ethics involve very large numbers.)

Broome, however, doesn't seem to suggest that intuition has no role to play in our moral theorizing. His point is rather that it's a mistake to hold it sacrosanct. Moreover, Broome may well agree that, when it comes to our moral theorizing, intuitions has at least some role to play. As Gideon Rosen put the point in conversation: Where else do we start?

One other important point. The first concerns the relation between what Persson calls *common-sense morality* and what I am here calling deeply held, widely shared *intuition*. Persson often seems to identify intuition with what he calls common-sense morality, dismissing both as products of the unreliable "gut" and favoring instead the "weighty philosophical argument" that derives from the "brain" (Persson 2017). As noted earlier, I find Persson's arguments against many of the edicts of common-sense morality highly

in advance, rule out that that won't be the fate of the basic existential intuition.

But if that's the path we take, then that will mean that a new platform of deeply held, widely shared intuition has been established that enables us to understand clearly just where our original intuition went wrong: a new platform that serves to loosen the hold the original intuition had on us and, in the end, eliminate it from our moral consciousness.

Thus the option of rejecting the basic existential intuition—*or* the basic maximizing intuition *or* one of the conceptual principles we seem to have no choice but to accept—remains on the table. And—as noted—weighty philosophical arguments have driven many moral philosophers to simply reject—that is, to *try* to reject—the basic existential intuition. But if that's the way they want us to go, then they owe us that aforementioned new platform of deeply held, widely shared intuition. They owe us an *understanding* of just how it has happened that we have so badly mistaken the basic existential intuition for a little piece of moral reality.

1.4 More than one way to maximize: Granulation versus aggregation, person-based consequentialism

Given the basic maximizing intuition, is there really any room left for the basic existential intuition? I think that there is.

The traditional total view—totalism—aggregates (i.e., sums up) the individual wellbeing levels of all the people who do or will

persuasive. But I see those same edicts as at odds with "intuition" as I use that term here. For example, my intuition—and I'm confident that it's both deeply held and widely shared—is that it makes the world morally worse, and is wrong, for the bystander not to save the child drowning in the shallow pond. But the view of common sense (whatever that is) may well be (as Persson suggests) that what we *don't* do, including the bystander's not rescuing the child, can't make things morally worse or be wrong. (The *child drowning in the shallow pond* case is from Singer 2009.)

exist in the various alternative futures that are to be compared.[22] If we assume that the basic maximizing intuition requires totalism, then we must reject the basic existential intuition. But the idea that moral law has that particular sort of *aggregative* structure isn't inherent in the basic maximizing intuition.

Thus, one way to explain why, other things equal, it makes things morally better to rescue five people stranded on a sinking ship than to abandon them is to say that that's what increases aggregate wellbeing—that's what makes things morally better for people *in the aggregate*.

But another way to explain that same evaluation is to say that that's what increases the individual wellbeing levels for *each and every one* of those five people *one at a time*—each of those individuals whose *only other accessible option* is to exist and suffer.[23]

And once we do that—once we focus on each person's plight and each person's options, once we *granulate* rather than *aggregate*—we put ourselves in a position to articulate a plausible account of still other cases including, critically, the case of Jaime versus Harry. We then have the room that we'll need to disentangle the *existential* details of a given case from its *wellbeing* details; to sort out the details of a given case in a way that totalism itself—that paradigm of the aggregative approach—can't even imagine. We'll then have the room that we'll need to say that Jaime's zero wellbeing level in f2 is just on a different moral plane altogether than Harry's zero wellbeing level in f1. The basic existential intuition, if it's to function at all, requires that we keep separate and not treat as morally indistinct the details of a given case that are in fact separate and distinct. A granulated approach allows for just such a maneuver.

How can we manage to disentangle the details of our cases given that we may not even know who the five people stranded on the

[22] So does averagism.
[23] See Roberts 2002, 2009a. See also Holtug 2012.

sinking ship are? Well, quantifiers help. Just as the universal quantifier enables us to talk about each member of an infinite collection of numbers one at a time without talking about them en masse and without talking specifically about any one of them, so can we say that, for *each member of the collection of five people*, the choice to rescue makes things better for *that member—for that person—* than the choice to abandon. Which is just to say that, for *each one* of those five individuals, the choice to rescue creates more wellbeing *for that person* than the choice to abandon.

Similarly, we are able to talk about the members of even a very large set—say, the set of "all men," or the (infinite) set of all integers, or all reals—*one at a time* and not en masse and not by specifically identifying them (naming them) one by one.

And that is something that we already know we often need to do. After all, it's true that the mass of all men weighs more than a ton. But we can easily make sense of the idea that, for each man *as an individual*, it's also true that that man weighs less than a ton.[24]

Accordingly, in what follows, the principles that will be introduced and that this book will stand behind—together, *person-based consequentialism*—will take a granulated approach to questions of moral betterness.[25] That collection of principles doesn't look at a given population as though it were a single massed object and the individual wellbeing levels of the members of that population as a single massed aggregate. Rather, it considers *each person at each future one at a time* and takes into account *both* that person's wellbeing level *and* that person's existential status at that

[24] Quantifiers, as a means of describing reality, have surely been there all along in our natural languages—and our brains. But they were formally brought to our attention by Frege (with, of course, the help of Russell) only around the turn of the last century.

[25] Now we may in the end *want* aggregation—addition—to play a role in our moral analysis (see Chapter 4 "The Addition Puzzle"). But, if we do, what will be added up won't be (per the traditional total view) *raw wellbeing levels* but rather will be what we will call *contributive values*: values that reflect not just our *maximizing* values, but also our *existential* values.

particular future *and* that person's wellbeing level *and* that person's existential status at each alternate accessible future.

In short, recognizing the principles that give voice to the basic maximizing intuition as principles that granulate rather than aggregate will enable us to accept the basic maximizing intuition without abandoning the basic existential intuition. It will give us the room we need to actually reconcile the one intuition against the other and thus to actually solve our puzzles and not just set them aside.

1.5 Are hormones to blame?

Why did so many moral philosophers fail to take the inquiry into how population variability bears on moral law seriously enough? Why did they set the puzzles aside without ever actually solving them?

Perhaps that mostly male population was driven by its own evolutionarily acquired moral—"moral"—inheritance to think that producing two offspring rather than none, or ten rather than two, really does make the world a morally better place even in the case where that production comes at a cost to the women who often (not always) do the lion's share of the work of all of that producing or to the earlier- and later-born siblings who are on occasion substantially burdened when an additional child is brought into existence.

I can't say. But my view is that they gave up on intuition—deeply held, widely shared intuition—too quickly. Instead of staying with the puzzles until they actually solved them, they set them aside, thus opening the door to the perhaps hormonally attractive idea that, yes, their work in producing the additional child, as long as that child has a life that is at least worth living and as long as not too much damage is done to anyone else (and it rarely is), really does make the world a morally better place.

1.6 Conceptual necessities also puzzle pieces; more inventive approaches on hold

As to those pieces of the puzzle beyond the basic maximizing intuition and the basic existential intuition, what are they? What other pieces of the puzzle do we need to concern ourselves with?

Obviously, the plausible moral theory will be consistent and cogent. But we can also at least aspire to construct a theory that is limited to principles (i) that we can *understand*—principles that aren't at odds with the various conceptual principles that we seem to have no choice but to accept—and (ii) that we can *test.*

My aim, in this book, will be to see how far we can go in solving the puzzles—and not just throwing out some of the puzzle pieces—*within the confines of those constraints.*

I am in awe of the philosophers who have invented new ways of making sense of how our moral theorizing is to take population variability into account. It's clearly the intent of those philosophers actually to solve the puzzles—to reconcile our two basic intuitions against each other—and not just set them aside.

But they themselves would be among the first to recognize that their more inventive approaches come with complications that it would be nice to avoid.

I'll briefly note here just why two such approaches worry me. We'll return to both, although also briefly, in what follows.[26]

The first is Larry Temkin's. Temkin retains a vestige of the basic existential intuition in the form of what he calls the *essentially comparative approach* to the matter of when one possible future is morally better—or, as he puts it, is *all things considered* better—than another. The theory he embraces defines betterness by reference to a *plurality of values*—values contemplated not just by the essentially comparative approach itself but also by what he calls the

[26] See Sections 3.3.2 and 3.3.3 (Temkin and Rabinowicz).

intrinsic aspects approach.[27] What isn't included in the theory—as it currently stands—is any significant precision regarding just what those values are and how they are to be weighed against each other.

Perhaps, in the end, we'll decide that moral law is complicated beyond any naïve hopes or expectations we might have had and find ourselves endorsing a plurality of values approach. Starting out, however, it's a problem that the approach doesn't generate any clear judgment whether any given future is better than any other. It's a problem that we don't know what that approach says about any of our test cases—cases, that is, with respect to which we think we already understand the results that any plausible theory will generate; cases that can help us determine whether a theory is consistent or not; cases that include Jaime versus Harry and many others to come as well. *How can we accept a theory we can't test?*

There's a second problem. If we accept the plurality of values approach as Temkin describes it, then we must also, according to Temkin, reject the *transitivity* of the all things considered betterness relation. According to transitivity, if, in a given case, we've determined that one future *y* is at least as good as another future *x* and that still another future *z* is at least as good as *y*, then it follows that *z* is at least as good as *x*. Now, transitivity may seem highly plausible—indeed, it may seem a conceptual necessity. But as Temkin observes there are plenty of cases—the much discussed *repugnant conclusion* case being but one[28]—where transitivity

[27] According to Temkin, a future's moral value is actually a composite of distinct values, and a given future may be *all things considered* morally better in virtue of the fact that it realizes values *beyond* wellbeing, including, for example values of equality, fairness, and "human flourishing" (see Temkin 1993, 2012). Persson, too, recognizes values that go beyond what he calls the *principle of beneficence*. Thus his own theory embraces both that principle as well as what he calls the *principle of equality* (Persson 2017).

[28] In Parfit's repugnant conclusion case, a future A contains a very large number of people, all of whom have lives well worth living, and a future Z contains all those people and many more besides, all of whom have lives only barely worth living. Various lines of reasoning generate the conclusion that Z is at least as good as A. But that conclusion seems clearly false—and, as Parfit says, *repugnant* (Parfit 1987, 381–390). In part to avoid the repugnant conclusion, both Temkin and Persson reject transitivity (see Temkin 2012, 132–143; Persson 2017, 17).

seems highly inconvenient: where we may—*may*—seem to want to say that *y* is at least as good as *x* and that *z* is at least as good as *y* but that *z* is worse than *x*. According to Temkin, the plurality of values approach enables us to make sense of those judgments. We can simply say that some values are relevant when it comes to some pairwise comparisons and others are relevant when it comes to other pairwise comparisons and still others are relevant when it comes to still other pairwise comparisons. The upshot for the repugnant conclusion? We avoid the result that the future we really do think is worse is, instead, at least as good as the future we really do think is better.

But can we abandon the transitivity of the morally *at least as good as* relation—or the morally *better than* relation or the morally *worse than* relation? Can we abandon the transitivity of moral betterness relation?

Can we really even grasp—conceptually understand—that *z* is worse than *x*, given that we've already figured out that *y* is at least as good as *x* and *z* is at least as good as *y*? *It's not clear to me that we can.*[29]

It's true that some of the various lines of reasoning that generate the repugnant conclusion rely on transitivity. But the ones that Temkin and Persson are worried about rely on other principles as well—including, for example, the *mere addition principle*, according to which a future (say, A+) that contains all the people in A and more people besides, all of whom have lives worth living, can't be worse than A: that A+ must be *at least as good as* A. We'll come back to that principle in Chapter 3. But, to avoid hiding the ball, I'll just say now that that's a principle we shall reject.

[29] Transitivity, indeed, seems to remain the sort of conceptually necessary principle we have no choice but to accept *even if* we happen to accept Temkin's plurality of values approach. Let's go back to the repugnant conclusion case (Chapter 1 note 28). We can certainly grasp that *A+* is at least as good as *A* in respect of one value (say, the maximization of aggregate wellbeing), and that *Z* is at least as good as *A+* in respect of a second value (say, the equal distribution of wellbeing across the population), and, at the same time, that *Z isn't* at least as good as *A* in respect of a third value (say, human flourishing). Then, on the plurality of values approach, we are to weigh (assuming that approach has now been extended to include the principle that tells us how that's to be done) those three values—and potentially others as well—against each other and arrive at an *all-things-considered* assessment of moral betterness. At that point, we may conclude that A+ is all-things-considered at least as good as *A* and that *Z* is all-things-considered at least as good as *A+*. To reject transitivity is to say at the same time that, for some such case, *Z isn't* all-things-considered at least as good as *A*: that Z, instead, is all-things-considered *worse*

Another among the more inventive approaches has been proposed by Wlodek Rabinowicz. Rabinowicz's approach is more testable than Temkin's—and preserves the transitivity of the usual value relations across futures (the *at least as good as*, *is worse than*, and *is better than* relations). But it has in common with Temkin's that it sets aside a certain conceptual principle. For Rabinowicz, the principle that must go is the *principle of trichotomy*.

According to trichotomy, if, in a given case, we've determined that one future isn't either morally better or morally worse than another, we are then committed to the position that the one future *is exactly as good as* the other. Rabinowicz, however, has argued—driven, I think, in part by the thought that we can't otherwise provide intuitively plausible accounts of even the most basic among the variable population cases—that trichotomy fails: that, when one of the two futures to be compared contains additional people and the two futures are otherwise alike, the two futures may be related in some *fourth* way; that, in such cases, the one future may simply be *incommensurate* with the other.[30]

Rabinowicz's view isn't simply that we may be *unsure* or *unclear* on which of the three more familiar relations in fact holds between the two futures. Nor is his view that the collection of principles that constitute the moral theory that we think is actually correct isn't complete and thus doesn't always tell us anything at all regarding whether one specific future is morally better than, morally worse than, or morally exactly as good as a second. His view is, rather, that

than *A*. Given, however, what we've already determined regarding how *A*+ relates to *A* and how *Z* relates to *A*+, I find it conceptually hard (not just hard, *impossible*) to grasp the idea that, at the same time, *Z isn't* all-things-considered at least as good as *A*. Since we think that last point is correct—since we think that *Z is* worse than *A*—the better strategy, I think, isn't to reject transitivity but rather to go back and unearth what went wrong earlier on: when we said that *A*+ is at least as good as *A* and that *Z* is at least as good as *A*+.

30 Rabinowicz 2009. In her work on parity, Chang as well has proposed a fourth way in which futures can be compared. Chang, 2022.

none of those three more familiar relations *in fact holds* between the two futures.

I find trichotomy very hard, at a conceptual level, to resist. Once we accept that there is such a thing as moral betterness between futures, and once we then determine that it's not the case that a given future is morally better than another, and that it's not the case that the one future is morally worse than the other, then how can that one future not be exactly as morally good as the other? *Where else is there to go?*[31]

I haven't begun to show here that the plurality of values approach or the incommensurability approach is doomed. I recognize that I can't say for sure that, in the end, we won't end up endorsing one of those more inventive approaches or another. After all, in this book I consider a scant five puzzles. And we can be sure that there are other puzzles out there as well.

But the aim of this book is to show that we can solve those five puzzles within the confines of consistency, cogency, and the handful of conceptual principles that we seem to have no choice but to accept, including transitivity and trichotomy.

The path this book goes down thus will be less inventive than some others. But my hope is that it will be more tractable.

Two final points. It's critical, if we are to make any progress in solving the existence puzzles at all, that we keep clearly in mind that not all the constraints—conceptual or otherwise—that have been proposed for work in population ethics hold up to scrutiny. At certain junctures, we'll need to display at least a little creativity to solve the puzzles. (They really wouldn't be puzzles otherwise.) It would be an unfortunate and potentially damning mistake to allow that creativity to be inhibited by constraints that don't really exist.

[31] When we try to answer that question—when we try to understand that fourth relation, the relation of incommensurability, itself—we come up against a more specific conceptual challenge (see Section 3.3.3).

And, second, the two more inventive approaches identified in this section far from exhaust the more inventive approaches philosophers have come up with as they try to say how population variability bears on moral law. And I will freely draw on some of those other more inventive approaches in what follows.[32]

1.7 The puzzle method, the role of intuition, the off ramp

Deeply held, widely shared intuitions—understood, when spelled out in the context of specific cases, simply as carefully considered *beliefs*; beliefs that we have, so to speak, internally adjudicated—taking us in opposing directions is a recipe for perplexity. The potential for collision—for inconsistency—that the basic maximizing intuition and the basic existential intuition give rise to has been outlined in its generic form in the Preface and in the earlier parts of this chapter. In the chapters that follow, we'll examine five more specific instantiations of the puzzle. We'll examine, that is, chapter by chapter the five *existence puzzles*.

The aim of this book then will be to work our way out of the perplexity that each of the five existence puzzles gives rise to. The aim of this book is to actually *solve* those puzzles.

All five puzzles are, I believe, in urgent need of solution. Until they are solved, we will not have in hand a moral theory we can actually accept—a moral theory we can actually believe at least might be correct. Why is that? Why not make our lives easier and just ignore intuitions we find inconvenient? They are, after all, *merely* intuitions—and we all know how sentiment can easily lead us all astray.

[32] See Chapter 3, "The Pareto puzzle."

As noted in the Preface, however, ignoring intuition in the context of our moral theorizing is to ignore a good chunk of the scant moral data that are available to us. Theories that ignore those data can't be counted on to tell us anything at all interesting about moral reality. If we ignore the data, we'll all too easily find ourselves taking our own moral theorizing in a direction that we ourselves find utterly confounding.

Thus the method I propose for the work of this book: we start with the supposition that the variable population cases explored in the chapters that follow are not counterexamples that prove that one or the other of our two basic intuitions must be false—that prove, that is, that our two basic intuitions can't be reconciled against each other—but rather give rise to puzzles that *we can solve.*

After all, we all understand that actually to solve a puzzle—to solve, at least, any good puzzle—is not a matter of simply tossing out some of the pieces of the puzzle. To actually solve a puzzle is to figure out how all the pieces of the puzzle fit together.

As noted in the Preface, even deeply held, widely shared intuitions sometimes need to be rejected. But solving any given puzzle will require more than simply rejecting—more precisely, *trying* to reject; *deeming* false—an inconvenient intuition in order to avoid an inconsistency. If we've done no more than avoid inconsistency, then we've done no more than fit some of the puzzle pieces together while throwing the rest into the fire.

We won't have actually solved the puzzle, in other words, if the original intuition still has a strong hold on us. Accordingly, any actual solution to the puzzle that includes the rejection of a deeply held, widely shared intuition will be accompanied by a *new platform* of deeply held, widely share intuition, one that enables us to understand just where our original intuition went wrong and that thus loosens its hold on us. Without that work, our original intuition will remain alive and well. Trying to reject it—or deeming it false or simply saying we must reject it—won't actually solve the puzzle but will instead function only to *set the puzzle aside* as something we shall find ourselves compelled to come back to if we ever want our own moral theory to make sense to us.

It thus—as noted in the Preface—can happen that even deeply held, widely shared intuitions must be rejected. But—as also noted in the Preface—I don't see that happening with the basic maximizing intuition or the basic existential intuition or, for that matter, with consistency or cogency or conceptual necessity. We'll need to do some careful tailoring of the principles that articulate those intuitions. To tailor a principle carefully is just to understand the underlying intuition more clearly. And—when that work is done—we'll find ourselves under no pressure at all to reject the intuition. Or so I shall argue in what follows.

One final methodological point is in order. There exists an off ramp for readers who authentically don't happen to have the intuitions—the beliefs—I claim to be deeply held and widely shared. Thus, if the intuition that you as the moral agent in Jaime versus Harry morally can't just do whatever you please isn't an intuition that you happen to have, then you'll likely confirm as well that, whatever precisely is the point the basic existential intuition is trying to make, it's not a point that you find, intuitively, to have any moral significance at all.

If that's your situation, then you just aren't going to be *puzzled* by questions like the implications of population variability for moral law or how the basic existential intuition is to be reconciled against the basic maximizing intuition. You just aren't going to see the problem that, in my view, we now need urgently to solve.

What counts as a puzzle is thus a relative notion. I'm not puzzled by the problem of evil since I don't start with the belief that God exists. But others do have that belief—and so for them the problem of evil is, well, *more* than a puzzle to be solved.

1.8 Accessibility relation, connection thesis

1.8.1 Distinction between accessible futures and logically possible futures

We noted that the futures displayed in Jaime versus Harry exhaust, not the case's *logically possible* futures, but rather its *accessible* futures. That convention will hold for all of the figures displayed throughout this book.

But we need to say a little more about when one future is *accessible* relative to another. A future *y* is accessible relative to a future *x* provided that agents in *x*, whether working alone or alongside other agents and whether in collaboration with those other agents or not, can (with any positive degree of probability) bring *y* about. Thus accessible futures are futures that agents have *the ability, the power*, and *the resources* to bring about, regardless of whether those futures represent futures that agents *want* to bring about, or *would* bring about, or are *likely* to be able to bring about.[33]

Control, then, regarding how the future will unfold under a particular choice isn't required for accessibility: an accessible future

[33] When we say that a choice is wrong in virtue of the fact that the future it gives rise to is morally worse than *other* futures, we take for granted that at least some of those other futures are futures that agents had at least some chance of bringing about. The morally *better* future, in other words, must be one that is *available* to agents—one that is *accessible* relative to the morally worse future—for that particular ranking of futures to make the *choice* that gives rise to the morally worse future wrong. That point reflects the widely acknowledged fact that moral law can't plausibly be thought to make it wrong for us to fail to accomplish that which we can't accomplish. Thus moral law doesn't make it wrong for agents to fail to change the laws of physics for the purpose of making things, going forward, better. The future in which I clap my hands and end gravity may be a *logically possible* future in the sense that nothing in logic or metaphysics rules it out. But much in science *does* rule it out. It's thus not an *accessible* future.

As I use the term here, what is *accessible* is not merely a matter of what *individual* agents can do on their own. It's also a matter of what agents (whether working collaboratively or not) can do *together*. If, for example, I am a member of a firing squad consisting of nineteen other individuals on the brink of killing an innocent person for no reason at all, the future in which that person survives unscathed remains *accessible* as that term is used here: it's well within the ability, power, and resources of the twenty of us to lay down our rifles and walk away.

may be highly improbable; it may be one that agents have no clear or informed idea at all just how to bring about at all.

1.8.2 Connection between evaluating choices and comparing futures in respect of moral betterness

I've so far taken it for granted that consequentialism includes the idea that choices are to be evaluated on the basis of their consequences: that what makes a choice morally obligatory, or permissible, or wrong is grounded in how the consequences that choice gives rise to compare against the consequences that alternate choices give rise to.[34]

Since I'm not at all sure what we are doing when we take up the project of comparing futures in respect of their moral betterness if we jettison that assumption, I retain it throughout. Thus I assume the *connection thesis*—that is, that there exists a *close*, though not perfect, connection between how futures are to be compared in respect of their moral betterness and how choices are to be evaluated from a moral point of view.[35]

[34] Here, I make use of the traditional concepts of deontic logic. In any given case, the *morally wrong* choice is a choice that brings about a future such that some other accessible future is morally better. The *morally permissible* choice is a choice that brings about a future that isn't morally wrong. The *morally obligatory* choice is a choice that brings about a *uniquely* morally permissible choice.

[35] Probabilities get in the way of any *perfect* connection between how consequences—how futures—are to be compared in respect of their moral betterness and how choices are to be evaluated from a moral point of view. When a given choice is only *improbably* related to a better future, the connection between the evaluation of that choice and how that future compares against others will loosen up (see Chapter 6, "The better chance puzzle").

It may seem that to accept maximizing consequentialism *just is* to accept the connection thesis. In fact, however, some consequentialists have distanced themselves from that thesis. They fully engage in the project of comparing possible futures in respect of their moral betterness. But they deny that such work has much to do with the evaluation of *choice*.

That strategy allows for the possibility that the moral permissibility of a given choice will be settled by principles that are distinctly *not* consequentialist at all, principles that evaluate choice *independently* of whether they make things better for people. Such principles may, instead, evaluate choices on the basis of the intent or character of the agent,

1.9 Five existence puzzles

The first of the five existence puzzles is the puzzle of the procreative asymmetry—the *asymmetry* for short (Chapter 2). This is a puzzle that has been circulating for decades without any clear resolution. The puzzle arises when two cases, the *miserable child case* and the *happy child case*, are set side by side. The argument is then made that what we clearly want to say about one of the two cases—that it's wrong to bring the miserable child into existence—commits us to a position about the other case—that it's obligatory to bring the happy child into existence—that immediately implies that the basic

adherence to Kant's categorical imperative, the act/omission distinction, or the doctrine of double effect—more generally, on the basis of Kantian ethics, or, alternatively, what is called common-sense morality. (For an especially acute refutation of the latter approach, see Persson 2017.)

But the better view seems to me to be that the connection thesis lies at the very heart of consequentialism. That idea seems critical to our making sense of what we are doing when we take up the project of comparing futures in respect of their moral betterness. After all, if comparing futures in respect of their moral betterness *isn't* connected with the evaluation of the choices that give rise to those futures in any close way, then why on earth are we comparing those futures to begin with? What is our purpose? What problem are we trying to solve? Are we doing it just for fun? Out of idle curiosity? Do theorists have the (mistaken) impression that, if they simply *deny* the connection thesis, no one will mistake their work on betterness as having any practical implications at all for contraception or abortion or for proposals that aim to address climate change by discouraging what most of us (though perhaps not the totalist) would consider overpopulation?

As Broome puts it: "If we are offered a concept of relative good, one thing we must be sure of is that it is genuinely a concept of good. It must retain much of the normal meaning of 'good.' Most importantly . . . it must be connected in an appropriate way to how one ought to act" (Broome 2004, 74).

Theorists who aim to say when one future is morally better than another but then disavow that their view on moral betterness has practical implications—that it has anything to do with what we morally ought to do, what is morally permissible for us to do, or what would be morally wrong for us to do—include MacAskill 2022, 169. Taking pains to say that, though confident that the worth-having existence of the additional child makes things morally better even when it makes things better for *no one* beyond that additional child, they won't "scold" us (MacAskill 2022, 188) for choosing not to have another child (*whew*!) or infringe on anyone's "autonomy" by forcing them to produce another child (Dean Spears in correspondence).

From a conceptual point of view, I find any such complete disconnect—though perhaps necessary to avoid the appearance of child neglect or an extreme misogyny—hard to defend. The more plausible and efficient approach is to attend *from the start* to the intuition that, other things equal, the worth-having existence of the additional child doesn't, on its own, make the world a morally better place.

existential intuition itself is false. Most consequentialists have taken the position that any attempt to fault the logic of that argument—to prize apart what we want to say about the two cases—will itself fall flat. Yet at the same time nothing in the argument even begins to loosen the hold the basic existential intuition has on us.

The second puzzle—the *Pareto puzzle* (Chapter 3)—arises out of the *three option case* first put forward by John Broome.[36] The case seemed originally meant by him to serve as a counterexample against the basic existential intuition and thus ultimately to steer the inquiry into population variability in a certain direction—specifically, in the direction of a traditional form of utilitarianism (i.e., totalism).

In the three option case, we see that, despite the basic existential intuition, which says that the additional worth-having existence doesn't, other things equal, make things morally better, some additional worth-having existences undeniably *are* morally better than others. Which surely means that they do add value. We seem, on the face of things, to have contradicted ourselves. For purposes of this book, however, the three option case will be considered to give rise not to a counterexample against the basic existential intuition but rather to a puzzle that we need to solve.

The first and second puzzles together, as we shall see, are particularly useful: solving these two puzzles takes us a long way in understanding just what the basic existential intuition itself is all about—and, in doing so, shows specifically that there's nothing in the basic existential intuition that rules out what we think we know about the basic maximizing intuition.

The third puzzle is the *addition puzzle* (Chapter 4). It arises in cases in which we seem forced to say that an additional quantity of wellbeing clearly both *does* and *does not* add to the moral value of a given future. Solving that puzzle will include recognizing a

[36] See, e.g., Broome 2004, 146–149. He discusses the case elsewhere as well.

conceptual trap that, whatever direction the variability inquiry takes us in, we must take care to avoid.[37]

The final two puzzles test the limits of our ability to solve the existence puzzles without throwing out any of the puzzle pieces. Those are the *anonymity puzzle* (Chapter 5) and the *better chance puzzle* (Chapter 6).

The anonymity puzzle questions whether the basic existential intuition commits us to an implausibly extreme form of antinatalism. Does the basic existential intuition force us to say that it makes things morally worse, and is wrong, *ever* to bring an additional person into existence in *any* case in which that person's wellbeing level isn't maximized? If we like the basic existential intuition, we'll hope that it doesn't have that implication. To see why it doesn't is to solve the anonymity puzzle.

The *better chance puzzle* (Chapter 6) poses the question why, given that a person's having a better *chance* of existence can make things morally better, the actual *fact* of that person's existence doesn't make things better. To solve the better chance puzzle is to show how it can be that the actual fact of the additional person's existence doesn't make a given future morally better even as we recognize that a person's better chance of existence can sometimes convert what would otherwise be a morally wrong choice into a choice that is perfectly permissible.

Notably, the better chance puzzle is closely related to what has been called the *nonidentity problem*. Indeed, those two problems are so closely related that, I suspect, they're often confused with one another. In fact, however, once we make the relevant distinctions, the nonidentity problem can be easily managed. The problem is

[37] Such traps include what's termed a "vicious cycling" across rankings of possible futures, cycles that can hypothetically turn agents into money pumps whereby they pay a small amount of money to obtain a second future over a first, a small amount more to obtain a third future over a second, and a small amount more again to obtain the first future over the third, ending up where they started but with less money in their pockets. For a discussion of money pump arguments, see Gustafsson 2022. For discussion of cycling generally, see Willenken 2012.

that managing the one doesn't help us manage the other: the better chance puzzle represents the far graver challenge to the basic existential intuition.

If we fail to solve any one of these five puzzles, then we will be left to accept—to *try* to accept; to *say* we accept—a moral theory that we are pretty sure is actually false. If we fail to solve any one of those puzzles, we'll find that our own moral theorizing has taken us in a direction that we ourselves at an intuitive level find utterly confounding.

Conclusions are summarized in Chapter 7. We can make sense of the deeply held, widely shared basic maximizing and basic existential intuitions within the context of a collection of principles that abide by the constraints of cogency, consistency, and the conceptual principles we seem to have no choice but to accept. The upshot? Our sense of what makes the world a morally better place and what we ought to do can flourish free of the concern that we are flirting with ideas that at base have nothing at all to do with morality or with moral law.

2
The asymmetry puzzle

2.1 The miserable child case, the happy child case, and some intuitions

Each of the five population puzzles explored in this book arises out of a tension between two deeply held, widely shared intuitions. We have the clear intuition that making things morally better is a matter of making things better for people—creating more wellbeing for people rather than less; bringing about consequences that make things better for people rather than worse. But we also have the clear intuition that making things better for a person *by way of* bringing that person into existence falls *outside* that moral dictum. In contrast to curing a child's terrible disease, bringing an additional person into existence to begin with just isn't, on its own, a way of making things morally better. Puzzles arise for us when we come to see that in any number of distinct contexts a collision between those two deeply held, widely shared intuitions—the *basic maximizing intuition* and the *basic existential intuition*—seems completely unavoidable.

The first of the five puzzles to be explored in this book is the puzzle of the *procreative asymmetry*—the *asymmetry* for short. It consists of a pair of cases, the *miserable child case* and the *happy child case*. In the first case, just two futures are accessible for a given child, Maija. In one future, Maija doesn't exist at all. And in the other, she exists and is completely miserable for the entirety of her life. Thus it's part of the case that in the future in which Maija exists she will have an overall lifetime wellbeing level that—at, let's say, −10—falls deeply into the negative range. Her life will be less

The Existence Puzzles. M. A. Roberts, Oxford University Press. © Oxford University Press 2024.
DOI: 10.1093/oso/9780197544143.003.0002

than worth living. And it's part of the case, too, that—whatever the source of Maija's misery—it can't be fixed. Nothing can be done, either before or after Maija begins to exist, that might enable her to have had any *better* existence.[1]

In the second case, the *happy child case*, two futures are accessible for another child, Haaken. In one of those futures, Haaken doesn't exist at all. But in the other he exists and is *perfectly happy*. More precisely (and to avoid the assumption for purposes of this book that "wellbeing" and "happiness" are one and the same), it's part of the case that in the future in which Haaken exists he will have an overall lifetime wellbeing level that—at, say, a fulsome + 10—is clearly positive. He, in other words, will have a *worth-having* existence. And it's part of the case, too, that nothing can be done that might make things any better for Haaken than they are at +10.

What are Maija's and Haaken's wellbeing levels in the futures in which they *never* exist? Taking nonexistence comparability for granted, we can say that Maija and Haaken have *no wellbeing at all*—that is, a *zero* wellbeing level—in the futures in which they never exist at all.[2] The future, then, where Maija never exists makes things *better for* Maija, while the future in which Haaken never exists makes things *worse for* Haaken. The future at which Maija *doesn't* exist is thus *maximizing* for Maija, and the future at which Haaken *does* exist is *maximizing* for Haaken.

The two cases are summed up in Figure 2.1.

The conventions established earlier for the case of Jaime versus Harry (Figure 1.2) apply here as well. Thus the accessible futures—the futures agents have the ability, the power, and the resources to bring about—for each of the two cases are exhausted by the futures displayed in the figure. The available choices, similarly, are

[1] In the law, imposing that kind of misery on an infant or a child, depending on the details of the case and on the state, would form the basis for a cause of action for wrongful life. See the Preface note 20.

[2] As noted earlier, I accept and, for purposes here, assume *nonexistence comparability*. See the Preface, Section 1.2, and Appendix A.

Figure 2.1: The asymmetry					
	Miserable Child Case			Happy Child Case	
	c1	c2		c3	c4
probability →	1	1		1	1
wellbeing ↓	f1	f2		f3	f4
+10					**Haaken**
+0	*Maija*			*Haaken*	
−10		**Maija**			

Figure 2.1 The asymmetry

exhausted by the displayed futures. Finally—and critically—other than Maija's and Haaken's, *no one else's wellbeing or existence* is at stake.[3]

To make sure that we all have in mind (roughly) the *same* cases, we need to add some additional detail before we start testing our intuitions. Let's start with the miserable child case. Suppose that you are a moral agent in that case and that, as a medical doctor and a fertility specialist, you have been given—by, let's say, the genetic parents—the job of making the choice whether to create an embryo via in vitro fertilization (IVF) and then transfer that embryo (ET) to the uterus of a surrogate "mother" (where, we assume, the pregnancy will continue uninterrupted). But there's a concern. The genetic materials you have to work with—the egg cell, or perhaps the sperm—are badly flawed and the wellbeing level of any child who might be produced out of those materials will fall deeply into the negative range.

[3] How could *that* be? Normally, after all, the existence of an additional child in a family or a community comes with *significant* consequences for other people. Here, however, we are to imagine that—and it's just part of the case that—for each person other than Maija and Haaken, that person's overall, lifetime wellbeing level isn't affected, at least on a net basis, by whether the additional child comes into existence or not. Thus there are plusses and minuses, in each case and for each other person, that come both with having the child exist and with having the child *not* exist. And those plusses and minuses balance out in the same way, whatever choice the agent happens to make.

You might then ask yourself a number of questions. Fully understanding that Maija will be completely miserable in the future in which she exists and that no one else's wellbeing or existence is at stake—not yours, not the genetic parents', not the surrogate mother's, not any earlier- or later-born sibling's, not anyone else's at all—you'll ask yourself what you, who have been left to make the choice, *morally ought* to do? Is it *permissible* for you to choose c1 and leave Maija out of existence altogether? Are you indeed *obligated*, for Maija's own sake, to choose c1 and step away from the lab table, leaving the genetic materials to die their own natural (not to mention painless) deaths? Or are you instead obligated to choose c2—*to choose life*—and thus to bring Maija into an existence that is *worse for her* than never existing at all?

In trying to answer these questions, it might be helpful for you to think about things in somewhat more abstract terms. Does bringing an additional child into existence—*regardless* of the cost to the child—make the world a morally better place? Is f2 morally better than f1? Or—given that no one else's wellbeing or existence is at stake—does everything turn on which future is *better for Maija*? Is f1, where Maija never exists at all, the morally better future and f2, where she exists and suffers, the morally worse future?

Running through the relevant questions may take a moment or two. But in this particular case coming up with the right answers doesn't seem that hard.

Thus I'm pretty sure we will all quickly agree that f1 is morally better than f2 and that c2 is morally wrong. We will all quickly agree that you are obligated instead to choose c1 and leave Maija out of existence altogether.[4]

[4] A very few theorists do, however, reject the underlying intuition. One such theorist is David Heyd. Because he rejects nonexistence comparability, he takes the position that it's a metaphysical or logical impossibility that bringing Maija into existence makes things *worse for* Maija (Heyd 1992, 2009). It's possible that Heyd still actually has the intuition but nonetheless feels compelled, on grounds of logic and metaphysics and in light of his further position (which I also hold) that making things morally worse requires making

Now, the principles that support those answers will be articulated and examined later. For the moment, it's the underlying *intuition* that's of interest—that deeply held, widely shared intuition that tells you that you just can't morally go through with the choice of IVF/ET—that you just can't do that to Maija.

That intuition itself is plausibly just an instance of the *basic maximizing intuition*. We ought to do the best we can for people—to bring about the best consequences for people that we can. The choice c2 brings about a future f2 in which the child Maija exists and is completely miserable, while the choice c1 brings about a future f1 in which Maija never exists at all. Given that no one else's wellbeing or existence is at stake, it seems clear that the choice that is *better for Maija* is the choice that is *morally better*.

Let's now turn to the happy child case. Suppose that you, as a medical doctor and fertility specialist, have again been given the job of making the choice whether to go ahead with IVF/ET. In this second case, there is nothing at all amiss with the underlying genetic materials. You can be certain that any child who might be produced out of those genetic materials will have a wellbeing level that will fall well into the positive range and thus will have a clearly worth-having existence.

You now face a series of questions similar to those you faced in the miserable child case. Would it make the world morally worse, and be wrong, for you *not* to bring Haaken into existence? Does Haaken's happy existence in f4 make f4 morally better than f3—and thus make f3 morally worse than f4? Given that no one else's wellbeing or existence is at stake, would it be morally wrong for you to *decline* to bring Haaken into existence and leave the genetic materials to die their own natural (and painless) deaths?

Or, instead, is c3 itself perfectly permissible? Is it permissible for you *not* to bring Haaken into existence? Does moral law allow us to

things *worse for* people—to *deem* it false. In any case, nonexistence comparability is assumed for purposes here.

decline to bring additional people into existence—to produce two children rather than three, or three rather than ten, or zero children rather than two—in cases in which what we do matters to no one else at all? Does moral law—when other things are equal, and often when they're not[5]—impose on us a *procreation obligation*?

I'm pretty sure that we can all quickly agree that it doesn't. I'm pretty sure that we can all quickly agree that here you may *do as you please*—that the additional existence of Haaken in f4 doesn't, on its own, make f4 morally better than f3 and that c3 and c4 are both morally permissible.

As before, the principles that would support that result will come later. For now, it's the underlying intuition that is important—that deeply held, widely shared intuition that is itself an instance of the *basic existential intuition*: the Narvesonian idea that, other things equal, while we're obligated to *make people happy*, we aren't, on top of that, also obligated to *make happy people*.

2.2 The puzzle

We now have before us two carefully considered, internally adjudicated (so to speak) beliefs regarding our two cases: two deeply held, widely shared intuitions.

> The intuition that it makes things *worse*, and is *wrong*, to bring Maija into existence; *and*
>
> the intuition that it makes things *neither better nor worse* to bring Haaken into existence, and that both choices are *permissible*.

[5] As when, for example, the wellbeing *cost* to a parent or an earlier- or later-born sibling is less than the wellbeing *gain* for the additional person.

Those two intuitions, laid side by side, form an *asymmetry*. In one case, the life the child will live (we can say) *counts against* bringing the child into existence, and, in the other, the life the child will live *counts neither against nor in favor of* bringing the child into existence. In one case, the life has moral significance: it makes the future that includes it worse. In the other, the life is morally inert: it doesn't make the future that includes it either better or worse. The two separate and distinct lives thus play *asymmetrical roles* in the two separate and distinct moral evaluations.

The puzzle emerges when we try to explain just why that's so. Why does one of the two lives have moral significance when the other one doesn't?

Wars (they say) can be triggered by boundary disputes, and that seems to be what started the war here. If the first half of the asymmetry—the half that says that it makes things worse, and is wrong, to bring Maija into existence—is indeed rooted in the basic maximizing intuition, and the second half—the half that says that it doesn't make things worse, and isn't wrong, to leave Haaken out of existence—is rooted in the basic existential intuition, then what is it *exactly* that stops the basic maximizing intuition from analyzing the happy child case just as it analyzed the miserable child case? What blocks the conclusion that f4, which makes things better for Haaken, a person, while making things worse for no one else at all, is morally better than f3? And what is it exactly that blocks the basic existential intuition from analyzing the miserable child case just as it analyzed the happy child case? What blocks the conclusion that, existence being *just different*, making things worse for Maija *by way of* bringing her into existence just doesn't register on our moral radar in the same way that failing to cure a child's terrible disease does? What blocks the conclusion that f2 after all isn't morally worse than f1?

If, in other words, it's better to make things better for Maija by leaving that child out of existence, why isn't it also better to make things better for Haaken by bringing that child into existence?

Alternatively: If existence is *just different* and bringing the happy child into existence doesn't make things better, why doesn't existence being *just different* also mean that bringing the miserable child into existence doesn't make things worse?

As Singer puts the challenge,

> It is more in harmony with the intuitive judgment most people have (I think) that [other things equal] couples are under no moral obligation to have children simply because the children are likely to lead enjoyable lives.... But how do we *square [that] view* with our intuitions about the reverse, when a couple are considering having a child who, perhaps because it will inherit a genetic defect, would lead a thoroughly miserable life and die before its second birthday?[6]

Early on in the discussion, it may have seemed to many theorists—including Narveson—that an explanation of the asymmetry could easily be provided. But that cheerful thought quickly came to seem naïve.[7]

Having surveyed what they (rightly) considered failed attempts to save the asymmetry (attempts we'll be taking a look at in Section 2.3), many theorists came to feel *compelled*—sometimes on grounds of consistency; sometimes not—to reject the asymmetry. Having taken that step, many of those same theorists then took the position—plausibly, I think—that, *if we must choose* between the two intuitions, it's the happy child half of the asymmetry that must go.[8]

[6] Singer 2011, 88–89 (emphasis added). See also McMahan 2009; McMahan 1981; MacAskill 2022, 172.

[7] Thanks to the work of McMahan 1981, among others.

[8] Certainly totalism would endorse that position. Not bringing Maija into existence and bringing Haaken into existence are, according to the totalist, just two different ways of making things morally better. But one doesn't have to be a totalist to take that position. Theorists don't need totalism to convince themselves that f3 is worse than f4 or that c3 is wrong. They can instead start from the position that it *just won't do* to avoid the asymmetry—the inconsistency—by rejecting the miserable child half of the asymmetry. Having accepted the miserable child half of the asymmetry, they then reason their way—I think incorrectly—to the happy child half of the asymmetry.

And where the happy child half of the asymmetry goes, so goes the basic existential intuition. And the matter was thus considered settled against the happy child half of the asymmetry: f4, where the happy Haaken exists, is morally better than f3, and c3, the choice not to bring the happy child into existence, is morally wrong.

But I think that is too quick. The problem with simply tossing the happy child half of the asymmetry is that it doesn't even begin to loosen the hold the relevant intuition—the basic existential intuition—has on us. That intuition still seems alive and well. That means that the puzzle itself is still alive and well. We can *say* that we are compelled to reject the happy child half of the asymmetry; we can *deem* it false. But it doesn't follow that that intuition isn't still thrashing around like an angry killer whale in the depths of our moral consciousness.

To put the point another way: *purporting* to solve the problem—the puzzle—by simply tossing the happy child half of the asymmetry isn't within the method of this book. We want *actual* solutions. To have an actual solution that includes tossing the happy child half of the asymmetry, we would need to have in place a *new platform* of deeply held, widely shared intuition, one that *loosens the hold* the original intuition has on us. Theorists may well reject the asymmetry—and then from there move to a traditional total view (totalism).[9] They may—by endorsing symmetry over asymmetry, by rejecting the happy child half of the asymmetry—*avoid an inconsistency*. And that's always a good thing. But—having never given us that requisite new platform of deeply held, widely shared intuition that would help us understand where our original

[9] See Section 1.2. According to totalism, just as it makes things worse and is wrong to bring Maija into existence, it also makes things worse and is wrong *not* to bring Haaken into existence. Alternatively, they may move to the position that nonexistence comparability is false. To reject nonexistence comparability would be to reject the idea that existence makes things worse for Maija or better for Haaken than nonexistence. Both approaches would thus simply reject one half of the asymmetry or the other: respectively, the half that says that it *doesn't* make things worse not to bring Haaken into existence or the half that it says that it *does* make things worse to bring Maija into existence.

intuition has gone wrong and thus loosen the hold that intuition has on us—they haven't actually *solved the puzzle*.

To simply reject either half of the asymmetry without having actually solved the puzzle—to just set aside a big chunk of the only data we have when it comes to our moral theorizing—is to take an unfortunate short cut, a short cut of Donner party dimensions, a short cut that ends in a moral theory we ourselves in point of fact *don't actually accept*. (The "moral" of the Donner story thus applies quite nicely to how we should approach the asymmetry: depart on time to avoid the risks that come with a long journey, and, for heaven's sake, don't take a short cut on the advice of a complete stranger.)

Now, as noted earlier, readers who, after reflection, simply don't share the relevant intuitions have an off ramp.[10] If their own deeply held intuitions tell them that symmetry is the end of the story—if the asymmetry itself has no hold on them—then for them *there is no puzzle* to be solved. Thus the point of this chapter—and this book—isn't to try to instill in readers intuitions they don't have. It's, rather, to solve the puzzles that arise out of the intuitions they *do* have.

2.3 Attempts to solve the puzzle that go nowhere

The various attempts to explain the asymmetry explored in this section agree that the key to a solution lies in our coming to a clear understanding of what the basic existential intuition itself is all about. They also all make the not implausible supposition that the key to that understanding is the idea that a person's *moral* status is grounded—in some way or another—in that person's *existential* status.

[10] See Section 1.7.

As we shall see, however, each proposed solution in effect oversteps: each generates results that in some cases run headlong into the basic maximizing intuition and that in other cases run headlong *back* into the basic existential intuition. Instead of solving the puzzle, they only intensify it.

2.3.1 Moral presentism

It might be thought that the basic existential intuition is best understood as follows. It, first, draws a distinction between people who *exist*—people who *now* exist, people who *at present* exist—and *possible future* people—people who won't exist, if they exist at all, until later. It, second, claims that all and only *existing* people—and that all and only what happens to *them*—matter morally.

It's those people and those facts that appear on our moral radar according to presentism. *Possible future* people and what happens to *them* have no role at all to play in our moral analysis: they are morally inert.[11]

The rationale for presentism would be this: *possible future* people *aren't here*. In point of fact, they aren't, as of *now*, *anywhere*. Moreover, it's always possible—indeed, arguably *likely*—that they'll never come into existence at all. How can we have any obligations at all in respect of *nothing*—or in respect of a highly iffy something?

According to presentism, when we face what seems to be a *hard* case—for example, a case involving a tradeoff between an *existing* person's wellbeing and a *possible future* person's wellbeing—we can reconfigure the case as an *easy* case, a case involving no *morally significant* tradeoff at all.

Our first case, Jaime versus Harry (Figure 1.2), was just such a case. There the agent can either cure the *existing* Jaime's terrible

[11] The term "moral presentism" is from Arrhenius. He rejects that view (see Arrhenius 2003b, 2009, and forthcoming).

disease or bring the *possible future* Harry into existence. According to presentism, Jaime, but not Harry, matters morally, and what happens to Jaime, but not Harry, matters morally. Now: to say that much isn't to provide a complete analysis of the case. The presentist picture of what matters morally doesn't, on its own, tell us much at all. It must first be combined with still *other* moral principles—principles that, on their own, we may well consider completely uncontroversial; principles, for example, fueled by the basic maximizing intuition; principles that tell us that it makes things worse, and is wrong, to make things *worse* for any person who matters morally when we could have, at no cost to anyone else, made things *better* for that person. What presentism adds is this: *not all people matter morally*—a person matters morally, and what happens to that person matters morally, *if and only if* that person, at present, *now*, *exists*.

It seems clear that presentism in combination with otherwise uncontroversial moral principles produces results for Jaime versus Harry that seem exactly right: the future in which Jaime is cured of his terrible disease is *morally better* than the future in which Jaime is left to suffer and Harry is made to exist, and the choice that brings about the one future is *obligatory* while the other is just *wrong*.

How does presentism apply to the asymmetry? To apply presentism, we must first know at just what point a person pops into existence. But we can add the relevant details to our two cases. We can stipulate that Maija *now* exists and suffers while Haaken *doesn't yet* but *may* exist. (The choice, in other words, to bring Maija into existence has already been made while the choice whether to bring Haaken into existence or not lies in the future.) Then, according to presentism, Maija matters morally while Haaken matters not at all. Thus what makes things better or worse for Maija will bear on the moral analysis, and what might make things better or worse for Haaken can be completely ignored.

Otherwise uncontroversial moral principles then kick in. Since Maija matters morally, and existence makes things worse for Maija, the future in which she exists is worse than the future in which she never exists, and the choice that brings about that future is wrong. Since Haaken *doesn't* matter morally, moral law just doesn't care what happens to him. And that's so, even given that the future in which Haaken never exists is worse for him than the future in which he eventually does exist.

But presentism faces clear obstacles. The first is probably obvious. Presentism produces perfectly fine results when we stipulate that *Maija* exists now and *Haaken* only later. The problem is that we can reverse that stipulation and generate a new pair of cases. Presentism then compels us to reject *both* halves of the asymmetry. We are then compelled to say that it's perfectly OK to bring the miserable Maija into existence *and* perfectly wrong to decline to bring the happy Haaken into existence.

A second obstacle arises when we consider a case in which a possible future child—call her *Missy*—will, if she exists at all, inevitably contract a terrible disease, a disease that, if left uncured, would render her life less than worth living. But you—again, a doctor and this time around also a research scientist, toiling away in your research lab—by taking certain steps now are in a position to make sure that a potent cure for that disease will be available to Missy once she comes into existence and falls ill. Assuming that choice would come at no cost to anyone else (i.e., that other things are equal) and assuming, too, that your *only* window of opportunity for securing a future cure for the future Missy is *now* and that anything you, or others, might do later, *after* Missy commences existence, would be completely ineffective, would it be *wrong* for you *not* to secure that cure now? Would it be wrong for you now just to walk away from your research lab?

Presentism seems to say that it's not: Missy doesn't *now* exist; therefore she *doesn't* matter morally; therefore *what happens to her* doesn't matter morally; therefore you *may do as you please.*

But that result seems clearly false. And—quite plausibly—what underlies our conviction that it's false is the basic maximizing intuition.

The presentist version, in other words, of the basic existential intuition infringes far too deeply into the territory properly governed by the basic maximizing intuition.

Does this evaluation change if we add that you can't be *certain* that it is *Missy* who will eventually exist and suffer the terrible disease? No. If the child who will exist and suffer doesn't happen to be Missy but is rather someone else entirely, you are surely still obligated to secure the cure for that nonidentical child. You are surely still obligated to secure the cure for *whatever child it is* who will eventually exist.

Does the evaluation change if we add that you aren't certain that any child at all will eventually exist? (That you aren't certain that, between now and then, a giant meteorite won't strike Earth and annihilate all forms of life forever?) No—at least not in this "other things equal" case. Taking probabilities into account sometimes complicates the moral analysis (as we shall see in Chapter 6). But, when other things are equal—as they are here—it's surely no more acceptable for you to put Missy's future wellbeing at risk than it is for you to put my future wellbeing at risk.

Thus it just won't work to say that the only people who matter morally *now* are the people who *now* exist and that possible future people matter not at all. Possible future people—even when we don't know precisely who they will be and even when their coming into existence isn't a certainty—matter morally, too.

Now, if our aim is to make sure that the basic existential intuition fails, then the claim that the basic existential intuition is best understood by reference to presentism may be one that we'll want to push hard. But that's not our aim. Our aim here is to understand what the basic existential intuition is all about—and thus to figure out whether it is capable of playing nicely with the basic maximizing intuition or not.

2.3.2 Moral actualism

Moral actualism (*actualism*) first draws a distinction between people who *do or will actually* exist (people, that is, who *do or will* exist in whatever unique future it is that will *in fact*, or *actually*, unfold) and *merely possible* people (people who could have, but as it happens never do, exist in the *actual* future at all). And it then claims that all and only *actual* people and what happens to *them* matter morally, while the *merely possible* and what happens to *them* matter not at all.

Actualism may seem almost a matter of common sense.[12] Actual people, whether existing or future, are clearly among the people we must—per the basic maximizing intuition—do our best for. But why should we worry at all about making things better for people who will never actually exist at all? Why would moral law care about how we comport ourselves in respect of a *completely empty* class of beings?

It's a plus for actualism that it understands that future people, just like people who exist now, matter morally. Beyond that, however, some of the problems we see with actualism closely track the problems we've already pointed out with presentism.

Let's go straight to the asymmetry. If we stipulate that Maija is actual and Haaken merely possible, then actualism—not on its own, but in combination with otherwise uncontroversial moral principles—produces entirely plausible results. But if we reverse the stipulation so that it's instead Haaken who is actual and Maija merely possible, then actualism fails in just the same way that presentism fails. We again find ourselves compelled to reject both halves of the asymmetry. We seem compelled to say both that it's *permissible* to bring the miserable Maija into existence but wrong *not* to bring the happy Haaken into existence.

[12] So some of its advocates seem to see it (Parsons 2002; Weinberg 2016).

Actualism faces a second challenge as well. Consider the case of *addition plus* (Figure 2.3.2a).

Figure 2.3.2a: Addition plus			
	c1	c2	c3
probability →	1	1	1
wellbeing ↓	f1	f2	f3
12		**Quinten**	
11	**Quinten**		
. . .			
6			**Quinten, Caddy**
. . .			
1		**Caddy**	
0	*Caddy*		

Figure 2.3.2a Addition plus

Let's stipulate that agents *actually* choose c1 and that f1 *actually* unfolds. Actualism then instructs that the only person in the case who has any moral status at all is the *actual* Quinten. We need not even have mentioned the non-actual, merely possible Caddy; what happens to her, according to actualism, is *completely irrelevant* to our moral analysis.

And then we simply note it would have been a plus for Quinten had the future f2 actually unfolded in place of f1—had, that is, Caddy actually been brought into existence and assigned a relatively low, though positive, wellbeing level. (Perhaps Caddy exists in f2 as one of the children in *Never Let Me Go*.[13]) Actualism—again, not on its own but in combination with otherwise uncontroversial moral principles—then quickly instructs that f2 is *better than* f1 and—even more obviously—that f2 is *better than* f3, that c2 is *obligatory*, and that c1 and c3 are *both wrong*.

But at least some of those results—at least the results that f2 is better than f3 and that c2 is obligatory—seem clearly false. And it's

[13] Ishiguro 2005.

the *merely possible* situation of the *merely possible* Caddy in f2 that grounds a more plausible analysis of the case. Yes, Caddy is merely possible and only Quinten is actual, and, yes, Caddy's existence in f2 is worth having. But what happens to the merely possible Caddy in f2—specifically, that f2 is worse for her than f3—clearly *bears on* the moral analysis. The more plausible analysis will recognize that the fact that f2 is worse for the merely possible Caddy than f3 is a point of high moral significance: potentially providing grounds for the position, not just that f2 isn't better than f3, but also that f2 isn't better than f1: not just that f2 is worse than f3, but also that f2 is worse than f1; for the position that c2 isn't after all *obligatory* but rather that it's *wrong*.

The case of *double wrongful life* (Figure 2.3.2b)) makes a similar point.[14]

Figure 2.3.2b: Double wrongful life		
	c1	c2
probability →	1	1
wellbeing ↓	f1	f2
+10		
+0	*Molly*	*Maggie*
−10	**Maggie**	**Molly**

Figure 2.3.2b Double wrongful life

Keeping in mind that there exists *no alternate accessible future* that would make things better for both Maggie and Molly—the die is, for whatever reason, already cast; a future in which neither exists is just not an option; either Maggie or Molly will inevitably come into existence and then proceed to have a life that is less than worth living (a *wrongful life*, in the terminology of the law of negligence[15])—what do we want to say about this difficult case?

[14] See Hare 2007; Parfit 2011; Parfit 2017.

[15] See Preface.

Given the parallels between the two futures, given that f1 and f2 are equally bad for at least one person, the judgment that f1 is exactly as *bad* as (i.e., exactly as *good* as) f2 seems clearly correct. The agent, thinking through the choices and their consequences in advance, will surely conclude that, from a moral point of view, there's no basis for choosing c1 over c2 or c2 over c1. That conclusion seems exactly correct. If we put that conclusion together with the idea that, in every case, agents always have at least one permissible option, we can add that c1 and c2 are both—however unfortunate, however horrible—*morally permissible.*[16]

Actualism, though, sees things very differently. While the agent may not *know*, just prior to choice, whether f1 or f2 will actually unfold, *the agent* knows, and *we* know, that it will be one and only one of those two futures. Let's suppose that it's f1—that the agent ends up choosing c1. Then, according to actualism (in combination with otherwise uncontroversial moral principles), Maggie being actual and Molly being merely possible, Maggie having full moral status and Molly having none at all, f1 is worse than f2 and c1 is wrong. If we suppose instead that it's f2 that is actual, then actualism will direct that, since Molly is actual and Maggie now merely possible, f2 is worse than f1 and c2 is wrong. *Whatever* the agent does, in other words, what the agent has done is *wrong.*

Like addition plus, this case shows that it's *just not plausible* to think that merely possible people don't matter morally. In the case where it's Maggie who is actual and Molly who is merely possible, what grounds our judgment that c1 is, as we said before, *permissible*, the reason it's OK, if unfortunate, to actually do the terrible thing to the actual Maggie—is that the *merely possible* Molly and what happens to her matters morally—and matters morally just as much as does Maggie and what happens to her.

[16] The idea that, in any case, there must exist at least one permissible choice—that there are no genuine "moral dilemmas," cases where *everything* that the agent might choose to do is *wrong*—seems clearly correct. Moral law is demanding, but it would seem not to be *that* demanding—to demand, that is, the *impossible.*

The cases of addition plus and double wrongful life bring to light a third problem with actualism and the last problem we shall note here. Let's go back to addition plus. We stipulated earlier that Quinten but not Caddy was actual—that is, that f1 is the future that will *actually* unfold. On that stipulation, actualism seems to say that f2 is better than f1 and also better than f3—and that c2 is obligatory.

But let's now stipulate instead that *both* Quinten and Caddy are actual—and that f2 will actually unfold rather than f1 or f3. Actualism can now plausibly be expected to generate a quite different set of results: depending on how we think that the tradeoff between Quinten and Caddy is to be handled, we'll now say, quite plausibly, that f3 is better than f2 and that c2 is *wrong*.

A problem is that a theory that generates those varying results—one set of result if f1 is actual and another set of results if f2 is actual—violates what Rabinowicz calls the principle of *normative invariance*: the idea that what we actually end up doing can't, on its own, make a future that is otherwise *better* than another future *worse* or convert a choice that would otherwise be *permissible* into a choice that is *wrong*.[17]

Double wrongful life raises precisely the same issue. As noted, actualism's analysis of that case will depend on what the agent *actually* chooses to do—on which future, as between f1 and f2, is actual. And that's a violation of normative invariance.[18]

2.3.3 Moral necessitarianism

Michael Otsuka sometimes sounds like a moral actualist. Thus he writes that it's a

[17] Carlson 1995 (crediting Rabinowicz).

[18] Normative invariance itself seems the sort of conceptual principle we may well have no choice but to accept.

> mistake to maintain that . . . a merely possible person might have any standing to complain about your failure to bring her into existence. A merely possible person is nothing more than the eternal absence of a person whose actual existence was also possible. . . . It's no one and nothing, and so lacks any moral standing to complain. To assume that an absence of a person is someone with moral standing is to take a metaphor—"possible person"—and transform it into a pale, ghostly person.[19]

Otsuka's later work, however, suggests that for a person to have full moral status—for, as Otsuka puts it, a person's *complaint* that that person is worse off in one future as compared against another to have *full moral weight*—isn't just a matter of that person's existing in the *actual* future.[20] It's also a matter of that person's existing (so to speak) *necessarily*—that is, existing in *each and every* one of the various futures that we are aiming to compare. I take it that that more restrictive position—we can call it *moral necessitarianism* (*necessitarianism*)—relates to the fact that, at a given time, it may be unsettled, or unclear, exactly which future, among many possible futures, will turn out to be actual—which future will actually unfold.[21]

Now, the complaints of people whose existence is—we might say—merely *contingent* do have some—though not full—moral weight, according to Otsuka. The contingent person's "complaints retain moral weight. But this weight is greatly reduced in

[19] Otsuka 2018. In this paper, Otsuka articulates the distinction he has in mind in terms of *choice-dependent* and *choice-independent* existences. In subsequent work, however, he puts the distinction in terms of *necessary* and *possible* existences (Otsuka 2021).

[20] Otsuka 2018.

[21] The term "moral necessitarianism" is from Arrhenius. He rejects that view (see presentism: Arrhenius 2003b, 2009, and forthcoming).

Otsuka may thus be thinking that we can finesse the issues raised by uncertainty—though it's unclear to me just what those are—by taking the position that a person's complaint has full moral weight *only if*, *whatever* the agents do, that person will exist—will exist, that is, at *whatever* future turns out to be the actual future. In this respect, Otsuka's position is similar to Heyd's (Heyd 1992).

comparison" against the "morally weighty" complaints of the necessary person.[22]

But to see the limitation of necessitarianism, it's enough to look back at addition plus (Figure 2.3.2a) According to necessitarianism, Quinten's complaint at f1 has full moral weight and his complaint at f3, given its magnitude, is weightier still. In contrast, the weight of contingent Caddy's complaint at f2 is, compared against Quinten's, "greatly reduced." One problem with necessitarianism—as Otsuka describes it—is that it seems highly plausible that on some version or another of the case we'll get the result that f2 is better than f1 and that c1 is, accordingly, wrong. (Perhaps it's one where we make Caddy's wellbeing level in f2 a little higher than it is in the original f2, thereby reducing the weight of her complaint relative to f3. Or perhaps it's one where we make Quinten's wellbeing in f2 itself a little higher than it is in the original f2, thereby increasing the weight of his complaint relative to f1.) We may even get that f2 is better than f3 as well—and that c2 is obligatory.

Necessitarianism faces an even deeper problem. As it stands, the view doesn't provide us with the information that we need to figure out how we are to weigh the complaints of necessary people versus the complaints of contingent people. Without that information, we can *speculate* what the theory, once it's more developed, might imply—and I've speculated, just above, that they'll count *against* that theory—but we can't do anything more than that. That we can't test a theory doesn't count in favor of that theory. To decide whether a theory is even plausible—and from there whether it's a theory we should accept or not—means that we must start with a theory that we can test.

Now, we could put forward our own version of necessitarianism—one that brings us much closer to a theory we can test. We can say that Quinten's complaints have *full* moral weight, while Caddy's have *none at all*. But that theory, just like

[22] Otsuka 2017, 15–16.

presentism and actualism, quickly fails. I leave it to the reader to say why that's so.

2.3.4 Moral existencism

On this approach, what determines a person's moral status is whether that person does or will exist *under the choice to be evaluated*, whether that choice and that existence happen to obtain in the actual future or not.

According to existencism, the people who matter morally for the purpose of determining whether one future is better than another, and, ultimately, evaluating any choice made at that one future, are just the people who *do or will exist under that choice at that future*. It's whether *those* people, and *only* those people, are made better off or worse off under that choice at that future that determines whether that future is morally better or worse than others and whether that choice is permissible or not.

Existencism, however, immediately runs into trouble. While any of the cases we've examined so far can help us see why that's so, double wrongful life (Figure 2.3.2b) does that work most efficiently. If our aim is to compare f1 against f2—and thus to evaluate c1—existencism seems to instruct that f1 is worse than f2 and that c1 is wrong. If our aim is to compare f2 against f1—and thus to evaluate c2—existencism seems to instruct that f2 is worse than f1.

But what if we aim—and surely we *do* aim—to ask and answer both questions? We then are compelled to say *both* that f1 is worse than f2 *and* that f2 is worse than f1. But that's a result that violates what may well be the most clearly correct of all the conceptual principles we seem to have no choice but to accept—that is, the principle of *anti-symmetry*. According to that principle, if a future x is worse than a future *y*, then it can't also be the case that the future *y* is worse than the future *x*.[23]

Thus existencism, as a way of understanding the basic existential intuition and thus as a basis for a solution to the asymmetry, fails, just as do presentism, actualism, and necessitarianism.

2.3.5 What has gone wrong?

The idea that the basic existential intuition in some way or another grounds a person's *moral* status in that person's *existential* status

[23] Existencism avoids a violation of anti-symmetry if it includes the idea that rankings of futures in respect of moral betterness are to be *relativized* on the basis of who in fact does or will exist at those futures. Thus Broome describes what I am calling *existencism* as proposing, not just one *categorical* betterness ranking of alternate futures, but rather multiple *relative* betterness rankings of alternative futures. Thus: "You might think betterness is relative to the population of people who exist . . . at any time" (Broome 2004, 73). (This is not, by the way, a view Broome endorses.) Applied to double wrongful life, that position instructs that, relative to the population that does or will exist in f1, f1 is worse than f2 but, relative to the population that does or will exist in f2, f2 is worse than f1. The permissibility of choice can be relativized along exactly the same lines. c2 is permissible, indeed, *obligatory*, relative to the population that does or will exist in f1, and c1 is permissible, indeed, *obligatory*, relative to the population that does or will exist in f2. But now we face a new problem. On this view, we've lost all sense of moral direction. We're now telling the agent that, depending on how we relativize, each of c1 and c2 will turn out to be obligatory. But surely we *don't* think we are operating in quite that much of a moral fog.

The four proposals noted in this section do not exhaust attempts to make sense of the asymmetry. Theorists have also proposed reasons-based approaches that aim to preserve, not the asymmetry as presented here, but a weaker form of the asymmetry: see, e.g., Algander 2011 (agents have a reason to bring the happy child into existence that is "favouring but non-requiring") and McMahan 2009 (distinguishing between "reason-giving" and "canceling" functions of goods and bads). Algander's approach, however, raises the question why favored choices, in the absence of *more* favored choices, aren't themselves obligatory. More critically, it isn't clear under his approach why the choice to bring the happy child into existence is merely favored but the choice not to bring the miserable child into existence is clearly obligatory. Understood in one way, McMahan's approach gives rise to parallel questions. Understood in another, it's not clear that the distinction he draws isn't contemplated within the consequentialist approach this book is working toward, one that recognizes both that in many cases the "goods" of a given life at least counterbalance the "bads," a detail of the case that bears on the permissibility of bringing an additional person into existence, and that it doesn't, other things equal, make things morally worse and isn't morally wrong *not* to bring that same person into existence.

may seem plausible at first glance. The four proposed solutions to the asymmetry we've just considered represent four different ways of making that connection. But each, as we've just seen, is highly problematic.

Each of the four solutions assumes that understanding the basic existential intuition and preserving the asymmetry will be a matter of first sorting the people who *do* matter morally into one class and sorting the people who *don't* matter morally into another class and then allowing various otherwise uncontroversial moral principles—principles largely fueled by the basic maximizing intuition—to go to work.

I propose, however, that that assumption is just a mistake. It seems, instead, that any moral theory capable of dealing in any plausible way with population variability will instead, *for each and every one of us*, for you, for me, and for the merely possible, take the things that make things *worse* for us (or, to go to the other side of the coin, *better* for us) into account in completing its moral analysis.

To put the point another way: moral theories that fail to take the *modal* effects—the *cross-future* effects—of what happens to people in one future for purposes of determining what is going on morally in still other futures do so at their peril.

We can see that modal effect at play in addition plus. We can't correctly determine how f1 compares against f2 or f3, or correctly evaluate c1, if we are barred from taking into account what is going on with Caddy in f2 as compared against what is going on with Caddy in f3—if, that is, we think that what is going on with Caddy in f2 and f3 is devoid of any *moral significance*. If, in virtue of the fact that Quinten already exists and Caddy doesn't, or that f1 is the actual future, or that Quinten but not Caddy exists in all three futures, our moral theory allows us to focus *only* on Quinten's plight, then we'll find ourselves defending the preposterous claims that f2 is better than f1 and f3 and that c2 is obligatory. More plausibly, what happens to Caddy in f2 as compared against what happens to her in f3 *bears on* what we need to say about f1 and c1. It, in effect, converts f2 from a future that we'd otherwise consider morally *better* than f1 into a one that we recognize as quite possibly *worse*—and a choice c2 that we'd otherwise consider *obligatory* into a choice that we think is just *wrong*.

That same modal effect is at play, too, in the case of double wrongful life. There, it seems clear that, in determining how f1 compares against f2 and in evaluating c1, we need to take into account not just what happens to Maggie in f1, but also what happens to Molly in f2. We need to recognize that the fact that things are worse for Molly in f2 than in f1 has *moral significance* for purposes of comparing f1 against f2 and for evaluating c1. We need to take into account the fact that what happens to Molly in f2 converts the future f1 that, due to its effects on Maggie, we'd otherwise consider *worse than* f2 into a future that we consider *at least as good as* f2, and convert the choice c1 that we'd otherwise consider *wrong* into a choice that is itself *perfectly permissible*. And all that's so, regardless of when Molly happens to come into existence, whether she happens to exist at the actual future or at an alternate, merely possible future, and despite the fact that she doesn't exist at all in one of the two futures involved in the case.

2.4 The existence-sensitive solution to the asymmetry

2.4.1 Where existential status matters and where it doesn't

The preceding discussion suggests that it won't work to divide possible people into those who matter morally and those who don't. Any plausible solution to the asymmetry will need to recognize that what happens to the people who do or will exist in *any* accessible future may have implications for our moral analysis—and far-flung implications at that. *Each person, merely possible or not*, matters morally for purposes of comparing not just futures in which they do or will exist but also futures in which they *never exist at all*.

What is interesting to me, and isn't, I think, always noticed, is that we can accept that point and still have plenty of room to insist that a given person's existential status has a critical role to play in our moral theorizing.

Thus a plausible account of the asymmetry—what I will call the *existence-sensitive account*—considers it a mistake to divide people into those who matter morally and those who don't. But we can still divide *the worse-making things that happen to any one person*—a person's being made *worse off* in one future as compared against another; the *losses* that a person sustains in one future *as compared against* another—into those that have *moral significance* and those that don't.

We thus discard the problematic idea that a person's *existential* status determines that person's *moral* status. And we instead take the position that a person's existential status *at a given future* determines whether *things being made worse for* that person at that future as compared against still other futures has *moral significance*. Specifically, the worse-making things that happen to you, me, *and* the merely possible, *and* that happen to us in futures in which we *do or will exist*, have *full moral significance*, while the worse-making things that happen to us in futures in which we *never exist* have *no moral significance at all*.[24]

[24] Why not just *discount*, rather than completely erase, the moral significance of worse-making things that happen to a person—the *losses* that person sustains—in futures in which that person never exists? I owe the need to answer that question to both an anonymous referee for this book and an informal discussion with Gustaf Arrhenius. That (seemingly more middle-of-the-road) variation on my proposal simply invites new puzzles. First, rather than actually solving any extant puzzle, it simply tosses out the basic existential intuition. To see that that's so, go back to the happy child half of the asymmetry. Discount Haaken's loss in f3 by *however much you want short of zero* and we still get the result that f4 is *morally better* than f3. Second, it's an approach that imposes a procreation obligation on the part of the agent that is more stringent than ever: to make up for, say, failing to do the best one can for an already existing child, the agent must produce not just one additional child but multiple additional children. Third, any specific discounting factor that might be proposed will inevitably seem, and likely be, arbitrary. Fourth, without numerical clarity on just what the discounting factor should be (is it 1/

* * *

That point can also be put in terms of the *losses* we face. Where we understand that a person sustains a *loss* in one future as compared against another just in case that person has less wellbeing in the one future than in the other (where we accept a widely comparative, modal account of loss), we can say that the losses we sustain in futures in which we do or will exist have *full moral significance* and that the losses we sustain in futures in which we never exist have *no moral significance at all.* To put the point still another way, the *ordinary* losses any of us (you, me, and the merely possible) face have *full moral significance,* while the *existential* losses we face have *no moral significance at all.*

Since, as a matter of conceptual necessity, we can surely accept the principle that, if one future is *worse* for a given person than that other, then that other future is *better* for that person than the one, we can also put the point we've just made in terms of *gains.*[25] Thus the gains that a person accrues in a given future that serve to reverse a morally significant loss themselves have *full moral significance.* If the loss is without moral significance, then so is the gain that reverses that loss.

Whether we put the point in terms of losses (or gains) or not, we can adopt the following generalizations—generalizations that are themselves entirely consistent with the far more precise principles we adopt in what follows: only the *morally significant* worse-making things that happen to a given person in a given future—only *morally significant* losses, only *ordinary* losses—*count against* the future

2? is it 1/3.5? is it, as Dean Spears recently, a little tongue-in-cheek, suggested in correspondence, 1/7832?), we don't have a principle we can *test.*

[25] Some theorists have disputed the principle asserted in the text on the ground that, if a person exists in one future *x* but not another future *y*, it makes sense to say that *x* is *better* for that person than *y* but *not* to say that *y* is *worse* for that person than *x*. Their dispute may be grounded in a rejection of nonexistence comparability. However, it seems to me that, *whatever* we think of nonexistence comparability, we can't get around the fact that that particular conceptual principle—at least as I am using the terms "better for" and "worse for" here—is one we have no choice but to accept.

in which they are sustained or, in a roundabout, cross-future, modal fashion, count in *favor* of a future in which they are avoided. Any other loss—any *existential* loss—may just as well, from the point of view of moral analysis, never have happened at all.[26]

2.4.2 The existence condition

We now have an account of the role a person's existential status plays in moral law—and, with that, a new way of thinking about what the basic existential intuition itself is all about. Whether a person does or will exist or not in a given future is critical, but not because it decides whether that person has moral status, but rather because it decides whether the *worse-making things* that happen to that person—that is, the *losses* that person sustains—in that future have *moral significance.*

Now, in that distinction there may already be enough to convey a highly plausible account of the asymmetry. Maija's being worse off in f2 compared against f1 has moral significance since she exists in f2, while Haaken's being worse off in f3 as compared against f4 doesn't have moral significance since he doesn't exist in f3.

But that distinction doesn't, on its own, tell us precisely what follows from the fact that the one loss has moral significance and the other doesn't. Given, however, that it's the basic existential intuition we are working to interpret, we can guess. Maija's loss in f2 counts against f2: it makes f2 worse than f1 and makes c2 wrong. Haaken's loss in f3 doesn't count against f3: it doesn't make f3 worse than f4, and c3 and c4 are both permissible.

We need, however, to do more than guess. We need a formulation of the basic existential intuition that we can test.

[26] The claims regarding how a person's existential status bears on moral betterness and moral obligations made in this section are reflected in what I have elsewhere called the *loss distinction thesis* (and, earlier on, *variabilism*). For further discussion, see Appendix B and Roberts 2011a, 2011b.

For that purpose, I propose the following condition—the *existence condition* (EC)—on when one future is morally worse than another and when a choice made at that one future is wrong. It, notably, provides only a *necessary*, not a *sufficient* condition on when one future is worse than another. But, as we shall see, it leaves just the right amount of room for us to introduce still other principles—including principles that give voice to the basic maximizing intuition and principles that hold as a matter of conceptual necessity—that, in combination with EC, will generate complete accounts of a wide array of the cases we are interested in here.

> *Existence condition (EC).* Where a future y is accessible relative to a future x, x is *morally worse* than y (i.e., y is *morally better* than x), and a choice made in x is *wrong*, *only if* there is a person p such that:
>
> (i) p does or will exist in x, and
>
> (ii) x is worse for p than y or there is a third accessible future z such that x is worse for p than z.[27]

One future is thus worse than another, and a choice made at that one future is wrong, *only if* there's something about that one future that makes things worse for a person who does or will exist in that one future than things could—*could*, not *would*—have been for that person.

If the *only* people the one future is worse for *never exist* in that future *or* if each person *who does or will exist* in that future is *at least as well off* in that future as in any other accessible future—in *either* the future we're comparing the one future against *or* another accessible future altogether—then EC's necessary condition is failed. And if the condition is failed, then, according to EC, the one future isn't worse than the other, and what the agents have done in that

[27] A conceptual principle we seem to have no choice but to accept is taken for granted here: if a future x is morally worse than a future y, then y is morally better than x.

one future isn't wrong. Which is just to say that the one future is *at least as good as* the other and that the choice that gives rise to that future is *permissible*.[28]

Before applying EC to the asymmetry, I want to underline two of EC's distinctive but highly convenient features.[29] The first feature won't come into play in connection with the asymmetry but will come into play later when we turn to still other cases. The inquiry EC has us undertake on occasion will be quite *expansive*. If our interest is in how *x* compares against *y*, EC will sometimes have us look *beyond y* to *still other futures z* to determine whether EC's condition on *x*'s being worse than *y* is satisfied. In other words: the condition on *x*'s being worse than *y* may be satisfied despite the fact that *x* isn't worse than *y* for a person who does or will exist in *x* but where *x* instead is worse for that same person than *a more far-flung z*. In any such case, EC leaves the door open for us consistently

[28] Thus I take the following to be among those conceptual principles we have no choice to accept: if a future *x* isn't worse than a future *y*, then it's at least as good as (and, of course, *may* also be better than) a future *y*. And another: if a choice isn't wrong, it's permissible (and, of course, *may* also be obligatory). See Chapter 1 note 34 (deontic logic).

[29] Many attempts to formulate the underlying intuition—the basic existential intuition, the Narvesonian idea that we *don't* favor making happy people, the intuition that curing a child's terrible disease and bringing a child into existence are intrinsically distinct from a moral point of view—make it a condition of *x* being worse than *y* that *x* is worse than *y* for a person who does or will exist in *x*. The *expansive inquiry* that EC requires—that is, the introduction of *z*, a future that may, but need not, be identical to *y*—distinguishes EC from those earlier attempts. That feature of EC comes into play in discussion of the case of *addition plus* in Sections 2.3.2 and 2.4.4 and discussion of the Pareto puzzle in Chapter 3.

Moreover, many attempts to formulate the underlying intuition make it a necessary condition of one future's being better than another that the one future make a person who does or will exist in the one future better off. EC's *narrower approach* again distinguishes EC from those other attempts. That EC *doesn't* require existence at the future that is to be deemed better is critical to its successful analysis of the miserable child half of the asymmetry (Section 2.3.3).

The principles that EC is to be distinguished from are often called *person-affecting* (see Parfit 2017; Hare 2007). As noted earlier, however, that term has been applied to so many different "intuitions"—so many *clearly false* claims—that the only purpose that term could have here would be to create confusion. (See Chapter 1 note 8 (list of failed attempts)). I therefore avoid that term altogether when referring to principles we might actually *want* to accept.

to say—by application of still other principles—that x is, after all, worse than y.

The second feature—as we shall shortly see—is critical to a plausible EC-based account of the asymmetry. EC *doesn't* require, for one future to be *better* than another, that the one future be better for a person who *does or will exist in* that one future. Consistent with EC, in other words, it can happen that one future is better than another *even if* that one future isn't better for anyone who ever exists in that one future at all. In that respect, EC *isn't* expansive at all but rather *very narrow*.

I believe that EC captures what lies at the heart of the basic existential intuition while leaving behind the (sometimes incredible and sometimes just very badly formulated) rest of what's been associated with the so-called "person-affecting intuition."

That EC itself is at least a *start* down the path of reconciling the basic existential intuition against the basic maximizing intuition should be plain. Indeed, EC itself incorporates a certain maximizing element. Thus an *alleged* victim is *not really a victim at all* at a given future, according to EC, if that person's wellbeing in that future has been *maximized*—if, that is, that person has *so much* wellbeing in that future that that person isn't better off in any other *accessible* future. (We take for granted that there are always *logically possible* futures that make things better for just about anyone!)

2.4.3 Application of the existence condition to the asymmetry, the Pareto reduction principle

Let's start with the miserable child half of the asymmetry. According to EC, f1 is *worse* than f2 *only if* f1 is worse than f2 for a person who *does or will exist* in f1. Since Maija *never exists* in f1, that necessary condition is failed, and we can infer that f1 *isn't* worse than f2 and that c1 *isn't* wrong—that is, that it's *permissible*.

And—just to underline again—EC *doesn't* require, for f1 to be *better* than f2, that f1 is better for a person who does or will exist in f1. That means that EC avoids the disastrous result that f1 isn't better than f2. We haven't yet produced, but clearly need to leave room for, the result that f1 *is* better than f2.

Of course, the result that f1 isn't worse than f2—our only solid result so far—leaves open the question whether f2 is worse than f1 and whether c2 is, accordingly, wrong. Here, EC is *completely silent*. It's silent in virtue of the fact that its necessary condition on f2's being worse than f1 is satisfied: Maija *both* exists in f2 *and* is worse off in f2 than in f1.

Is it a problem that EC, on its own, *doesn't* provide a *complete* account of the miserable child case? No. EC is not designed to map out the whole of moral law or even the whole of the basic existential intuition. By remaining silent at various critical points, EC leaves room for otherwise plausible moral principles—principles plausibly fueled by the basic maximizing intuition—to step in to produce the intuitive results we want.

We'll shortly turn to how the comparison between f1 and f2 can be completed. But first let's finish with EC. Let's see what it has to say about the happy child half of the asymmetry.

According to EC, f3 is worse than f4 *only if* a person does or will exist in f3 and f3 is worse for that person than f4. Though f3 is—per nonexistence comparability—worse for Harry than f4, since Harry *never exists* in f1, EC's necessary condition is failed. And we infer that f3 *isn't worse* than f4 and that c3 is permissible.

EC provides, moreover, that f4 is worse than f3 *only if* a person does or will exist in f4 and f4 is worse for that person than f3. Harry, of course, exists in f4. But his wellbeing in f4 is maximized; no other accessible future makes things better for Harry than they are in f4. EC thus implies that f4 *isn't worse* than f3, and that c4 is, just like c3, perfectly permissible.[30]

[30] As it happens, we can also infer that f3 *is exactly as good as* f4. Here we appeal to another conceptual principle we seem to have no choice but to accept, *trichotomy*: if *x* isn't

So far, so good.

We've pulled all that we can out of EC. Let's now go back and complete the comparison of f1 against f2.

As already noted, EC implies that f1 isn't worse than f2. That's a start. But what principle tells us that f2 is worse than f1 *without also* telling us that f3 is worse than f4?

Let's first just note that, if the case at hand were a *same population* case rather than a *variable population* case—if, specifically, Maija *existed* in f1, even if at a zero wellbeing level—a certain widely accepted Pareto principle would immediately instruct that such a *reworked* f1—call it *f1**—is better than f2.

We can call that widely accepted principle the *same people Pareto principle.*

> *Same people Pareto principle.* Where a future *y* is accessible relative to a future *x* and *exactly the same people* do or will exist in *x* and *y*, *x* is *morally worse* than *y* (*y* is *morally better* than *x*) *if*
> (i) *x* is worse than *y* for at least one person who does or will exist in *x*, *and*
> (ii) *x* is better than *y* for no person who does or will exist in *x*.

Same people Pareto maps out its own fair share of moral law and indeed of the basic maximizing intuition.[31] But it *doesn't* apply to the miserable child half of the asymmetry since the two futures to be compared in that case contain *different people.*

Still, the idea that inspires same people Pareto seems entirely apropos for use in the miserable child case. There, f1 makes things better for a person who does or will exist in f2 without making

morally worse than *y*, and *y* isn't morally worse than *x*, then *x* is morally exactly as good as *y*. For discussion of Rabinowicz's more skeptical look at trichotomy, see Section 3.3.3.

[31] Like many other articulations of Pareto principles, same people Pareto establishes *only* a sufficient condition—*not* a necessary condition—on when one future is worse than another. But this principle is also *explicitly* restricted in a way that articulations of other Pareto principles often are not: it applies *only* in the case in which *exactly the same people* do or will exist in each of the futures to be compared.

things worse for anyone who does or will exist in f2 at all. It achieves that end by leaving Maija out of existence altogether.

But so what? If that's what it takes to make things *better for* Maija, and given that no one else's wellbeing or existence is at stake, then that's what makes things *morally better*.

The following principle makes exactly that Pareto-inspired point. Leaving a person *out* of an existence can sometimes make things *morally better*. Which is just to say that bringing that same person *into* existence can sometimes make things morally *worse*. Thus the *Pareto reduction principle*:

> *Pareto reduction principle*. Where a future *y* is accessible relative to a future *x* and each person who does or will exist in *y* also does or will exist in *x*, *x* is *morally worse* than *y* (*y* is *morally better* than *x*) *if*
>
> (i) *x* is worse than *y* for at least one person who does or will exist in *x*, *and*
>
> (ii) *x* is better than *y* for *no* person who does or will exist in *y*.

Given that f1 (which here goes in for "*y*") is better for Maija than f2 (which goes in for "*x*"), and that f2 is better than f1 for no one who does or will exist in f1, this (fairly blunt) principle immediately implies that f2 is worse than f1—that is, that f1 is better than f2.

Now, the Pareto reduction principle doesn't explicitly say what the implications of the result that f2 is worse than f1 are for the evaluation of *choice*. But given the assumption that c1 *with certainty* gives rise to f1 and c2 to f2, we can here freely rely on the *connection thesis*. According to that thesis, the comparison of futures in respect of their moral betterness is *closely connected* to the evaluation of choices as to their moral permissibility. We can say, in other words, that f2 being morally worse than f1 means that c1 is not just *permissible* but *obligatory*—that is, that c2 is *wrong*.

The final step is to make sure that, in introducing the Pareto reduction principle into the picture, we haven't contradicted ourselves.

What, in other words, does that principle say about the happy child case? Does it say anything that's inconsistent with what we've already said about the second half of the asymmetry?

The answer is: it says nothing at all. We've already determined from EC that f3 is *at least as good as* f4. We can now just note that the Pareto reduction principle *doesn't* generate the problem result that f4 is *better than* f3. It's silent on that point since no person who *does or will exist in f3* is made worse off in f3 than in f4.

We now have highly intuitive, complete, and consistent account—the *existence-sensitive account*—of the asymmetry. It makes things *worse*, and is *wrong*, to bring the *miserable* child into existence, but *doesn't* make things worse, and *isn't* wrong, *not* to bring the *happy* child into existence.

Critically, we've solved the puzzle of the asymmetry *without* throwing out any of the puzzle pieces. We've shown how the two puzzle pieces—the basic existential intuition at work in EC and the basic maximizing intuition at work in the Pareto reduction principle—instead fit nicely together. And we've done so within the confines of consistency, cogency, and the conceptual principles we seem to have no choice but to accept.

2.4.4 Application of the existence condition to addition plus and double wrongful life

I won't be able to give a complete account of addition plus here.[32] But we can note that the existence condition—EC—leaves the door open for a plausible account of that case.

Specifically, EC leaves the door open for the result that f2 is not just worse than f3 but also worse than f1.

32 Ultimately, a complete account of addition plus will depend on how tradeoffs are to be made when the futures to be compared contain *exactly the same people*. Does moral law allow Caddy to be made *much* worse off than she could otherwise be *just so* that Quinten's wellbeing (along with total wellbeing) can be maximized? I think not. But I set

We can start with the comparison of f2 against f3. Since Caddy does or will exist in f2 and f2 is worse for Caddy than f3, EC remains silent on whether f2 is worse than f3. Consistent with EC, we are thus free to say that f2 is worse than f3.

That much seems straightforward. But now let's consider how f2 compares against f1. As noted earlier, any determination whether EC's condition on worseness is satisfied often requires an *expansive* inquiry. And so it is for the comparison of f2 against f1. Since Caddy exists in f2 and f2 is worse for Caddy than f3, EC remains silent on whether f2 is worse than f1. EC thus—and in contrast to many other attempts to formulate the underlying intuition—comes with no automatic endorsement of the *mere addition principle*, a principle that immediately insists that f2 *can't* be worse than f1 and a principle that we'll find good reason to question in the next chapter. In contrast, EC leaves open the possibility that f2 is indeed worse than f1, not because f2 is worse than f1 for Caddy, but because f2 is worse than f3 for Caddy.

Let's turn to *double wrongful life*. There, EC is silent on whether f1 is worse than f2 and whether f2 is worse than f1. Its necessary condition on worseness is, in other words, satisfied on both sides: Maggie exists in f1 and is worse off in f1 than in f2; Molly exists in f2 and is worse off in f2 than in f1. EC thus leaves the door open for otherwise plausible principles to step in to complete the account. Ditto, by the way, the Pareto reduction principle. That principle doesn't apply when we both add a person to one of our two futures *and also add* a person to the other of our two futures.

What otherwise plausible principles might we introduce, then, to complete the account of double wrongful life? Here, just as in addition plus, we face a tradeoff scenario: Maggie's wellbeing against Molly's. But here the depth and the degree of the losses of wellbeing

aside, for purposes of this book, substantive issues of equality and priority. (I'll just note that, due to the leveling down objection against a strict equality principle, I favor a priority principle.)

each sustains in the future in which she exists are identical. Surely, then, any plausible principle equipped to deal with tradeoffs will instruct that f1 is exactly as good as f2, and that c1 and c2 are both permissible.[33]

2.5 Objections and replies

This section considers objections against the existence-sensitive solution to the asymmetry. Still other objections that specifically target EC independent of what it says about the asymmetry will emerge—and be addressed—in the chapters that follow.

2.5.1 Doesn't the existence-sensitive solution relocate, rather than solve, the puzzle?

It might be objected that the existence-sensitive account of the asymmetry doesn't genuinely solve the puzzle but rather simply *relocates* it. f2 makes things worse for Maija than f1; f3 makes things worse for Haaken than f4; *on what basis* does the proposed account make much of the fact that f2 is worse for Maija but nothing at all of the fact that f3 is worse for Haaken?

Reply. It seems to me that we can easily explain why things being worse for Maija in f2 and things being worse for Haaken in f3 play very different roles in our moral analyses. Things being made worse for Maija is a matter of making things worse for a real, live, flesh-and-blood, existing or future person (whether that person happens also to be an *actual* person or not!). Things being made worse for Haaken is a matter of making things worse for a person who never exists at all. The only loss one person sustains is in a future in which

[33] In other words, any plausible principle that addresses issues of equality and priority will surely instruct that f1 is exactly as good as f2.

she *does or will exist*. The only loss the other person sustains is in a future in which he *never* exists.

I can't see that we need to say more than that to explain why the distinction between Maija's situation in f2 and Haaken's situation in f3 is perfectly reasonable, indeed, compelling.

2.5.2 Doesn't the existence-sensitive solution assume an irrational (ad hoc, arbitrary) distinction?

Applied to first half of the asymmetry—the miserable child half—EC states that, if f2 is *worse* than f1, it must be the case that a person *does or will exist* in f2 and that f2 is *worse for* that person than f1. Given the facts of the case, the only person that can be is Maija. That raises the question of whether it's irrational (or arbitrary or ad hoc) *not* to accept as well, *if* we accept EC, a *parallel* necessary condition on f1's being *better* than f2—specifically, the condition that, if f1 is *better* than f2, then it must be case that a person exists in f1 and that f1 is *better for* that person than f2.

If that parallel necessary condition, on pain of irrationality, *must* be absorbed into the existence-sensitive solution to the asymmetry alongside EC itself, then that solution will immediately fail. We would then be forced to say that f1 *isn't* better than f2. But if f1 *isn't* better than f2, then f2 *isn't* worse than f1. But if f2 *isn't* worse than f1, then there's no asymmetry: the miserable child half of the asymmetry, the half that says that it makes things worse to bring the miserable child into existence, is false.

Things get worse. We haven't merely *lost the asymmetry*. We've also *contradicted* ourselves. For we earlier—appealing to EC in combination with the Pareto reduction principle and certain conceptual principles—took the position that f2 *is* worse than f1, and we're now saying that it *isn't*.

Reply. This objection against the existence-sensitive account of the asymmetry is certainly worth raising. But the reply perhaps needn't go on at length. The account of the asymmetry this book offers is one that includes EC, a necessary condition on *worseness*, and doesn't include the parallel necessary condition on *betterness*. If readers want an account that abandons the asymmetry and also manages to contradict itself, then the theory that includes *both* conditions is for them. But if readers want a solution to the asymmetry—an account that preserves both halves of the asymmetry; that reconciles the two halves of the asymmetry against each other—and avoids inconsistency, then the existence-sensitive account might be of interest to them.

What are we to make of the related objection that the following is a valid inference—and thus that, if we accept EC's condition on *worseness*, we are forced *by logic* to accept the parallel condition on *betterness* as well? For a clear picture of how the inference is supposed to work, it's helpful to restate EC itself—and the parallel condition EC is supposed to rationally require—a bit more casually.

1. If a future *x* is *worse* than a future *y*, then a person must *exist* (now or later) in *x* and be worse off than that person is elsewhere.

---

2. If a future *x* is *better* than a future *y*, then a person must *exist* (now or later) in *x* and be better off than that person is elsewhere.

Again, the reply can be quick. (1) doesn't entail (2) (and no complete, consistent first-order theory in the world will say otherwise). We can consistently accept—our brains do *not* explode if we accept—(1) but reject (2).[34]

[34] *Many* formulations of the underlying intuition—the basic existential intuition—make the mistake of requiring existence in a given future *both* for that one future to be *worse* than a second *and* for that one future to be *better* than a second. See e.g., Parfit 2017; see generally Chapter 1 note 8 (list of failed attempts). The principle they then aim to test—which they call, not the *existence condition*, but rather the *person-affecting intuition*—then of course immediately fails!

3

The Pareto puzzle

3.1 The three option case

The *Pareto puzzle* arises when we try to put both the basic maximizing intuition and the basic existential intuition to work in providing an account of the *three option case*.[1]

In that case, each of three futures f1, f2, and f3 contains exactly the same people at exactly the same well-being levels with one exception: the child Charlotte never exists in f1 but does or will exist in both f2 and f3 and is worse off in f2 than in f3. Thus while the futures the case involves may contain people other than Charlotte, no one else's well-being or existence is at stake (Figure 3.1).

Figure 3.1: Three option case			
	c1	c2	c3
probability →	1	1	1
wellbeing ↓	f1	f2	f3
+10			**Charlotte**
+5		**Charlotte**	
+0	*Charlotte*		

Figure 3.1 Three option case

[1] The three option case tracks the case that Broome introduced to show that what he called the *neutrality intuition* is false. The neutrality intuition represents Broome's own attempt to interpret the Narvesonian idea that we favor *making people happy*, not *making happy people*—that is, what I am here calling the basic existential intuition (Broome 2004, 145–149). Looking ahead, I will accept Broome's argument against the neutrality intuition but reject the neutrality intuition as a correct formulation of the basic existential intuition (see Section 3.3.1).

The Existence Puzzles. M. A. Roberts, Oxford University Press. © Oxford University Press 2024.
DOI: 10.1093/oso/9780197544143.003.0003

The conventions we've adopted for earlier figures apply here as well. Thus the choices displayed in the figure exhaust the agents' choices, and the futures displayed in the figure exhaust the futures that (with some degree of probability; here, a probability of 1) may arise out of those choices.

What do we want to say about this case? In keeping with the basic *existential* intuition, we *don't* think it makes things morally worse, or is wrong, to fail to bring Charlotte into existence to begin with. We *don't* think that f1 is *worse* than f2 or f3. Nor do we think that leaving Charlotte out of existence is itself a moral obligation: we *don't* think that f1 is *better* than f3. At the same time, in keeping with the basic *maximizing* intuition, we *do* think it makes things morally worse, and is wrong, to bring Charlotte into existence and do less for her when, at no cost to anyone else, we could have done more. We *do* think that f2 is clearly worse than f3.

That account of the three option case seems highly intuitive. And especially so if we apply the existence condition (EC)—and, more generally, the connection thesis—to the evaluation of each of the available choices. The choices of c1 and c3 are both perfectly *permissible*, but the choice of c2 is *wrong*. The agents may bring the additional child into existence or not as they please. But they can't bring her into existence and do *less* for her when they could have done *more*. What could be more intuitive than that?

The problem is that a close look at that collection of highly intuitive claims may seem—*seem*—to show that they can't all be true—that consistency requires that at least some of them must go.

Now: what we've said so far isn't—I hope—enough to convince anyone that we face an actual inconsistency or that we have an actual puzzle on our hands.

Things change, however, when we try to *articulate the principles that stand behind those intuitions* and apply those principles uniformly across the case. It's then that we recognize the seriousness of the challenge that we face: how to avoid inconsistency without jettisoning any component of the highly intuitive account of the case we've just given.

3.2 The puzzle

In Chapter 2, I proposed that the existence condition (EC) captures a core component of the basic existential intuition.

> *Existence condition (EC).* Where a future *y* is accessible relative to a future *x*, *x* is *morally worse* than *y*, and a choice made in *x* is *wrong, only if* there is a person *p* such that:
> (i) *p* does or will exist in *x*, *and*
> (ii) *x* is worse for *p* than *y or* there is a *third* accessible future *z* such that *x* is worse for *p* than *z*.

Let's now consider what EC says about how f1 compares against f3. It immediately implies that f1 isn't worse than f3. That's so, since there's *no existing* or *future person*—no *existing or future Charlotte*—in f1 such that f1 is *worse* for that person than any other accessible future is.

EC also instructs that f3 isn't worse than f1. That's so, since there's no person who does or will exist in f3 such that any other accessible future makes things *still better* for that person than they are in f3. Since, in other words, f3 does as much for Charlotte as accessibly *can* be done—since it *maximizes* well-being for Charlotte—and given that no one else's well-being or existence is at stake, EC sees no moral deficiency at all in f3 as compared against f1.

Combining those two results (that f1 isn't worse than f3 and that f3 isn't worse than f1) with a conceptual principle we seem to have no choice but to accept—*trichotomy*, according to which if *x* isn't either better or worse than *y*, then *x* is exactly as good as *y*—we can infer that f1 is exactly as good as f3. So far, so good.

And now let's look at what EC tells us about how f1 compares against *f2*. According to EC, f1 isn't worse than f2. That's so, since there's *no existing* or *future person*—no *existing or future Charlotte*—in f1 such that f1 is *worse* for that person than any other accessible future is.

What EC *doesn't* tell us is how to complete the comparison of f1 against f2. It doesn't tell us that f2 is worse than f1, and it doesn't tell us that it isn't. On that issue, EC is completely silent. EC thus leaves the door open for the result that f2 *is* worse than f1.

It's worth pausing to confirm why that's so. It's cases like the three option case that trigger the more expansive inquiry that EC on occasion requires. We are aiming to compare f2 against f1. According to EC, if f2 is worse than f1, it must be the case that a person who does or will exist in f2 is worse off in f2 than that same person is in still another accessible future—a future that may, *but need not*, be identical to f1. In the three option case, there exists just such a future—f3. Since Charlotte exists in f2 and f2 is worse for Charlotte than f3, EC's necessary condition on f2 being worse than f1 is satisfied. That means that EC never instructs that f2 *isn't* worse than f1. And that's what leaves the door open to the possibility that f2 *is* worse than f1.[2]

But it may well seem that that door is quickly to be slammed shut. After all, is it really credible to claim that f2 is *worse* than f1? When we take a close look at how f2 compares against f1, it seems hard to see anything in f2—any moral deficiency in f2—that would *count against* f2 as compared against f1. f2, after all, changes *nothing* in f1 for *anyone* other than for Charlotte. And f2 clearly does *more for Charlotte* than f1. f2 thus makes things better for at least one person while making things worse for no one at all. Under those conditions, how could f2 possibly be *worse* than f1? As Parfit put

[2] Competing formulations of the basic existential intuition don't remain silent on that question. Those include what Broome calls the *neutrality intuition*, discussed in Section 3.3.1, and what Parfit calls the *person affecting intuition* (Parfit 2017).

it, how could the *mere addition* of a worth-having existence make things worse?

Supporting Parfit's point is the seemingly completely innocuous and unassuming *mere addition principle*, a very modest sufficient condition on a very modest result: not that f2 is *better than* f1, but only that f2 *isn't worse than* f1.

> *Mere addition principle*: Where a future *y* is accessible relative to a future *x*, *y isn't worse than x* (*y* is *at least as good as x*) *if*
> (i) for each person who does or will exist in *x*, *y* is at least as good for that person as *x*, *and*
> (ii) each person who does or will exist in *y* but not in *x*—each *additional* person—is such that that person's existence in *y* is worth having (i.e., *y* isn't *worse* for that person than *x*).

We can now complete the comparison between f1 and f2. According to the mere addition principle, f2 isn't worse than f1; rather, f2 is at least as good as f1.

Combining the results that f1 isn't worse than f2 and that f2 isn't worse than f1 with trichotomy, we infer that f1 is exactly as good as f2.

A quick application of still other conceptually necessary principles—*transitivity* (if *x* is exactly as good as *y* and *y* is exactly as good as *z*, then *x* is exactly as good as *z*) and *symmetry* (if *x* is exactly as good as *y*, then *y* is exactly as good as *x*)—tells us that f2 is exactly as good as f3.

At this point, alarms should sound and red lights flash. For surely f2 *isn't* at all at least as good as f3; surely—as noted earlier—f2 is *worse* than f3. The principle that supports that result—and that gives the Pareto puzzle its name—is the *same people Pareto principle*. We noted that principle in Chapter 2 and just restate it here.

> *Same people Pareto principle*. Where a future *y* is accessible relative to a future *x* and *exactly the same people* do or will exist in *x* and *y*, *x* is *morally worse* than *y* (*y* is *morally better* than *x*) *if*

(i) *x* is worse than *y* for at least one person who does or will exist in *x*, *and*
(ii) *x* is better than *y* for no person who does or will exist in *x*.

Since exactly the same people exist in both f2 and f3, and f3 makes things better for Charlotte than f2 and worse for no one, same people Pareto immediately implies that f2 is *morally worse* than f3. Which is just to say that f3 is *morally better* than f2.

We now do have both an inconsistency and a puzzle—the Pareto puzzle. EC—reflecting the basic *existential* intuition and, a little bit, the basic *maximizing* intuition—is still telling us, loudly and clearly, *both* that f2 and f3 aren't better than f1 *and* that f3 (having maximized well-being for Charlotte) isn't worse than f1. And the *mere addition principle*—so innocuous, so unassuming, so carefully *not* claiming that the additional worth-having existence makes things morally better but merely that it doesn't make things morally worse—is still telling us, loudly and clearly, that f2 isn't worse than f1. The conceptual principles that we've applied—including transitivity and trichotomy—all (for the moment) seem nicely to hold their own as principles we have no choice but to accept. And then same people Pareto steps in to say, loudly and clearly, that f2 is surely *worse* than f3.

It can't be the case both that f2 is exactly as good as f3 and that f2 is worse than f3. Something clearly has gone wrong. But what?

3.3 Attempts to solve the puzzle by tossing out some of the puzzle pieces

3.3.1 Reject the basic existential intuition, reject the existence condition

The Pareto puzzle makes use of some of the same logic that we see in Broome's argument against what he calls the *neutrality intuition.*[3] According to the neutrality intuition, if a person's existence falls within what Broome calls the *neutral range*—if it's, presumably, neither miserable nor glorious—and no one else's well-being or existence is at stake, then the addition of a person to a given future is morally (Broome says *ethically*) neutral, making that future neither morally better nor morally worse.[4]

We can stipulate that Charlotte's existences in both f2 and f3 fall within the neutral range. Given that stipulation, the neutrality intuition, when combined with the conceptual principles we've already put to work and same people Pareto, generates roughly the same argument to inconsistency we produced above.

Broome argues—correctly, I think—that the neutrality intuition is false. But the neutrality intuition—which, for well-being levels that fall within the neutral range, *combines* EC and the mere addition principle—says a lot. It says both that f2 isn't better than f1 and that it isn't worse, and both that f3 isn't better than f1 and that it isn't worse. Which of those several components of the neutrality intuition does Broome mean to target?

Given that Broome explicitly puts the neutrality intuition forward as an interpretation of the Narvesonian idea that *making happy people* isn't the sort of thing that, other things equal, makes things morally *better*,[5] it's not implausible to suppose that the parts of the neutrality intuition that his argument is designed to target are the parts that reflect *that* idea. If that's correct, then his way out is to reject the claims that f1 isn't worse than f2 and that f1 isn't worse than f3—to reject, that is, EC—and to take the position instead that Charlotte's existences in f2 and in f3 makes f2 *or* f3 *or* both *better* than f1.

[3] And in constructing the Pareto puzzle in Section 3.2, I relied on a good portion of the logic that Broome uses in constructing that argument (Broome 2004, 140–150). A distinction? What he sees as a refutation of a certain (highly intuitive) claim, I see as a *puzzle*.

[4] Broome 2004, 145–146.

[5] Broome 2004, 145.

We, of course, could apply that same strategy and thus avoid the inconsistency involved in the Pareto puzzle—the inconsistency laid out in Section 3.2. We could reject the claims that f1 isn't worse than f2 and that f1 isn't worse than f3. We could reject EC. We could instead say that one or the other of f2 and f3—perhaps just f3—is better than f1. And then applying the connection thesis we could say still more: that c2 or c3—perhaps just c3—is permissible and that c1 is wrong.

But that won't solve the puzzle. Broome himself acknowledges that he finds the intuition that "adding a person to the world is very often ethically neutral" "strongly attractive."[6] Now, to be fair, Broome doesn't claim to be in the puzzle-solving business. He's, rather, in the inconsistency-avoiding business.

In contrast, we *are* in the puzzle-solving business *and* the inconsistency-avoiding business.

To avoid the inconsistency, it thus works well to reject EC and to say instead that f2 is better than f1 *or* that f3 is better than f1 *or* that both. Any one of those three options will do the trick. But as solutions to the puzzle, they fail.

Broome's strategy would have us reject not just the neutrality intuition but specifically the *most intuitive parts of the neutrality intuition*—the parts that coincide with EC; the parts reflected in the Narvesonian idea that what we are in favor of is *making people happy*, not *making happy people*; the parts reflected in the basic existential intuition itself. But nothing in Broome's own discussion works to loosen the hold that *those* parts of the neutrality intuition seem clearly to still have on us. The fact that rejecting *those* parts of the neutrality intuition avoids inconsistency *isn't enough*—on its own—to dislodge the intuition that EC itself so nicely captures from our moral consciousness. We would need more. We would need a new platform of deeply held, widely shared intuition that helps us understand just

6 Broome 2004, 143.

where we went wrong in accepting the original intuition to begin with. And that *more* we don't yet have.

This is not a critique of Broome's work. I'm asking for something in this book that there's no reason to think Broome meant to provide: an actual *solution* to the puzzle and not just a way of avoiding an inconsistency.[7]

3.3.2 Reject transitivity of betterness relation

The principles that generate the Pareto puzzle include a handful of conceptual principles that we at least seem to have no choice but to accept. We haven't heretofore questioned those principles. In Temkin's view, however, that was a mistake.[8]

Thus Broome avoids inconsistency by rejecting the neutrality intuition—and, it seems, the *most intuitive parts* of the neutrality intuition: those captured by EC itself; those that say that Charlotte's worth-having existences in f2 and f3 *don't* make f2 or f3 morally better than f1.

In contrast, Temkin aims to retain at least some vestige of those intuitions in what he calls the *essentially comparative approach.*

[7] A distinction between my approach and Broome's—and a distinction that may help to explain in part why he isn't as focused on actually solving the puzzle—is that his main interest is explicitly in how futures (or outcomes or worlds) compare in respect of their overall betterness and less in how choices are to be evaluated. Thus he seems to disavow the connection thesis—and it's when we apply the connection thesis that we obtain the highly counterintuitive results that c3 is *obligatory* and that c1 is *wrong*. But, as noted earlier, he also argues that if "we are offered a concept of relative good, one thing we must be sure of is that it is genuinely a concept of good. It must retain much of the normal meaning of 'good.' Most importantly . . . it must be connected in an appropriate way to how one ought to act" (Broome 2004, 74). I agree. If the connection between the projects becomes too attenuated, it's not clear in respect of *what* we are aiming to rank futures.

For still another concern raised by Broome's argument against the neutrality intuition, see Appendix C.

[8] The suggestion I have outlined here for how Temkin might address the three option case isn't the suggestion Temkin himself outlined in Temkin 2012. The suggestion I outline here, rather, extrapolates from what Temkin says about a closely related problem,

And—as noted earlier[9]—he thinks that, as a pluralist, he can do that while also giving voice to what he calls the *internal aspects approach*, an approach that—like the traditional total view—values the maximization of aggregate well-being.

But to achieve both those goals—within the confines of consistency—there's a price to be paid. And that price, according to Temkin, is the *transitivity* of what he calls the *all-things-considered betterness relation.*

To see what a Temkinian account of the three option case might look like, let's start with the claims that f2 and f3 *aren't* better than f1. Those claims would seem to have the support of Temkin's essentially comparative approach, given its focus on how *particular* people fare across an array of futures in which they do or will exist.[10] Since Charlotte never exists in f1, the essentially comparative approach can take the position that f2 and f3 aren't better than f1—that f1 is at least as good as f2 and f3.

Could f2 or f3 be *worse* than f1 on Temkin's view? Temkin seems to think not. While he raises questions in other contexts about both the mere addition principle and the same people Pareto principle, he doesn't challenge the idea that f2 and f3 are each *at least as good as* f1.[11] And the position that both f2 and f3 are at least as good as f1 would seem to find support in the intrinsic aspects approach, which surely includes the idea that, absent other factors, bringing about more well-being in the aggregate *isn't* something that makes things *worse.*

Finally, we turn to whether f2 is worse than f3. Here, the essentially comparative approach and the intrinsic aspects approach

the *mere addition paradox* (Temkin 2012, 364–383). My reason for making that switch is that it's my understanding that Temkin himself has renounced his 2012 account of the three option case—which account would *allow* us to retain transitivity—and that he now favors the sort of account I attribute, by extrapolation, to him here.

[9] See Section 1.6 (Temkin; plurality of values).

[10] Temkin 2012, 416–422.

[11] Neither the mere addition principle nor same people Pareto are principles that Temkin categorically accepts. When, for example, mere addition, or the fact that one

would seem to agree that (again), absent other factors, f2 is indeed worse than f3.

Those claims in hand, application of the same old conceptual principles we deployed earlier—including transitivity—now generates the same old inconsistency: that f2 is exactly as good as f3 *and* that f2 is worse than f3.

But now the crux of Temkin's proposal: we can avoid the inconsistency if we simply reject *transitivity*, a conceptual principle that we may have accepted out of habit and without any clear ground. So let's (he proposes) reject transitivity.

Temkin's broader point? *Nontransitivity* is a position that is itself made at least tenable once we accept a plurality of values approach, an approach that Temkin himself considers capable of generating highly plausible accounts not just for the three option case but also for a wide array of still other variable population cases, including perhaps the most recalcitrant of them all: the repugnant conclusion case.[12]

Problems with nontransitivity. A solution to the puzzle that requires us to reject transitivity seems highly problematic. I'll outline three concerns here.

(a) If the rejection of transitivity is rooted in a plurality of values approach, then, as noted in Section 1.6, that approach as it's been developed to date is hard to test and just as hard to apply in the context of any concrete case.

Thus in this Section 3.3.2 I have only *speculated* what a plurality of values account of the three option case would look like.

person is made better off at no cost to anyone else, creates a significant *inequality*, Temkin's plurality of values approach may reject the results of the relevant principle. In the present context, however, we can easily imagine that the people who do or will exist beyond Charlotte have well-being levels that are all over the place: some closer to what Charlotte has in f2 and some closer to what she has in f3. In that context, it seems that Temkin would hold that both principles reflect values that his account of all things considered betterness would need to reflect.

[12] See Temkin 2012, 217–230.

Temkin is clearly on the record as having rejected transitivity. But beyond that we can't with any certainty say much else. Just to take one example: for all we know, the fact that aggregate well-being is significantly greater in f3 than in f1 may *swamp* the fact that f3 makes things better for no one who does or will exist in f1.

(b) *Can* we really reject transitivity? Is that move really within our conceptual repertoire? Once we conclude that (as Temkin puts it) f2 is *all things considered* at least as good as f1 and that f3 is *all things considered* better than f2, it is still very unclear just why—even if the betterness relation is *complex*, even if the plurality of values approach is *correct*—we aren't then *compelled* to conclude that f3 is *all things considered* better than f1.

Transitivity seems to take over at some point in the analysis of the three option case *regardless* of any mental resistance we try to get going against it in our own little minds. Transitivity, in other words, remains one of those conceptual principles we seem to have no choice but to accept. As such, it remains a piece of the puzzle.

What the account needs to get over this hurdle is a new platform of deeply held, widely shared intuition—one that would serve to loosen the hold that the deeply held, widely shared intuition of transitivity continues to have on us.

(c) Why are we so reluctant to reject transitivity? One reason may be that we appreciate, at some very deep level, just how problematic *nontransitivity* would be for our moral theorizing. Thus the account of moral betterness that includes transitivity protects against the risk of *cycling*: of turning the do-gooder into a money pump, the agent who pays \$5 to bring about *y* over *x* (because *x* is worse) and another \$5 to bring *z* about over *y* (because *y* is worse) and another \$5 to bring about *x* over *z* (because *z* is worse)—and ending up back at *x*, exactly where we started, with the do-gooder *both* \$15 poorer without having done any good at all *and* on a hamster wheel (back at x, with y still there advertising its moral betterness relative to x, the do-gooder cycles yet again. And again. And again . . .).[13]

This is not to argue that nontransitivity *necessarily* leads to cycling: that principles *can't* be fashioned and added to the account that would block the sort of cycling involved in the simple case I've just described. But we need those principles.

3.3.3 Reject trichotomy in favor of incommensurability

Like Temkin, Rabinowicz aims to preserve the *most intuitive parts* of the neutrality intuition: those captured by EC itself, those that say that Charlotte's worth-having existences in f2 and f3 *don't* make f2 or f3 morally better than f1.

And, like Temkin, Rabinowicz proposes that we avoid inconsistency by rejecting one of the conceptual principles that we seem to have no choice but to accept. But for Rabinowicz, it's trichotomy, not transitivity, that is the weak link.

According to trichotomy, we are limited to three possible claims in determining how two futures compare against each other in respect of their moral betterness: that the one future is *worse than* the other, that it's *better than* the other, and that it's *exactly as good as* the other. The better view, according to Rabinowicz, is that there exists a fourth possibility: that the one future is *incommensurate* with the other.

In fact, Rabinowicz considers cases like the three option case to ground a plausible argument against trichotomy. Thus, in response to such cases—cases, that is, in which inconsistencies arise when we try to say, for example, that two futures that contain additional existences at different well-being levels within the neutral

[13] Temkin discusses money pump challenges but doesn't directly counter (but rather seems to accept as potentially not irrational) the money pumping that I've described here (Temkin 2012, 183–193).

range are both *exactly as good as* a future without those additions—Rabinowicz writes that the "obvious answer is that the world with added people at neutral levels *must be incommensurate* with the world without those additions."[14]

Now, as a matter of definition, a future *x* is *incommensurate* with a future *y if and only if x isn't* worse than *y* and *x isn't* better than *y* and *x isn't* exactly as good as *y*. But as a substantive matter what triggers incommensurability is any scenario in which the additional worth-having existence is a *mere* addition—when the addition doesn't make things better or worse for anyone other than the person whose existence is at stake. Under those conditions, the future "with added people at neutral levels *must be incommensurate* with the [future] without these additions."

A plus of the principle just stated—let's call it the *additional person incommensurability principle*—is that we can readily see what it says about the three option case. It immediately implies both that f2 is incommensurate with f1 and that f3 is incommensurate with f1. That means, by definition, that f2 *isn't* better than f1 and f3 *isn't* better than f1, and that f1 *isn't* better than f2 and that f1 *isn't* better than f3.

What the incommensurability approach *denies* is that those facts together prove that f1 is exactly as good as f2 or that f1 is exactly as good as f3. That's so, given that the fact that *x* isn't better than *y* and *y* isn't better than *x* isn't enough, once we reject trichotomy, to establish that *x* is exactly as good as *y*. We thus never get to the problem result (via, among other principles, transitivity) that f2 is exactly as good as f3.

Moreover, while Rabinowicz accepts transitivity for the standard three betterness relations (*x* is *better than y*, *x* is *worse than y*, and *x* is *exactly as good as y*), transitivity *isn't* preserved for the relation of incommensurateness. We thus never get to the problematic result

[14] Rabinowicz 2009 (emphasis added).

that f2 is incommensurate with f3. We are thus free to accept—per same people Pareto—that f3 is better than f2.

Problems with rejecting trichotomy. (a) I noted earlier that one concern I have about the incommensurability approach is whether we *can* really reject trichotomy. Is that move really within the purview of our conceptual capabilities? If *x* isn't better than *y* (if *y* is at least as good as *x*) and *x* isn't worse than *y* (if *x* is at least as good as *y*), how can *x not* be *exactly as good as y*? *Where else is there to go*?

(b) A related concern: it's true that we avoid inconsistency if we, as Rabinowicz proposes, reject trichotomy. But that in itself doesn't solve the Pareto puzzle. For us to accept the incommensurability approach as a solution to the puzzle, we would need to understand what it is about addition that is so special—that so *disables* us from making the sorts of comparisons we often readily can make in same-people cases. *Why* does the mere addition of a person to a future take us beyond any of the three relations that trichotomy itself prescribes and in the direction of a conceptually difficult relation that is most precisely spelled out for us in terms that are themselves entirely negative (if *x* is incommensurate with *y*, then *x isn't* better than or worse than or exactly as good as *y*)?

To say that variable population cases—like the three option case, like the two cases that make up the asymmetry—have challenged moral philosophers to the limits of their patience doesn't answer that question. Until we answer that question of *what makes addition so special* we will not have actually *solved* the puzzle.

(c) If two futures are incommensurate in value, then surely the one future's value is at least *in the same vicinity as*—though not identical to—the other future's value. It seems we need to say *something* like that since, if the distance between the moral values of the two futures were very great—at least as great as or greater than some distance D— then the one future would be either better or worse than the other.

But that way of understanding the fourth relation seems not to work. Consider two *fully commensurate* futures *x* and *y*. Those two futures contain exactly the same people but *x* makes things *much better* for a certain collection of people, and worse for no one at all, than *y*. On those grounds—and we can add whatever details to the case we need to add to make sure that this next stipulation clearly holds—we can say that *x* is *much better* than *y*, that the value of *x* is *much greater* than the value of *y*, that the distance in moral value between *x* and *y* is—let's say—not just D but *three times D*.

But now consider a third future *z*, a future just like *x* and *y except* that the collection of people *x* is better for than *y never exist at all in z*. Given those facts, additional person incommensurability implies that *z* is incommensurate with both *x* and *y*.

If that means that the value of *z* is *in the vicinity of* the value of *x and also* in the vicinity of the value of *y*, then we have a problem. Consider Figure 3.3.3.

Figure 3.3.3: Geometry of incommensurability

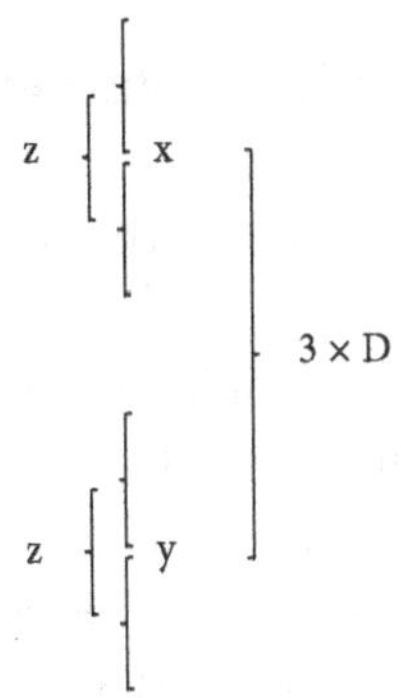

Figure 3.3.3 Geometry of incommensurability

The tall right-hand bracket indicates the clear distinction in the moral values of *x* and *y*. The multiple shorter left-hand brackets are meant to show that *z isn't* better than, worse than, or exactly as good as *x*. We don't want to say that the value of *z* is "jumping around"—we just want to show that it's *in the vicinity of* the value of *x* but still *incommensurate* with the value of *x*. Ditto for *y*.

But if the value of *z* is *both in the vicinity of* the value of *x and also in the vicinity of* the value of *y*, then, since *x*'s value is itself very far apart (three times D apart) from *y*'s value, it will turn out that *z's value* is *not* in the same vicinity of *z's value* (*z*'s value being *both* in the same vicinity as *x*'s much higher value *and* in the same vicinity as *y*'s much lower value). And that, surely, can't happen: *z*'s value isn't merely in the *same vicinity as z*'s value: it's *identical* to *z*'s value.

What I've just said about the case I've just described likely presumes more in the way of geometry than the incommensurability proposal itself anticipates, which means that the case doesn't show us much at all about whether we should reject incommensurability. But it does show that the incommensurability proposal is conceptually challenging. But we already knew that—and Rabinowicz would likely be the first to acknowledge that that's so.

3.4 The Pareto minus solution to the Pareto puzzle

3.4.1 A skeptical look at the mere addition principle

What role does the mere addition principle play in generating the Pareto puzzle? Let's first note that we don't *need* that principle to generate the result that f3 is at least as good as f1 (i.e., that f3 isn't worse than f1). Thus EC itself, as we have seen, tells us both that f3 isn't worse than f1 and that f1 isn't worse than f3. Conceptually necessary principles then step in to complete the picture: f1 is exactly as good as f3.

EC also tells us, as we have also seen, that f1 isn't worse than f2—that is, that f1 is at least as good as f2.

What EC *doesn't* tell us is that f2 isn't worse than f1—that is, that f2 is at least as good as f1.[15] For that result, the mere addition principle is critical. And, as we've seen, once we have that result, conceptual principles then generate the result that f1 is exactly as good as f2. At that point, we are well on our way to inconsistency.

As noted earlier, the mere addition principle itself is seemingly completely innocuous. It's so unassuming, so carefully *not* claiming that the additional worth-having existence makes things morally *better* but *only* that it *doesn't* make things morally *worse*! Again from Parfit: How can the *mere addition* of the worth-having existence make things *worse*? How can the worth-having existence of the additional person Charlotte in f2 make f2 *worse* than f1?

The mere addition principle says that it *can't*. The purpose of this Section 3.4.1 is to lay out an intuitive foundation for the position that it *can*.

If we can *come to understand* that the idea that f2 *isn't* worse than f1 is a mistake—if we can *accept* that it's false that f2 isn't worse than f1; not just *deem* it false, but it *accept* it as false—then we can avoid inconsistency *without* throwing away any of the puzzle pieces. The claim that f2 isn't worse than f1—that f2 is at least as good as f1—will no longer be a piece of the puzzle.

Of course, to reject the claim that f2 isn't worse than f1 is to reject the mere addition principle. Thus for this strategy to work we shall also need, not just to *deem* that principle false, but also to *accept* that principle as false. We will need to come to understand just *why*

[15] We made that point earlier and can simply restate it here. Since a person—Charlotte—exists in f2, and f2 is worse for Charlotte than *some accessible future or another*—namely, f3—EC's necessary condition on f2's being worse than f1 is satisfied. The requirement under EC for one future to be worse than a second thus isn't that a person exists and is worse off in the one future than in the second, *but rather* that the person exists and is worse off in the one future than in some *third* future, where that third future can, *but need not*, be identical to the second. That, in turn, leaves EC with nothing at all to say on the question whether f2 is *worse* than f1.

the mere addition principle fails on those occasions when it does fail and just *where* it goes wrong.

Two points work to dislodge the mere addition principle from our moral consciousnesses. (a) The narrow inquiry that the mere addition principle employs to reach the result that f2 isn't worse than f1 seems, on inspection, *arbitrarily* narrow. Why *not*, in comparing f1 against f2, take into account what is going on in f3? How can the appreciation of *more* of the details of a particular case render our moral analysis of that case *less* credible? And (b) the mere addition principle itself—*seemingly* so innocuous, so unassuming, so carefully *not* claiming that the additional worth-having existence makes things morally *better* but *only* that it *doesn't* make things morally *worse*—in fact packs a very hard punch.

Here, we take up points (a) and (b) in turn.

(a) *Arbitrary to bar the more expansive inquiry.* Let's start by noting why someone might *mistakenly* think that, having accepted that f3 is at least as good as f1, we should also automatically accept that f2 is at least as good as f1.

It's part of the three option case that Charlotte's existence in f3 is worth having. Which is not to say that her life in f3 is *perfect.* Let's suppose it isn't—that into Charlotte's life, just like any other life, some rain must fall; that things *could* be better for her than they are in f3. We *don't* think that that's enough to show that f3 is *morally worse* than f1. Comparing f3 against f1, we see no moral deficiency in f3 that could credibly account for the result that f3 is *worse* than f1. We may think—the basic existential intuition and EC at work—that it's not *morally better.* But we don't think it's *morally worse.*

We can now just note that *everything* we've just said about how f3 compares against f1 also applies to the question how f2 compares against f1. After all, it's part of the case that Charlotte's existence in f2 is worth having. It isn't *perfect*—things *could* be better for her than they are—but neither is her existence in f3. Just as we, in comparing f3 against f1, see no moral deficiency in f3 that could credibly account for the result that f3 is worse than f1, we now, comparing f2 against f1, seem to see no moral deficiency in f2 that could credibly account for the result that f2 is worse than f1. We may think—again, the basic existential intuition and EC at work—that it's not *better*. But we may also seem to have no grounds for thinking that it's *worse*.

Thus it might seem that what we say about how f2 compares against f1 should automatically track what we say about how f3 compares against f1.

In fact, however, a more expansive inquiry—simply glancing up from the cursory comparison of f2 against f1 that we've just completed—immediately underlines a clear distinction between f2 and f3.

It's true that for both f2 and f3 there's a *logically possible* future in which Charlotte's wellbeing is greater than it is in f2 and greater even than it is in f3. The distinction between f2 and f3 is that it's part of the case that such a *logically possible* future in which things are better for Charlotte is *accessible* relative to f2 but *not* relative to f3. While more *can* accessibly be done for Charlotte in f2, more *can't* accessibly be done for Charlotte in f3. A future in which Charlotte has a stunningly good life that goes on forever is *logically possible* relative to f3. But such a future—given science, given the laws of physics—remains entirely *inaccessible* relative to f3.

Now, we may willfully blind ourselves to that distinction *if* we are convinced that in comparing one future against a second future we have no need at all even to glance at what is going on in any third future. The problem with that blindered view is that the moral deficiency in f2 comes into relief, not when we compare f2 against f1, but only when we compare f2 against f3. (More precisely—and we return to this point in Section 3.5—it comes into relief only when we take a close enough look at f2 to see that f3 exists as an accessible future relative to f2. For now, however, plainer terms will do.) We then have to question why that moral deficiency *doesn't count against* f2 for purposes, not just of comparing f2 against f3, but also of comparing f2 against f1.

It is not as though the moral deficiency we see in f2 when we take into account what is going on in *f3 just goes away* when we return to the task we started with—that of comparing f2 against f1. That deficiency *doesn't come and go* as we shift our attention back and forth between comparing f2 against f3 and comparing f2 against f1. Yes, it's when we compare f2 against f3 that the deficiency jumps out at us. But the deficiency is *there to stay* whether we happen at the moment to be comparing f2 against f3 or not.

The upshot for the mere addition principle is this: As soon as we recognize that a more expansive inquiry, one that has us compare f1 against f2 *with an eye on* f3, may produce different results than the blindered inquiry insisted on by the mere addition principle, the mere addition principle itself is thrown into question. As is the result that had only the support of the mere addition principle to begin with: the result that f2 isn't worse than f1. Both rest firmly on an *assumption* that the preceding discussion shows that we must *seriously doubt*: that the comparison of f2 against f1 can proceed by taking into account *just* what is going on with Charlotte in f1 and f2 and *without* taking into account what is going on with Charlotte in f3.

Now, we can still conclude that, *if* the mere addition principle is true, then f2 *isn't* worse than f1. But that *conditional* conclusion isn't what we would need to generate the inconsistency—or the puzzle. Can we produce a good argument for the mere addition principle at all beyond the fact that it seems on its face so innocuous, unassuming, so modest? Can we produce a good argument for the *unconditional* result that f2 isn't worse than f1? It's not clear that we can.

(b) *Mere addition principle implies Pareto plus.* The mere addition principle may well seem completely innocuous and unassuming on its face. After all, it's capable only of generating the result that, other things equal, the addition of the worth-having existence doesn't make things *worse*. It will *never* try to tell us that that additional existence makes things *better*.

In contrast, consider a much stronger principle we can call *Pareto plus.*[16] Pareto plus and the mere addition principle apply under the same conditions. But where the mere addition principle would tell us only that f2 *isn't worse than* f1—that Charlotte's existence in f2 *doesn't* make f2 worse than f1—Pareto plus tells that f2 *is better than* f1; that is, that Charlotte's *nonexistence* in f1 makes f1 *worse* than f2.

> *Pareto plus principle.* Where a future *y* is accessible relative to a future *x*, *y is better than x* (*x* is *worse than y*) *if*
> (i) for each person who does or will exist in *x*, *y* is at least as good for that person as *x*, *and*
> (ii) each person who does or will exist in *y* but not in *x*—each *additional* person—is such that that person's existence in *y* is worth having (i.e., *y* isn't *worse* for that person than *x*).

The contrast between the weaker mere addition principle and the stronger Pareto plus may mollify us into thinking that the assumption of the mere addition principle *isn't* really anything we want or need to challenge. After all, Pareto plus explicitly contradicts EC as well as the basic existential intuition itself and the most intuitive parts of the neutrality intuition. Where EC implies that f1 *isn't* worse than f2, Pareto plus implies that f1 *is* worse than f2.

We could therefore quite reasonably challenge Pareto plus on the ground that it *begs the question against* EC. But we couldn't, it may well seem, challenge the *mere addition principle* on that same ground. The mere addition principle doesn't *seem* to contradict EC at all. Thus, where the mere addition principle asserts that f2 *isn't* worse than f1, EC *doesn't* assert that f2 *is* worse than f1. Instead, EC is *completely silent* on that point. There's no contradiction between

[16] Dasgupta 1993.

the claim, on the one hand, that f2 isn't worse than f1 and, on the other, silence.[17]

Thus it was a surprise to me to see that the mere addition principle a few steps into its own logic *in fact does* directly contradict EC and, thus begs the question against EC, just as effectively as Pareto plus does.[18]

To make that point, we'll prove the conditional that, if the mere addition principle is true, then EC is false. And we'll prove that conditional by, first, assuming that the mere addition principle is true. We'll then make the further assumption that EC is *true*. Since—as we'll see—that further assumption leads to inconsistency, we'll know that that further assumption must have been *false*. And we'll then know, too, that, if the mere addition principle is true, then EC is false.

1.	Mere addition principle	Assumption for conditional proof
2.	f2 isn't worse than f1	(1), facts of three option case
3.	f3 isn't worse than f1	(1), facts of three option case
4.	EC	Assumption for *reductio ad absurdum*
5.	f1 isn't worse than f2	(4), facts of three option case
6.	f1 isn't worse than f3	(4), facts of three option case
7.	f1 is exactly as good as f2	(2), (5), conceptual necessity
8.	f1 is exactly as good as f3	(3), (6), conceptual necessity
9.	f2 is exactly as good as f3	(7), (8), conceptual necessity
10.	f2 is worse than f3	Same people Pareto
11.	Inconsistency	(9), (10)
12.	EC is false	(4)–(11), conclusion of *reductio*

Therefore,

13.	If the mere addition principle is true, then EC is false	(1)–(12), conclusion of conditional proof

[17] The fact that Broome and Parfit appeal, not to Pareto plus, but to the seemingly—*seemingly*—innocuous mere addition principle is part of what makes their arguments so interesting.

[18] See Roberts 2020, 76.

The upshot? If we accept the mere addition principle, we must reject EC.

Of course, in proving that conditional, we've relied on same people Pareto and various conceptual principles that we seem to have no choice but to accept, including transitivity and trichotomy. We've already seen the difficulties we face if we reject those conceptual principles, and nothing we've seen gives us any reason (and I think we have no reason) to reject same people Pareto. The upshot is clear: the mere addition principle contradicts—and begs the question against—EC just as effectively as Pareto plus does.

We've established that the mere addition principle and Pareto plus are *of a piece*: they both quite effectively—though the mere addition principle does so more quietly—rule out EC and thus the basic existential intuition. Once we realize that that's so, it seems clear that the mere addition principle isn't, after all, one of the puzzle pieces we are bound to fit together for purposes of solving the Pareto puzzle. The mere addition principle is no more a piece of the puzzle than Pareto plus itself.

A second, related proof makes the point that, *completely independently* of whether the mere addition principle begs the question against EC, the mere addition principle implies some surprisingly strong Pareto plus-type results, showing, yet again, that the mere addition principle isn't innocuous at all—that it, instead, packs a very hard punch.

This time, the conditional to be established (now *without* the help of EC) is that, if the mere addition principle is true, so are the Pareto plus results that f1 is worse than both f2 and f3 (i.e., that f2 and f3 are each better than f1). All we need is the additional supposition that, under Pareto plus, the claim that f3 is better than f1 and the claim that f2 is better than f1 are *related*—and specifically that, if one of the two claims Pareto plus supports is false, so is the other.

1.	Mere addition principle	Assumption for conditional proof
2.	f2 isn't worse than f1	(1), facts of three option case
3.	f3 isn't worse than f1	(1), facts of three option case
4.	Pareto plus is false	Assumption for *reductio ad absurdum*
5.	f2 isn't better than f1	(4), supposition noted above
6.	f3 isn't better than f1	(4), supposition noted above
7.	f2 is exactly as good as f1	(2), (5), conceptual necessity
8.	f3 is exactly as good as f1	(3), (6), conceptual necessity
9.	f2 is exactly as good as f3	(7), (8), conceptual necessity
10.	f2 is worse than f3	Same people Pareto
11.	Inconsistency	(9), (10)
12.	Pareto plus is true	(4)–(11), completion of *reductio*

Therefore,

13.	If the mere addition principle is true, so is Pareto plus	(1)–(12), completion of conditional proof

The supposition that justifies the inference from (4) to both (5) and (6) in place, the mere addition principle turns out to be a *far stronger principle* than its meek presentation might have been taken to suggest: it still yields that either f2 or f3 *is morally better* than f1, a result that on its own directly contradicts and arguably begs the question against EC and, in any case, goes far beyond the innocuous, unassuming result that we thought it had committed us to: merely that f2 and f3 *aren't morally worse* than f1.

Important puzzles are interesting puzzles, and interesting puzzles start with cases we can understand and claims and principles that strike us as highly intuitive. But by now it should be clear that the mere addition principle doesn't meet that high bar. Maybe it *seemed* almost trivial starting out. (And maybe that's why it worked its way into Broome's own neutrality intuition without comment.) But on further inspection it's clear that the mere addition principle is far more than what meets the eye: *if* we accept it, we are on the hook to accept Pareto plus or its close kin as well.

3.4.2 When the additional worth-having existence makes things worse

The mere addition principle at first may seem highly innocuous. However, between noticing the mere addition principle's arbitrarily narrow perspective and realizing just how far out on the limb in the direction of Pareto plus the mere addition principle actually goes, we are now in a position to resist that principle.

We can now say that, on occasion, even when nothing at all changes for anyone else, bringing the additional person into a worth-having existence can make things *morally worse*. That recognition forms the core of what I'll call the *Pareto minus* solution to the Pareto puzzle.

The Pareto minus solution accepts that making things better for a person often makes things morally *better*. It accepts the same people Pareto principle and thus that f3 is better than f2 (that f2 is worse than f3).

And it accepts that, sometimes, making things better for a person leaves things morally *as they are*. It accepts EC and thus that f1 and f2 aren't worse than f3 *and* that f3 isn't worse than f1. Applying, then, various conceptual principles that we seem to have no choice but to accept—principles that the Pareto minus solution itself accepts—we infer that f1 is exactly as good as f3.

What the Pareto minus solution now notes is that, sometimes, making things better for a person makes things morally *worse*. And thus f2 is worse than f1.

On what grounds?

The results we've just noted—that f1 is exactly as good as f3 and f2 is worse than f3—in combination with still other conceptually necessary principles together entail that f2 is indeed worse than f1. While f1, then, is exactly as good as f3, f2 is worse than both.

The connection thesis allows us to say still more: that c1 and c3 are both permissible and that c2 is wrong.

Thus we permissibly can, other things equal, bring the additional child Charlotte into existence or not. But it would be wrong to bring Charlotte into existence and make things worse for her when we could have made things better. What could be more intuitively exactly right than that?

But, now, on top of preserving our intuitions, we have also avoided the seemingly intransigent inconsistency. EC—given the more expansive inquiry it requires in order to produce any results at all—*never gets* to the problem result that f2 *isn't* worse than f1—that f2 is at least as good as f1. It *never gets* to the problem result *required* under the (now rejected) mere addition principle or indeed under Broome's neutrality intuition. Thus, a highly intuitive and perfectly consistent account of the three option case.[19]

3.5 Objection and reply: Doesn't the Pareto minus solution violate the principle of the independence of irrelevant alternatives?

According to the *principle of the independence of irrelevant alternatives*, any comparison between possible worlds or futures *x*

[19] The Pareto minus solution to the Pareto puzzle comports perfectly with the results we can obtain from what we can call the *loss distinction thesis*. For further discussion, see Appendix B. For earlier discussions of Broome's argument against the neutrality intuition, see Roberts 1998 and Roberts 2003b.

and *y* is to be completed on the basis of features *internal* to *x* and *y*—that is, *independent* of information regarding the features included in any possible third future *z*. If it's been determined, for a given case that includes *x*, *y*, and *z* as possible futures, that *y* is worse than *x*, then *subtracting z* from the case—eliminating *z* as a possible future—will not *change* that original determination.

The independence principle, thought to capture a basic feature of rationality, is sometimes motivated by cases bordering on the trite. Thus, if you find that you prefer (on a given occasion, in a given case) vanilla ice cream over chocolate and you are then informed that pistachio, too, is available, you might rationally choose the pistachio over the vanilla *and* the chocolate (though, ugh). But what you *can't rationally* do, when informed that pistachio, too, is available, is switch your preference from *vanilla* over *chocolate* to *chocolate* over *vanilla*. If you are rational, your ranking of *vanilla* over *chocolate* doesn't *depend* on whether you happen to learn that *pistachio* is available or not.

Does the Pareto minus solution to our puzzle violate the independence principle? At first glance, it might seem that it does. After all, EC requires us, in comparing f2 against f1, to take into account—to keep an eye on—what is going on with Charlotte in f3. According to EC, how f2 compares against f1 *depends* on what is going on with Charlotte in f3. But the independence principle seems to say that what is going on in f3 *can't bear on—can't be relevant to*—how f2 compares against f1.

The independence principle thus *rules out*—as outside the bounds of rationality and indeed as arguably inconsistent—the position that (i) f2 *is* worse than f1 in case in which f3 *is* an accessible alternate future but (ii) f2 *isn't* worse than f1 in the (very distinct) case in which f3 *isn't* an accessible alternate future.

We've already seen that the Pareto minus solution endorses (i). The *two option case* (Figure 3.5) shows why the principles that make up that solution might seem to endorse (ii) as well.

Figure 3.5: Two option case		
	c1	c2
probability →	1	1
wellbeing ↓	f1	f2
+10		
+5		**Charlotte**
+0	*Charlotte*	

Figure 3.5 Two option case

EC tells us that f1 isn't worse than f2. But, now that f3 isn't in the picture, EC's necessary condition on when f2 is worse than f1 is failed (there being no existing or future person in f2 such that any other accessible future is better for that person than f2). We can then infer that f2 isn't worse than f1. Conceptual principles that we seem to have no choice but to accept then complete the picture: f1 *is exactly as good as* f2.

The two cases together may seem to show a violation of Independence. When f3 *doesn't* exist as an alternate accessible future, we decide that f2 *isn't* worse than f1 and in fact that f1 *is* exactly as good as f2. When f3 *does* exist as an alternate accessible future, we decide that f2 *is* worse than f1 (i.e., is *not* exactly as good as f1). How we compare f1 against f2 seems clearly to depend on whether f3 exists as an alternate accessible future or not.

Reply. Let's back up. The pairwise comparisons we are interested in completing are not between simple *distributions of well-being across particular populations* but rather between *possible worlds* or *futures* in *all their detail.*

But to change—to "change"—*even a single detail* in a given possible world or future is to change *futures.* That's so in virtue of the fact that possible futures have all their properties *necessarily.* The possible future in which you wear your *old* Grateful Dead t-shirt to teach next Thursday is a *distinct future* from the possible future in which you instead wear your *new* Grateful Dead t-shirt to teach next Thursday, *even if* the distribution of well-being across the population and the populations themselves are *identical* between the two futures.[20] After all, if we know nothing else, we know that there's no *one* possible future in which you *both* wear your old Grateful Dead t-shirt to class on that particular Thursday and don't wear that same shirt to that same class on that same Thursday.

That thought in mind, let's just recall what it is to say that one future is *accessible* relative to another. The relation in question being that of *moral* betterness, to say that a future *y* is *accessible* relative to a future *x* is to say that the agents in *x* (whether working as individuals or in groups, and whether in collaboration or not) have the ability, the power, the resources to bring about *y* in place of *x*. Thus, the future in which I instantly cure a child's terrible disease by clapping my hands, though certainly a *possible* future (a *logically* and *metaphysically* possible future), isn't an *accessible* future relative to the actual future. In contrast, the future in which I wade into a pond and save a drowning child *is* perfectly accessible to me.[21] Whether or not I in fact *choose* to make that future unfold or *want* to make that future unfold or (counterfactually) *would* instead have made some *still worse* future unfold in place of *that* future if barred from making the future I happen to prefer unfold, I have the ability, the power, the resources to wade into the pond and save the child.

Accordingly, to say that f3 is *accessible* relative to f1 in the three option case is just to say that agents in f1 have the ability, the power, the resources to bring about f3: to bring Charlotte into existence and make things better for her than they are in f2. To say that f3

[20] On that basis, we can then explain what it means to say things like "X *might* be true, but X *might* be false": it's to say there is some possible future at which X is true, and there's some other possible future at which X isn't true.

[21] Singer 2009 uses the case not to demonstrate the accessibility relation but rather to give a clear example of some of the moral obligations we intuitively consider ourselves to have. But part of the reason he can so persuasively argue that we ought to wade into the pond to rescue the child is that that's something we *accessibly* can do.

isn't accessible relative to f1 in the two option case is to say that agents in f1 *don't* have that ability. But—as the t-shirt case shows—to "change" even one little thing about a given future is to change *futures*. Agents in f1 *can't* both *have* the ability to bring about f3 and *not* have the ability to bring about f3. f3 *can't* be both *accessible* relative to f1 and *not* accessible relative to f1.

Ditto f2: f2 can't be both *accessible* relative to f1 and *not* accessible relative to f1.

Does this mean we've contradicted ourselves? No. It just means that we need to clean up our language. The "f1" we are making a claim about in the three option case and the "f1" we are making a claim about in the two option case *aren't* one and the same future. And the same is so for "f2."

To clean up our language—to adopt a more precise vocabulary—is to introduce distinct names for our two cases. And that's easy to do: we'll stay with f1 and f2 for purposes of talking about the three option case and introduce f1* and f2* for purposes of talking about the two option case.

We now have the resources to make sure that our accounts of our two cases are not mutually inconsistent—a first step toward rationality. We can consistently take the position *both* that, for the three option case and given the accessibility of f3, Charlotte's existence in f2, per the Pareto minus solution, *does* make f2 worse than f1 *and* that, for the two option case and now without any "f3" in the picture, Charlotte's existence in f2* *doesn't* make f2* worse than f1*.

Now, the independence principle on its face requires more than mere consistency. It also requires the following: that the determination of whether f2 is worse than f1 be settled *solely* by reference to features *internal* to f2 and f1; that whether f2 is worse than f1 or not is *independent* of features of any further alternate accessible future f3.

But the work that we've just done to show that the Pareto minus solution is consistent also shows that that solution isn't in violation of that further requirement. After all, the accessibility of f3 relative to f1 and f2 in the three option case is a *feature of f1 and f2*—it's a feature *built into* f1 and f2 and a feature reflecting the fact that agents in f1 and f2 have the ability, the power, the resources to bring about f3 in place of f2. And possible futures, as we've already noted, have all their features *necessarily*.

Those points together entail what we can call the *accessibility axiom*:

> *Accessibility axiom*: For any two possible futures x and y, if y is accessible relative to x, then *necessarily* y is accessible relative to x.

The accessibility axiom, in turn, tells us something about still other cases, including the two option case: that it *just can't happen* that f2 *is* worse than f1 when f3 *is* accessible *and* f2 *isn't* worse than f1 when f3 *isn't* accessible. For it *just can't happen* that, relative to f1 and f2, f3 *isn't* accessible.

To put the point another way: the morally critical features of f1 and f2 provide us with all the information we need to complete the comparison of f2 against f1—including the fact that, relative to f1 and f2, f3 is accessible. Thus to say that we need to "keep an eye on f3" when comparing f2 against f1 is just a heuristic: a reminder not to blind ourselves to any of the morally critical details of our case as we complete our comparison. To "keep an eye on f3" *just is* to attend to all the morally critical details of the three option case, including the accessibility of f3 relative to f1 and f2.

Clearly, the concept of *accessibility* is doing much of the work here. We have relied on that concept to show that the Pareto minus solution both avoids inconsistency and satisfies the independence principle. That strategy, however, raises the following very general question: Why *accessibility* rather than *possibility*?

Consider, again, whether f1 is exactly as good as f3 in the three option case. EC says that it is, there being no further accessible future that makes things better for Charlotte than f3. What happens if we amend EC's necessary condition to require, not just that there exists no further better-for-Charlotte *accessible* future, but instead that there exists no further better-for-Charlotte *possible* future? EC then would remain silent: for there will always be a further *possible* future, a future consistent with the demands of *logic*, in which things are better for Charlotte than they are in f3. (However inconsistent with the demands of the laws of nature and however limited the ability, the power, the resources of the agents, Charlotte's having a longer life, or a happier life, or both, remains a *logical* possibility.) If we want to retain the connection thesis—the idea that the evaluation of choice is closely connected with how the futures those choices give rise to compare in respect of their moral betterness—in any robust form, then the key concept needs to be not mere *logical* possibility but rather *accessibility.* And that's so, whatever we think about the Pareto minus solution or EC itself.

4
The addition puzzle

4.1 The puzzle

To introduce the addition puzzle, we won't need a new hypothetical. The three option case (Figure 3.1) developed in Chapter 3 will work perfectly for that purpose.

In that case, Charlotte doesn't exist in f1, she exists and has a wellbeing level of +5 in f2, and she exists and has a maximized wellbeing level of +10 in f3. For purposes here, we have agreed that Charlotte's existing in f2 or in f3 is better *for Charlotte* than her never existing at all in f1.[1] According, however, to the existence condition (EC), that fact doesn't make either f2 or f3 morally better than f1. That result comports nicely with the basic *existential* intuition. We then applied the same people Pareto principle to determine that f3 is morally better than f2—a result that comports nicely with the basic *maximizing* intuition. To solve the Pareto puzzle—and avoid the looming inconsistency—the Pareto minus solution then takes the position that making things *better for* a person by bringing that person into existence can, on occasion, make things *morally worse*. And so it does in f2: f2 is morally *worse* than f1.

Thus an intuitive account of the three option case: bringing the additional child into existence, on its own, makes things *neither morally better nor morally worse*. But bringing the additional child into existence and making things *worse* for that child when things could have been made *better* does make things morally worse—and is wrong.

[1] We have, that is, assumed nonexistence comparability.

The Existence Puzzles. M. A. Roberts, Oxford University Press. © Oxford University Press 2024.
DOI: 10.1093/oso/9780197544143.003.0004

But let's now step back. It seems that we can pull the following points out of what we have just said. The additional dollop of wellbeing that Charlotte has in f3—the five additional units of wellbeing she has in f3 as compared against what she has in f2—makes f3 morally better than *f2*. It *adds* to the moral value of f3. But that *very same* additional dollop of wellbeing in that *very same* future—those *same* five units of wellbeing in f3—*fails to add* to the moral value of f3: it *fails* to make f3 better than f1.

The Pareto minus solution to the Pareto puzzle thus appears to countenance a certain instability in the value that a given increment of wellbeing can add to the moral value of a given future. One and the same increment of wellbeing—what Charlotte does have in f3 and doesn't have in f2—both *adds* to the value of f3 and *doesn't* add to the value of f3. How can that happen? How can the same five units of wellbeing be both *moral-value-enhancing* in the future in which they have been bestowed on Charlotte and *morally inert* in that *very same* future?

We can put the point another way. The Pareto minus solution to the Pareto puzzle seems to rely on addition but at the same time to ignore addition. We *rely* on addition when we say that Charlotte's additional five units of wellbeing in f3 makes f3 better than f2. But we then *ignore* addition when we say that Charlotte's additional five units of wellbeing in f3 doesn't make f3 better than f1.

Normal arithmetical addition gives us perfect confidence that when we add things up—provided that it's the *same things* we are adding up—we always get exactly one result and don't sometimes get one result and sometimes another. Addition being a function, it *just can't happen* that we sometimes add 2 to 3 and get 5 and sometimes add 2 to 3 to get something other than 5. That's because the values of what is to be added up (2 and 3) are *stable*.

We need that to be so when it comes to the overall moral value of a given future as well. No plausible moral theory, in other words, can have it that the moral value of a given future is the sort of thing that can shift around—move either up or down—depending on what comparative task we ourselves happen to have taken on: increasing when we happen to compare f3 against f2, not increasing when we happen to compare f3 against f1. The plausible moral theory will instead have it that the value of any given future is itself *fixed*.

But for that to be so the values of *whatever it is* that constitutes the overall moral value of a given future must themselves be stable. But that latter requirement—the *requirement of the stability of the values of the parts*; for short, the *stability requirement*—seems to be failed under the Pareto minus account. How much Charlotte's additional five units of wellbeing in f3—how much that *part* of f3—adds to the moral value of f3 seems not to be stable at all: it adds a *lot* when we compare f3 against f2 but *nothing at all* when we compare f3 against f1.

Thus the addition puzzle. We want to talk in terms of what makes one future morally better than another—to talk, that is, in terms of what *adds to* the moral value of one future as compared against another. And we say that what makes f3 better than f2 is the fact that f3 is better for Charlotte than f2—that is, that the extra increment of wellbeing Charlotte has in f3 is *moral-value-enhancing*. We want to talk in terms of *addition*.

But, at the same time, and even as we recognize that the extra increment of wellbeing Charlotte has in f3 is *there to stay* regardless of the comparative task we ourselves happen to be undertaking, we want to say that that extra increment *may not* add to the moral value of f3. When we turn to compare f3 against f1, we want to say that that extra increment of wellbeing Charlotte has in f3 *doesn't* do any moral-value-enhancing work for f3 at all: that it's morally *inert*. We want *not* to talk in terms of addition.

But how can we have things both ways? How can we, per the basic maximizing intuition, often avail ourselves of addition—and, per the basic existential intuition, on occasion seem to proceed as though moral analysis has nothing to do with addition at all?

Here as elsewhere the method of this book applies: to solve the puzzle without throwing out any of the puzzle pieces.

4.2 Why we love addition

Let's start, in Section 4.2.1, with why it might seem that we should just reject addition. We'll then turn, in Section 4.2.2, to why we may not want to do that at all—to the critical role addition at least arguably plays in our moral theorizing.

4.2.1 The raw addition principle, inconsistency with existence condition

Let's back up. The *raw addition principle* is itself an axiom of the traditional total theory—of, that is, totalism. It immediately avoids the tension we've just brought to the surface in the Pareto minus solution.[2]

> *Raw addition principle.* The *moral value* of a possible future *x* is just the summation of the individual wellbeing levels for all those people who do or will exist in *x*; *and*
>
> where *x* and *y* are possible futures and *y* is accessible relative to *x*, *y* is *morally better* than *x if and only if* the moral value of *y* is greater than the moral value of *x*.

The raw addition principle understands the *moral value* of a given future to be *additive* in nature and specifies that what is to be added up are the individual wellbeing levels of each person who does or will exist in that future. Since within a given future those individual wellbeing levels can't themselves change, the raw addition principle easily meets the stability requirement.

[2] An analogous raw addition principle holds for averagism. As noted earlier, however, averagism seems clearly to fail. See Chapter 1 note 13 (Hell Three). We therefore don't bother saying anything more about it here.

Why do we call it the *raw* addition principle? Because under that principle—under, that is, the traditional total view, or *totalism*—the individual wellbeing levels—the *utilities*—at a given future are to be added up *without any adjustment* to reflect values that go beyond the value for the particular person of having more wellbeing rather than less—values that go beyond the value of things being made *better for* a given person. The raw addition principle thus doesn't propose that what is to be added up is the individual wellbeing levels *as adjusted for* any value beyond the value of wellbeing itself (*as adjusted for*, e.g., equality or fairness or desert).[3]

The glaring problem with the raw addition principle is that it leaves no room at all for the basic existential intuition.

The *two paths to zero wellbeing level* case (Figure 4.2.1) makes that point clear.

Figure 4.2.1: Two paths to zero wellbeing			
	c1	c2	c3
probability→	1	1	1
wellbeing↓	f1	f2	f3
+10			**Fiona**
...			
+0	*Fiona*	**Fiona**	

Figure 4.2.1 Two paths to zero wellbeing

To calculate the value of a given future, the raw addition principle adds up dollops of wellbeing scattered across that future and determines that f2 isn't either better or worse than f1: that f2 is exactly as good as f1. It thus sees *no moral distinction* between f1 and f2—*no moral distinction* between Fiona's having a zero wellbeing

[3] More sophisticated addition principles have been proposed. Thus proposals from Broome and Feldman are outlined in Section 4.3.2. The principles those philosophers propose are designed to address deficiencies in the raw addition principle relating to equality, fairness, priority, desert, and justice. But they do nothing to address the raw addition principle's *existential* deficiencies.

level in f1 and Fiona's having a zero wellbeing level in f2, between Fiona's *never existing at all* in f1 and Fiona's existing at a perfectly avoidable and miserably low wellbeing level in f2.

If something seems off about that result to you, that may mean that the basic existential intuition has been awakened somewhere within your moral consciousness.

And—as an articulation of that very intuition—EC supports a very different account of the case.

> *Existence condition (EC).* Where a future *y* is accessible relative to a future *x*, *x* is *morally worse* than *y*, and a choice made in *x* is *wrong, only if* there is a person *p* such that:
> (i) *p* does or will exist in *x*, *and*
> (ii) *x* is worse for *p* than *y or* there is a *third* accessible future *z* such that *x* is worse for *p* than *z*.

EC immediately instructs that f1 is *at least as good as* f2. Then—in contrast to the raw addition principle—EC is silent on whether f2 is *worse* than f1. That silence then opens the door for the result that f2 is *worse* than f1, a result that EC in combination with same people Pareto and various conceptual principles we seem to have no choice but to accept—together, person-based consequentialism—quickly produces.[4]

Which account of the case seems more plausible? The account that says that f2 is *exactly as good as* f1? Or the account that says that f2 is *worse than* f1?

I favor the latter. Theorists who like the raw addition principle for this case face the challenge of accepting—of *trying* to accept—the deeply counterintuitive results it generates for this case. Ditto for almost all of our other cases as well, including Jaime versus Harry,

[4] The Pareto minus solution, specifically, continues as follows: EC implies that f1 is exactly as good as f3, and same people Pareto implies that f2 is worse than f3. Conceptual principles then instruct that f2 is worse than f1. See Section 3.4.

the happy child case, and the three option case. (Though not for all: the raw addition principle—totalism—and the principles that we shall accept here agree on the miserable child case.)

If theorists rest content with the raw addition principle but still find the basic existential intuition alive and well in their moral consciousnesses, then they haven't actually solved the puzzle but have instead simply set it aside.

4.2.2 Obstacles to doing away with addition

Why not, then, just reject any critical role for the addition function in our moral theorizing? Why not just say that the moral theory that consists of EC, same people Pareto, the Pareto reduction principle, and no doubt (once completed) some other substantive moral principles to be introduced on an as-needed basis along with a handful of conceptually necessary principles offers a very good start at solving the puzzles rather than just setting them aside?[5] Why not just reject out of hand addition as having any role at all to play in the form of maximizing consequentialism—specifically, *person-based consequentialism*—that this book is working to develop?

The fact is that there is much to be said for addition. Four considerations favoring addition are outlined here.

(a) *Addition helps to satisfy skeptical concerns.* To say that a person exists in a future in which the existence that person has is *worth having* is just to say that that person's *individual wellbeing level* in that future is *positive.* If that person's existence at a given

[5] Thus in earlier chapters we've alternately introduced principles that have given rise to puzzles and principles we've accepted for the purpose of solving those puzzles. The substantive *moral* principles we've introduced and accepted include the following: the existence condition (EC), same people Pareto, and the Pareto reduction principle. The mere addition principle, in contrast, is *out*. And the conceptual principles we have accepted include if a future x is better than a future y, then y is worse than x; if a future x isn't worse than a future y and y isn't worse than x, then x is exactly as good as y (*trichotomy*); and, if a future x is better than a second future y, and y is better than a third future z, then x is better than z (*transitivity*).

future is *worth having*, then that future is *better for that person*—it has *more value for that person*—than a future in which that person never exists at all.

It's, moreover, undeniable that, other things equal, the future that contains the additional worth-having existence contains more wellbeing *in the aggregate* than the future that doesn't. We add one more drop of water to a bucket of water, and, other things equal, we *can't not* have ourselves more water. We *add* one more dollop of that which has value for people to a future, and, other things equal, we *can't not* have more *value for people* in that future.

Moreover, for purposes of determining how much wellbeing in the aggregate a given future contains, it obviously *just doesn't matter* whether that additional dollop of wellbeing derives from an *ordinary* benefit (from, e.g., curing a child's terrible disease) or from an *existential* benefit (from bringing an additional person into a worth-having existence).

None of what we have just said seems at all controversial. But nor does it try to make the leap from a future's containing *more value for people in the aggregate*—that is, *more wellbeing in the aggregate*—to that future's having *more moral value*.

But is that much of a leap? What could the moral value of a given future consist in beyond the value that future has for people? What magical, mystical thing could moral value then consist of? The empiricist in us—the Humean in us—is highly skeptical that the moral value of a given future could subsist in anything over and above the *value that future has for people*.

If we think the inference from a future's containing *more value for people*—that is, *more wellbeing*—and a future's being *morally better* is trivial, then we have already accepted that addition plays a critical role in determining the moral value of a given future.

In the end, I think we will want to reject the raw addition principle—that is, the traditional total view, or totalism. To make sense of our cases, I think we need to accept that a future's containing an additional worth-having existence (like Charlotte's in f2 in the three option case) on occasion doesn't make things morally better and can even make things morally worse. At the same time, I find the point just made on the question on addition itself compelling.

For me, then, the challenge will be to specify the values of the various existences (present and future) in a given future such that the summation of those values represents the overall moral value of a given future and *at the same time* to make sure that those specifications themselves comply with the stability requirement.

(b) *Addition explains many cases. Whatever* moral value is, case after case suggests that it must be the kind of thing that is governed by addition. It's that fact that explains why the future in which the agent pulls a switch and diverts the trolley from the one track to the other, thereby causing the death of only one person rather than five, is the morally better future.[6] It's that fact that explains why the future in which ten people enjoy an additional unit of wellbeing is, other things equal, morally better than the future in which only five people enjoy an additional unit of wellbeing—that explains why, that is, the *numbers count*.[7] It's that fact that explains why, when the population of a given future is finite and each person who does or will exist in that future has a hellish existence—an existence *far less* than an existence worth having—adding even one more person who will also have a hellish existence makes things morally worse.

It's not, then, just a coincidence, or the reflection of bias or prejudice, that we might see moral value as additive. Moral value surely *is*, in some way or another, additive in nature.

(c) *Addition protects against irrationality.* The accounts we have proposed of the cases we've already considered routinely appeal not just to *moral* principles but also to various *conceptual* principles that we seem to have no choice but to accept.

[6] Foot 1967; Thomson 1985.

[7] Taurek 1977.

Let's focus on the latter for a moment. *Conceptually necessary principles* are principles we seem to have no choice but to accept *even after* careful inquiry and however hard we try. (We've seen nothing that works to dislodge them from our thinking.) We accept them—and put them to work in our accounts—because we seem unable *not* to accept them. In effect, they, too, along with our deeply held, widely shared intuitions, are pieces of the puzzle: we can't just toss them out and still consider ourselves to have actually solved the puzzle.

But conceptually necessary principles play another role as well. Abiding by them, we abide by the demands of consistency and cogent analysis. Abiding by them, we safeguard the accounts we offer of even the most puzzling of our cases—even the cases in respect of which we could most easily fall into failures of consistency or cogency—against *irrationality*.[8]

Of course, simply adding a given conceptually necessary principle to a collection of moral and conceptually necessary principles doesn't even begin to make sure that that collection itself abides by that conceptually necessary principle. For example, we have accepted, as a matter of conceptual necessity, the transitivity of the relation of moral betterness. We've thus included transitivity in our collection of moral and conceptually necessary principles we've proposed for purposes of analyzing variable population cases. But, depending *on what other principles we consider included in that*

[8] Adding one more drop of water to the bucket, other things equal, *can't not* increase amount of water in the bucket—by exactly one drop. Moreover, having such an arithmetically clear approach at hand for identifying the overall moral value of a given future means that we can make sure that our ranking of futures in respect of their moral betterness satisfies the requirement of transitivity as well as certain other logical and conceptual requirements. It, after all, provides us with a well-defined way of cleanly correlating overall moral values against, e.g., the set of natural numbers, and we know in advance that the natural numbers themselves satisfy any logical and conceptual requirements that might be thrown at us (if bucket x, which contains 9 cups of water, contains more water than bucket y, which contains 7, and y contains more water than bucket z, which contains 5 cups of water, we know that x is sure to contain more water than z does *because we know* that, 9 being greater than 7 and 7 being greater than 5, 9 is *sure* to be greater than 5).

collection, the results that those principles all taken together generate may leave transitivity in the dust.

How can we make sure that our moral theory—the collection of principles we in the end accept—won't do that? That it won't suffer from nontransitivity and all the perils that come with that?[9] How can we make sure that the results we derive from that collection won't fail to comply with transitivity?

A plus of an addition principle is that it—*thanks to addition*—leaves no doubt at all on that point: the betterness results that we derive by application of addition will clearly satisfy transitivity.

(d) *Addition ensures the assignment to each future of no more than a single, fixed moral value.* Here again it helps to go back to the three option case. In that case, Charlotte doesn't exist in f1, exists and has a wellbeing level of +5 in f2, and exists and has a wellbeing level of +10 in f3.

The Pareto minus solution to the Pareto puzzle appeals to both EC and same people Pareto while avoiding (by virtue of having rejected the mere addition principle) any implication that f2 is at least as good as f1. Those points, in combination with conceptual principles we seem to have no choice but to accept, imply Charlotte's existence in f2 makes f2 *worse* than f1.

As noted earlier, the Pareto minus solution instructs both that Charlotte's existence at +10 in f3 makes f3 better than f2 (per same people Pareto) *and* that Charlotte's existence at +10 in f3 *doesn't* make f3 better than f1 (per EC). Relative to f2, Charlotte's existence at +10 in f3 *does* make things better; relative to f1, Charlotte's existence in f3 at +10 *doesn't* make things better.

But how can the additional dollop—the additional five units—of wellbeing that Charlotte accrues in f3 relative to f2 both make a *positive* contribution to f3's moral value relative to f2 and make *no contribution at all* to f3's moral value relative to f1?

[9] As noted earlier, among the perils we should worry about are money pumps. See Section 3.3.2 and Chapter 3 note 13.

Suppose that we try to insist that *that's just what it does*: that the additional dollop of wellbeing Charlotte has in f3 plays dual and opposing roles in the case: one role when it comes to comparing f3 against f2 and another when it comes to comparing f3 against f1.

The problem with insisting on that position is that it seems to preclude *any settled conclusion* on just what the moral value of f3 itself is. It seems to preclude the assignment of any *fixed* moral value to f3 itself. For the betterness ranking of f1, f2, and f3 to be settled, we need our calculation of the moral value we assign to f3 not to consist in a *multiplicity* of moral values but rather in a *single* moral value.

But for that to happen, the values that are to be added up—the values of the parts that constitute the overall moral value of the particular future; the values that contribute to, that *add* to, the moral value of the future under scrutiny—can't themselves come in multiples.

Thus the *stability requirement*: the values of the parts that are to be added up must themselves be fixed (i.e., *stable*). When it comes time to determine what the parts together contribute to the moral value of the future that contains it, we must have just *one* value, just *one* number, for each person who does or will exist, to add up. We can have *no more than one moral-value-enhancing increment per person per future.*

> *Stability requirement.* The existence of a person at a wellbeing level in a given future in a given case adds to the moral value of that future by the same amount *regardless* of which other future accessible in that same case that one future happens to be compared against.

Back to the bucket analogy: to say anything else would be like saying that the single drop of water both *has* and *lacks* any dimension: that it both *adds* and *doesn't add* to the quantity of water in the bucket. If that's the information we start with, we obviously can't reach any conclusion at all whether adding the drop of water leaves us with more water or not.

As noted, the raw addition principle easily complies with the stability requirement. In contrast, the Pareto minus solution doesn't—on the face of things—seem to work that way at all. It instead seems to consider Charlotte's existence at +10 in f3 both to add to the value of f3—for the purpose of comparing f3 against f2—and not add to the moral value of f3—for the purpose of comparing f3 against f1. The Pareto minus solution seems, in other words, *inherently incapable* of complying with the stability requirement.

4.2.3 Summing up

We should now feel the full force of the addition puzzle.

We've just outlined the critical role that the addition function plays in our moral theorizing. We've just seen why we love addition—why, specifically, we're worried that without addition we are on our way into irrationality. We can't just dig our heels in on the basic existential intuition or EC or the Pareto minus solution and make that worry go away.

At the same time, we've seen, in case after case, starting with Jaime versus Harry, just how deep a hold the basic existential intuition has on us. Nothing in our itemization of the plusses of the raw addition principle even begins to dislodge from our moral consciousness the idea that curing a child's terrible disease and bringing a child into existence to begin with are, from a moral point of view, quite distinct. Nothing in that itemization provides us with the requisite new platform of deeply held, shared intuition that it would take to dislodge that intuition. Nothing in that itemization provides us with that new way of looking at things that would help us understand just how the basic existential intuition itself went so wrong.

Of course, as we've already seen, the basic existential intuition—in the form of EC—is inconsistent with the raw addition principle!

Nonetheless we may well have the sense that (*I* at least have the sense that) the two discussions together are less an argument to inconsistency and more on the order of two ships passing in the night.

Which should give us some sense that we can after all solve the puzzle without rejecting any of the puzzle pieces.

4.3 Inversive existence-sensitive solution to the addition puzzle

4.3.1 Perennial concerns about the raw addition principle

We've noted the many plusses that come with the raw addition principle, itself an axiom of the traditional total view (i.e., totalism). If it seems that we are being unduly squeamish when we don't immediately endorse that principle and abandon the basic existential intuition, let's just note that *no one* (I *think* no one) thinks that the raw addition principle comes with no minuses at all. The doubts we have about the raw addition principle, in other words, aren't at all limited to the fact that it's at odds with the basic existential intuition.

(a) *Repugnant conclusion.* One widely recognized difficulty for the raw addition principle is Parfit's *repugnant conclusion.* As Parfit observes, the raw addition principle often forces us to say that a future *A* in which *many, many* people all have lives well worth living is morally *worse* than another future *Z* in which those very same people and still others besides all have lives only *barely* worth living. Parfit describes that conclusion as "repugnant"—as, that is, a conclusion that no plausible moral theory can seem to sustain. On that point, most theorists are in agreement.[10]

[10] See Parfit 1987, 381–390 (chapter 17). The line of reasoning Parfit himself puts forward for the conclusion relies, not on the raw addition principle, but on a combination

(b) *Infinite population problems.* A second difficulty the raw addition principle faces comes in the form of *infinite population problems.* In one such case, we imagine two futures each containing an infinite number of people and each containing exactly the same people. The problem is that each person in the first future is much better off—at, say, a wellbeing level of +10—than each person in the second future—at, say, a wellbeing level of +5.[11] Since each future contains an infinite number of units of wellbeing, the summation of such units for each future is exactly the same: aleph-zero. The raw wellbeing principle then generates the result that the one future is *exactly as good as* the other. Surely, however, that result is false; surely the first future, which makes things better for each person who does or will exist in it than the second, is morally better than the second.

Infinite population problems are not always taken very seriously. Some philosophers have suggested that our intuitions fall apart when the cases we are aiming to evaluate involve very large numbers. But does that point have any application here? Could it be that the one future *really is exactly as good as* the other but that our little minds are just too limited to see that that's so?

I don't think so. The facts here are just too clear, the chance of misunderstanding any critical detail of the case virtually non-existent. Moreover, we deal quite capably with infinite classes all the time. (Quantifiers help us with that; we don't need to *list*

of the mere addition principle and various conceptual principles, including transitivity. We, of course, have already rejected the mere addition principle.

Not everyone agrees that the conclusion that *A* is worse than *Z* is repugnant (see Huemer 2008). Nor does everyone agree that the fact that a theory implies the repugnant conclusion demonstrates that the theory is false; see Budolfson and Spears 2021 (arguing that *all* theories—or perhaps all *credible* theories—produce a version of the repugnant conclusion and thus that the repugnant conclusion doesn't provide adequate grounds to reject any theory).

[11] Kagan and Vallentyne 1997. Are infinite populations even *possible*? As both a physical and a conceptual matter, it seems that they are: it's hard to rule out the prospect of generations of people rolling along, one after the other, forever into the future.

the natural numbers when we can *quantify over* the set of natural numbers.)

Of course, we can *say* "the one future is exactly as good as the other." But it is hard to see how we can actually make ourselves accept the proposition that we thereby assert.[12]

(c) *Equality; priority.* Here, I'll just note a more traditional objection against the raw addition principle. Consider two futures that contain exactly the same two people. One future assigns one of those people a life far *less* than a life worth living and the other a truly amazing, very long life. Let's say the wellbeing levels are, respectively, −10 and +100. The other future assigns both people very good lives—wellbeing levels of, say, +40.

The raw addition principle will favor the first future. *It doesn't care* that one person has in effect served as a human sacrifice for the other. But we might care. We might even think that such a case is enough to show that the raw addition principle is itself *false*. If the case just described doesn't happen to be such a case, there are plenty of others—cases that motivate us to point out that moral law has something to say about *equality* and perhaps specifically about *priority*; that moral law directs that the plights of the *least* well off in a given future are those that should be remedied *first*—and all it takes is one.

4.3.2 Strategy: Addition without raw addition

At this point, we know enough to say that we'd like to see the basic maximizing intuition articulated with reference to addition but not

[12] Other philosophers gesture toward work in mathematics that suggests that the two futures don't in fact contain the same number of units of wellbeing. I think, however, that that's a proposition that *is* hard to grasp. It's hard to see how the infinite number of units of wellbeing in the one future isn't *identical* to the infinite number of units of wellbeing in the other future. Here, the critical point is that both sets are countable: both are exactly the same size as the set of natural numbers.

with reference to a principle that—like the raw addition principle—rules out the basic existential intuition.

Broome and Feldman outline theories that share an underlying strategy that can, I think, help us do just that. The core principles they propose still *add things up* to determine the moral value of a given future. But the values that those principles add up are values *other than* levels of raw wellbeing.

Broome's concept of the personal good. Thus, in the context of his interpretation (in effect, his defense) of a certain addition principle—specifically, Harsanyi's theorem—Broome observes that philosophers need not reject addition in order to leave room in their theories for values that go beyond the value of an individual's having more wellbeing rather than less. They can instead take the position that what is to be added up to determine the value of a given future are not the values we assign to units of *raw wellbeing* but rather the values we can instead assign to units of what Broome calls the *personal good.*[13]

According to Broome, it would be a mistake to think that Harsanyi's theorem

> is opposed to strict egalitarianism. Each person's betterness relation might itself be influenced by the person's standing in comparison to other people. For example, suppose that in some outcome a person is worse off than other people who are no more deserving than her. This may be an unfairness she suffers. Suffering an unfairness is presumably bad for her, so it will influence her personal betterness relation, and will be registered in her own utility.[14]

[13] Broome 2015.

[14] Harsanyi's principle, Broome thinks, doesn't rule out the idea that a person's wellbeing in combination with how equally wellbeing has been distributed to that person and others may contribute to the overall good (what he calls the "general good") of a given future. But it "does rule out communal egalitarianism [that is, egalitarianism *apart* from the additional personal good it creates for each person in the particular future]. Harsanyi's [t]heorem is opposed to strict communal egalitarianism about good." Broome 2015, 252.

And again:

> [Harsanyi's theorem] means recognizing fairness [or equality or perhaps priority] as a personal good and unfairness [or inequality or a failure of priority] as a personal harm. When a distribution of good among people is unfair in some way, this unfairness diminishes the good of individual people.[15]

Broome thus thinks that philosophers have the option of retaining the addition principle but insisting that what is to be added up—the values of units of the *personal good*—requires a good deal of further discussion. Thus, for the traditional totalist, the personal good just is wellbeing. But for the egalitarian, the personal good may be wellbeing as adjusted to take into account the value of equality. If we think equality, fairness, or priority are critical values, then, according to Broome, we can construct our concept of the personal good to reflect that fact without rejecting the critical role the addition function itself has to play in our moral theorizing.[16]

Feldman's concept of desert-adjusted utility. In his attempt to fashion an additive theory that meets the challenge of the repugnant conclusion, Feldman has proposed the notion of *utility adjusted for desert.*[17] He accepts that, as between a future *A* that contains a very large number of people, all of whom have lives well worth living, and a future *Z* that contains all those people and many more besides, all of whom have lives only barely worth living, *Z* is worse

[15] Broome 2015, 257.

[16] In Broome 2015, Broome uses the term "personal good" as described here and without reference to any more basic concept (e.g., a concept of raw, unadjusted *wellbeing*). I should note, however, that Broome often seems to use the terms "wellbeing" (in 2004) and what he calls the "personal good" (in 2015) as synonyms: both terms, for him, designate a potentially *adjusted* value. In contrast, for purposes here, we'll continue to use the term "wellbeing" exclusively to designate the *raw, unadjusted* value that a given future has for a given person (what it is that makes life so precious for the one who lives). In what follows, I will distinguish (raw, unadjusted) *wellbeing* from the *contributive value* of a given existence at a given future.

[17] Feldman 1995a, 1995b.

than *A*. His object, then, is to explain how, within the context of an additive approach, that result can hold.

Feldman's basic insight is that, as the repugnant conclusion case is typically described, there is no reason to think anyone in *Z deserves* the very low wellbeing level—the very low *utility*—that person has in *Z*. To determine, then, the contribution each such person's existence in fact makes to the *moral* value of *Z*, we plausibly must adjust the utility each such person has *for desert*. Since their utilities are very low and undeservedly so, we can anticipate that the adjusted utilities will fall into the negative range. In contrast, the people who exist in *A* have at least the utility they deserve in *A*. Their utilities, then, adjusted for desert, plausibly remain within the positive range. Since the summation of the adjusted utilities in *Z* is less than the summation of the adjusted utilities in *A*, Feldman's approach generates the result that he and we want: that *Z* is worse than *A*. Of course, in another case, one in which the people who exist in *Z* for some reason *deserve* their very low utilities, or where the people in *A don't* deserve their very high utilities, the analysis will proceed differently.

The challenge for any philosopher who accepts Broome's suggestion on how the values of fairness and equality may be reflected within the context of an additive approach will be to define the relation between *raw wellbeing* and the *personal good* and thus to produce a theory that generates actual results when applied to concrete cases. A theory that can't do that is not a theory that we can test. Philosophers who find Feldman's approach more credible face a similar challenge: to say just when, and by how much, individual utilities are to be adjusted to reflect considerations of desert and justice.[18]

[18] A second problem arises for Feldman's theory as well. Consider two futures, a future Z^* that contains a large number of people all of whom undeservedly have lives *less* than worth living—have, that is, utilities that fall into the negative range—and another future Z^{**} that contains all of those people and more besides, all of whom (just like the people in the original *Z*) have lives that are worth living but only barely so. In many such cases, the utilities adjusted for desert for both futures will surely fall into the negative range.

But all that means is that we can't yet say—since we can't yet test—whether their approaches serve the purposes for which they are designed: to help fashion a theory that clearly recognizes our maximizing values while also accommodating the values of equality, fairness, priority, justice, and desert.

Now, in this book, those *aren't* the values we are aiming to accommodate. It's not that I'm not concerned with equality, fairness, priority, justice, and desert (though I might on another occasion propose we can narrow the list to priority alone). Rather, it's that the values that we are aiming to accommodate here—the values we are aiming to reconcile against our *maximizing* values—are just our *existential* values.[19]

And—conveniently—it seems that our *existential* values can be far more easily defined—in, for example, the form of EC—than the values of equality, fairness, justice, and desert.

To sum up: I have ongoing concerns regarding how Broome's and Feldman's own proposals are to be worked out in the form of principles we can test. But that doesn't mean that the *common underlying strategy* those two philosophers have described can't help solve the addition puzzle.

But if the population of Z^{**} is sufficiently larger than the population of Z^{*}, Feldman's theory will instruct that Z^{**} is morally *worse* than Z^{*} despite the fact that each person in Z^{**} has a life worth living and each person in Z^{*} has a life *less* than worth living. And we think that that's a mistake. Each person in both futures *deserves* more wellbeing. But, that said, we think that the future in which everyone has a life at least worth living is morally better than a future in which many of those same people have lives *less* than worth living. The problem I describe here derives from Arrhenius 2003a. He aptly calls his own version of the result that Z^{*} is better than Z^{**} the *sadistic conclusion*. Whether or not Feldman's theory can be amended to address the challenge—and my understanding is that Feldman at this point thinks that it can't—Arrhenius's point serves as a very nice objection against critical level utilitarianism.

[19] My aim here is *exclusively* on accommodating our existential values. Doing so will simplify our discussion, which is nice. But, as it happens, accommodating our existential values goes at least part of the way toward accommodating all those other values as well. What is the fairness, or desert, in being assigned a life only *barely* worth living when, but for massive overpopulation, that same life would easily have been *well* worth living?

4.3.3 Implementation: Contributive value and value inversion

The aim of this section is to do for our *existential* values what Broome has done for the values of equality, fairness, and priority and what Feldman has done for the values of justice and desert while keeping the stability requirement firmly in mind.

The solution I want to propose comes in two stages (a) and (b). First, we accept addition but take the position that what is to be added up to determine the moral value of a given future must reflect our existential values. Thus: *existence-sensitive addition.* We then employ a strategy of *value inversion* as a way of assigning moral values to individual existences—to the values, that is, that are to be added up—that satisfies the stability requirement. Thus: *inversive existence-sensitive addition.*

(a) First stage: Contributive value and existence-sensitive addition. I won't use Broome's term "personal good" for purposes here. It's too close in ordinary meaning to the term "wellbeing," and it's hard for me to see how we won't, in the end, need both the *raw, unadjusted* concept and a new *adjusted* concept. Nor will I use Feldman's "utility adjusted for desert," since, as noted earlier, desert isn't one of the values we are keeping an eye on for purposes of this book.

Instead, since the term "contributive value" seems most clearly to describe what this new value is meant to do—to tell us the value that the additional person's existence at a certain wellbeing level contributes to—literally *adds to*—the moral value of the future in which that person does or will exist—I'll use that term here. *Wellbeing,* then, will continue to mean *raw, unadjusted* wellbeing. And to say that one future is *better for* a person than another will continue to mean that that person has *more wellbeing* in one future than that person has in another.

Anticipating, then, that *contributive value* will be spelled out in a way that reflects not just our *maximizing* values but also our *existential* values, we can abandon the *raw addition principle* in favor of the *existence-sensitive addition principle.*

> *Existence-sensitive addition principle.* The *moral value* of a future *x* is just the summation of the individual contributive values for all the existences of all the people who do or will exist in *x*; *and*
>
> where an alternate future *y* is accessible relative to a future *x*, *y* is *morally better* than *x if and only if* the moral value of *y* is greater than the moral value of *x*.

Under that principle, *more* contributive value always makes things morally *better*; *less* contributive value always makes things morally *worse.*

The task then becomes to spell out just how—taking both our maximizing values *and* our existential values into account—a person's wellbeing level in a given future in which that person does or will exist translates to the *contributive value* of that person's existence in that future.

Now, it's no surprise that a person's having more wellbeing in a given future will often mean that the contributive value of that person's existence at that future is *greater*, while less wellbeing will often mean that the contributive value of that person's existence in that future is *lower*. Thus we make room for our *maximizing* values.

Consistent, however, with the idea that more wellbeing often means more contributive value and less wellbeing often means less contributive value, we can also take the position that more wellbeing doesn't *always* mean more contributive value. Thus under nonexistence comparability a future in which a person has a worth-having existence is *better for* that person than a future in which that person never exists, then that person has *more wellbeing* in the one future than in the other. But it doesn't follow that that person's existence in the one future comes with any contributive value at all; it doesn't follow that the contributive value of that person's existence in that future makes any positive contribution to—that it *adds* to—the moral value of that future. We thus leave room for our *existential* values.

Now, those general comments don't, on their own, solve the addition puzzle or show how we can meet the stability requirement. What they fail to explain is how, for the very same person and the very same future, the very same increment of wellbeing can be both moral-value-enhancing and *not* moral-value-enhancing. They fail to explain how what is to be added up—units of contributive value—can *remain stable* even as we move from one pairwise-comparison (of, e.g., f3 against f2 in the three option case) to another (f3 against f1 in that same case). To explain how we can meet the stability requirement, we move the second stage of the proposal.

(b) Second stage: Value inversion. What we now need to do is show how the existence-sensitive addition principle together with the concept of contributive value we've just described can both accommodate our basic intuitions *and* satisfy the stability requirement.

In the three option case, to satisfy the stability requirement is to assign a single contributive value to Charlotte's existence in f3. And that single contributive value must both *add* to the moral value of f3 when we compare f3 against f2 and *not add* to the moral value of f3 when we compare f3 against f1.

But how can we do that without abandoning one or the other of our two basic intuitions? If we limit ourselves to just one contributive value, and if that one value, together with existence-sensitive addition, tells us that f3 is better than f2, then it may at first glance seem that that same contributive value, together with that same principle, must tell us that f3 is also better than f1. Which is to reject the basic existential intuition. Which is not to solve the puzzle but rather just to throw out one of the puzzle pieces. Ditto if we limit ourselves to one contributive value and that one value, together with existence-sensitive addition, instructs that f3 *isn't* better than f1. Then it seems that that same one value, in combination with the same principle, will tell us that f3 *isn't* better than f2. Which is to reject the basic maximizing intuition. Which is, again, not to solve the puzzle but rather just to throw out one of the puzzle pieces.

* * *

Here, it helps to wean ourselves away from any idea that adjusting raw wellbeing in light of our existential values is in some way like adjusting raw wellbeing in light of—for example—equality.

The picture of the sort of adjusting that needs to take place in order to take equality into account (in my mind at least) is just this: the adjustment to be made when everyone's wellbeing is exactly the same would shift the individual wellbeing level up a notch or so; the adjustment to be made in the face of a significant inequality would shift the individual wellbeing level down a notch. But neither perfect equality nor serious inequalities would necessarily shift the individual wellbeing levels in any *dramatic* way.

We must tinker with the numbers to adjust for equality. But we don't up-end the scale: if the individual wellbeing level is *positive* starting out, then wellbeing adjusted for equality will often be *positive* as well.[20]

But if we try to solve the addition puzzle by merely *tinkering* with the numbers—if, e.g., we say that the contributive value of Charlotte's existence in f3 isn't +10 but rather is +9 or even +5 or +1—then existence-sensitive addition will instruct that f3 is better than f1. And that's the very result we want to avoid.

So let's not merely tinker with the numbers. Instead, let's boldly go to the number that we shall need in the end to secure the result that f3 is exactly as good as f1. Let's say that, notwithstanding the fact that Charlotte's wellbeing level in f3 at +10 has been maximized, the *contributive value* of Charlotte's existence in f3 is +0.

[20] Just to note: Feldman's solution to the repugnant conclusion—utility adjusted for desert—doesn't just tinker with the numbers but rather up-ends the scale at least in some cases; on Feldman's view, a positive wellbeing level, once adjusted for desert, may become negative. My own up-ending of the scale comes with sharper corners—introduced as *inversion* in the text following this note—but owes much to Feldman's insight.

And let's not merely tinker with the numbers in connection with f2, either. After all, we can hardly say the value of Charlotte's existence in f2 *decreases but remains positive* since the last thing any of us want is the result that, contra the same people Pareto principle, f2 is *better* than f3. But that's just the result that sort of tinkering around gets us given a commitment to the position that the contributive value of Charlotte's existence in f3 is +0.

Let's instead take advantage of the fact that we are confident that f3 is better than f2—that is, that we are confident that same-person Pareto is true. We can then quite naturally take the position that the contributive value of Charlotte's existence in f2 is, accordingly, for some natural number *n*, −*n*.

And now we need just one other point. We need to understand that a person's *nonexistence* in *any* future—including Charlotte's nonexistence in f1—comes with *no* contributive value at all: that is, *zero* contributive value.

Those contributive values in hand, we can now confirm that we've met the stability requirement. We've assigned *exactly one contributive value* for Charlotte in each of f1, f2, and f3—zero for her nonexistence in f1; −*n* for her existence at a less-than-maximized wellbeing level of +5 in f2; and zero for her existence at a maximized wellbeing level of +10 in f3 (Figure 4.3.3).

Figure 4.3.3: Three option case with contributive value n is a natural number			
	c1	c2	c3
probability →	1	1	1
wellbeing ↓	f1	f2	f3
+10			**Charlotte**
+5		**Charlotte**	
+0	*Charlotte*		
contrib. value ↓			
+0	*Charlotte*		**Charlotte**
-n		**Charlotte**	

Figure 4.3.3 Three option case with contributive value

Those assignments of contributive values in place, we are now in a position to apply existence-sensitive addition. And it produces just the results we want and, critically, just the results we earlier obtained by application of the Pareto minus solution to the Pareto puzzle: f1 is exactly as good as f3, and f2 is worse than both. Appealing to the connection thesis, we can then say still more: c1 and c3 are both perfectly permissible, but c2 is wrong.

* * *

In moving from raw wellbeing levels to contributive values, we used a strategy of inversion, which, in turn, enabled us to satisfy the stability requirement. We assigned for each person at each future *exactly one contributive value*. We avoided assigning one contributive value to Charlotte's existence in f3 in connection with our comparison of f3 against f1 and another to Charlotte's existence in f3 in connection with our comparison of f3 against f2.

That, in turn, means that—given how the addition function itself works, that it's a *function*—we can be confident that the moral value of f3 itself is *perfectly fixed*. We can say that f3 is exactly as good as f1 and better than f2 without making the mistake of endorsing the idea that the moral value of f3—or indeed of *any* future—is the sort of thing that can shift—that can move up or down—depending on what comparative task we ourselves happen to have taken on: increasing when we happen to compare f3 against f2 and not increasing when we happen to compare f3 against f1.

Tinkering may—*may*—work when it comes to equality or fairness. Adjusting a positive wellbeing level in light of equality or fairness perhaps will still yield a value in the positive range. But adjusting wellbeing in a way that preserves both the basic existential intuition and the basic maximizing intuition requires the bolder approach we've just described. By taking that bolder approach, we've succeeding in assigning a single, stable contributive value for each person in each future. We've succeeded in satisfying the stability requirement.

Is it a problem that we haven't said exactly *which* natural number *n* stands for? No: *whatever* that number is, existence-sensitive addition, as we've just seen, produces exactly the right results.

We've described a certain *inversion* as we move from *raw wellbeing levels* to *contributive values*. The additional person's wellbeing level might be +10, +100, +1,000. Such a *positive* wellbeing level in a given future will often—including, but not limited to, when a person's wellbeing is maximized in that future—be reduced to a contributive value of zero. And positive wellbeing levels will sometimes translate to *negative* contributive values—as when things could have been made better for a given person, a person who does or will exist in the future in which things are worse—at no cost to anyone else. Either way, there will always be an upper limit on how much that additional existence will contribute to the moral value of its future—*and that upper limit will always be zero.*

It's like turning over a kayak, where for a few desperate moments all of the important activity takes place below the water's surface rather than above. Here, for purposes of determining contributive value, all of the interesting analysis takes place below the zero level *despite* the fact that the individual wellbeing levels themselves are—in many, many cases—*at* or *above* the zero level.

4.4 Objection and reply: Isn't inversive existence-sensitive addition circular?

In determining the contributive values of Charlotte's existences in f2 and f3, it's true that we used some "backward engineering."[21] Specifically, we used EC and same people Pareto, along with

[21] Wlodek Rabinowicz notes that the proposal here is reminiscent of G. E. Moore's approach to determining the value of an organic unity and that Moore, too, was accused of engaging in some backward engineering. The accusation doesn't, however, in itself prove that there is anything amiss about backward engineering. As noted in this section, backward engineering and circularity are two very different things.

inversion, to determine the contributive values of Charlotte's existences in f2 and f3.

But it would be a mistake to see any *circularity* in the inversive existence-sensitive addition solution. For the aim and function of that solution is not to determine the betterness ranking across a given domain of futures. It's rather to make sure that the rankings that emerge from the collection of moral and conceptually necessary principles that we *already accept* abide by addition—which in turn is a way of making sure that those principles themselves *don't go off-track in a way that signals irrationality.*

Thus it's left to us to make sure that our collection of moral and conceptual principles doesn't produce assignments of *more than one* contributive value for the existence of any person at any future. It is, in other words, left to us to make sure that that collection of moral and conceptual principles satisfies the stability requirement. *Only after* we've made sure that that's so can we apply the existence-sensitive addition principle.

What if our collection of moral principles and conceptual principles we seem to have no choice but to accept isn't robust enough to assign *even one* contributive value to each such existence? That won't mean that the ranking itself—if incomplete—isn't rational. Rather, it will mean that existence-sensitive addition doesn't generate results for every case. While it does a fine job in the three option case and many others, that's not a guarantee that it will do any job at all in still other cases. Rather, at least until we add to that collection of principles, existence-sensitive addition may well remain silent in those other cases.

Given the aim and function of the proposed solution, backward engineering, in other words, doesn't mean circularity. We don't, for example, use same people Pareto to establish existence-sensitive addition and then use that existence-sensitive addition to confirm same people Pareto. Rather, we use same people Pareto (with inversion) to assign any contributive values that we can. We use EC (with inversion) to assign *other* contributive values. And—though we didn't need it for purposes of analyzing the three option case—in other cases we can use the Pareto reduction principle (with inversion) to assign *still other* contributive values. If that work produces a complement of contributive values for the particular case that meets the stability requirement, we can then use existence-sensitive addition to demonstrate that our results have all features that—given our love of addition—we hoped that they would have.

If our moral principles and our conceptual principles we seem to have no choice but to accept together *already* generate a completely satisfactory ranking for our problem cases, why do we need to bother with inversive existence-sensitive addition? Why do we need to bother with the backward engineering? We obviously have other ways of testing to make sure that our moral theory passes our formal tests—that it satisfies the demands of consistency, cogency, and conceptual necessity.

Does, in other words, inversive existence-sensitive addition really have any role to play in the formulation of a moral theory we might actually want to defend?

Two points weigh in favor of the view that we need to make room for addition. First, we seem to concede that addition is important when we take the position that the additional increment of wellbeing Charlotte has in f3 as compared against f2 is *moral-value-enhancing*—which is just to say that it *adds* to the value of f3. We can't arbitrarily, then, take the position that addition isn't important.

And, second, inversive existence-sensitive addition satisfies the four considerations noted in Section 4.2.2 favoring addition just as well as the raw addition principle does. Thus, among other things, it's an additive approach that ensures against failures of transitivity—and that gives concrete meaning to the idea that the *numbers count*, which surely they do.[22]

[22] Taurek 1977.

It's true that, to make inversive existence-sensitive addition work, every time we face a new case that requires us to add a new principle to our collection of moral and conceptual principles, we'll have to check everything all over again—including each and every assignment of contributive value—to make sure that the stability requirement is (still) met. Our results for any given case, accordingly, won't be completely settled until we *close the collection*. But it's always good to have a goal in life: ours can be closing that collection.

4.5 Applications of inversive existence-sensitive addition

4.5.1 The two paths to zero wellbeing case

The two paths to zero wellbeing case, just like the three option case, can be analyzed using EC and same people Pareto. In Figure 4.5.1, we quickly infer that f1, where Fiona never exists, is exactly as good as f3, where she exists and her wellbeing is maximized, and, moreover, that f2 is worse than both.

Figure 4.5.1: Two paths to zero wellbeing with contributive value n is a natural number			
	c1	c2	c3
probability→	1	1	1
wellbeing ↓	f1	f2	f3
+10			**Fiona**
...	...	...	...
+0	*Fiona*	**Fiona**	
contrib. value ↓			
+0	*Fiona*		*Fiona*
−n		**Fiona**	

Figure 4.5.1 Two paths to zero wellbeing with contributive value

We can then backward engineer to an assignment of contributive values. Notably, the zero that represents Fiona's wellbeing level in f1 and the zero that represents her wellbeing level in f2 don't translate to the same contributive values for Fiona in f1 and in f2. The contributive value of her nonexistence in f1 is just zero, while the contributive value of her existence in f2 is (given inversion) $-n$ (for some natural number n). Finally, the contributive value of her existence in f3, where her wellbeing has been maximized, is also zero.

Having assigned exactly one contributive value for Fiona in each future, we've met the stability requirement. Existence-sensitive addition then instructs that f1 is exactly as good as f3, while f2 is worse than both f1 and f2.

The connection thesis then completes our account of the case. Moral law doesn't obligate agents to bring Fiona into existence. But if they do bring her into existence, they must make things better for her rather than worse.

4.5.2 Infinite population problems

The infinite population problem described earlier had us imagine two futures each containing exactly the same infinite population. In that particular case—let's call it *infinite population case (a)*—each person in the first future is much better off (at a wellbeing level of +10) than each person in the second future (at a wellbeing level of +5). The raw addition principle instructs that the one future is exactly as good as the other. But that result seems clearly false.

Applying inversive existence-sensitive addition, we can first note that same people Pareto immediately implies that the one future—let's call it f1—is morally better than the other—f2.

We then turn to the task of assigning contributive values (and here is our backward engineering at work).

With the emboldened inversion strategy dictating that even the best of all possible existences is to be assigned a contributive value of no more than +0, we assign the value of +0 as the contributive value of the existence of each person in f1. And we'll assign as the contributive value of the existence of each person in f2 the value of $-n$, where n is a natural number. The case described by Figure 4.5.2a makes that point.

Figure 4.5.2a: Infinite population case (a) with contributive value s1 = {p|p is a person who does or will exist in f1} s2 = {p|p is a person who does or will exist in f2} s1 = s2 s1 and s2 are countably infinite n is a natural number		
	c1	c2
probability→	1	1
welbeing↓	f1	f2
+10	**p1 . . . (all and only members of s1)**	
+5		**p1 . . . (all and only members of s2)**
+0		
contrib. value↓		
+0	**p1 . . . (all and only members of s1)**	
-n		**p1 . . . (all and only members of s2)**

Figure 4.5.2a Infinite population case (a) with contributive value

Having checked to make sure the stability requirement is met—that we have just one contributive value per person per future—we then apply existence-sensitive addition to generate the result that f2 is worse—indeed, *infinitely* worse[23]—than f1. The connection thesis now completes our account of the case. The choice of c1 is permissible, indeed, obligatory, and the choice of c2 is wrong.

[23] I owe thanks to Wlodek Rabinowicz for underlining this point to me.

So far, so good. Now, we need to note that there also exist infinite population cases in which we seem to find that same people Pareto and any inversion strategy that we might attempt going in different directions.[24] Thus consider infinite population case (b) (Figure 4.5.2b).

Figure 4.5.2b: Infinite population case (b) with contributive value s2 = {p|p is a person who does or will exist in f2} s3 = {p|p is a person who does or will exist in f3} s2 = s3 s2 and s3 are countably infinite m, n are natural numbers			
	c1	c2	c3
probability →	1	1	1
welbeing ↓	f1	f2	f3
+10	p1 . . . (all and only members of s2 and s3)		
-5		p1 . . . (all and only members of s2)	
-10			p1 . . . (all and only members of s3)
contrib. value ↓			
+0	p1 . . . (all and only members of s2 and s3)		
-m		p1 . . . (all and only members of s2)	
-n			p1 . . . (all and only members of s3)

Figure 4.5.2b Infinite population case (b) with contributive value

Same people Pareto immediately instructs that f2 is morally worse than f1 and that f3 is morally worse than f2. We assign contributive

[24] The infinite population case (b) is very similar to a problem case that Wlodek Rabinowicz has pointed out to me. Johann Frick identified a similar problem case in connection with an earlier instantiation of the proposal discussed in this chapter.

values accordingly, specifying, in particular, that $n > m$. Still, however boldly we work the inversion strategy, existence-sensitive addition is going to disappoint us. Since the summation of the contributive values for f2 will be exactly the summation of the contributive values for f3, addition-sensitive addition implies that f2 is exactly as good as f3.

Do we restrict same people Pareto? I don't think so: f3 really does seem clearly worse than f2. Do we restrict existence-sensitive addition to cases in which the populations *aren't* infinite? A solution that would (correctly, I think) leave same people Pareto untouched? The problem there is to say what alternative addition principle we are to put in its place. (The raw addition principle, of course, fails in this case.) Do we amend the notion of contributive value to discount to nothing the contributive values for some infinite segment of the populations in f2 and f3—say, the segment that includes people ordered by the number one trillion and above—leaving us with a more tractable *finite* population, one that existence-sensitive addition can make sense of? The problem there is that discounting seems completely at odds with moral law: whatever else is the case, my own bad existence in either f2 or f3 surely doesn't count *more* against those futures than the existence of person number one trillion and one.

At one level, the result that f2 is exactly as good as f3 isn't troubling. After all, that result leaves untouched the arguably more critical result that both f2 and f3 are worse than f1. And the connection thesis easily then instructs that c2 and c3 are both wrong and that c1 is permissible, indeed, obligatory. At the level of the evaluation of choice, in other words, existence-sensitive addition still performs well.

Nonetheless, the result we've obtained at the other level—the level of the ranking the futures—is disturbing. We may have to say, for the moment, that infinite population case (b) has given rise to a puzzle that we haven't managed to solve in this book.

4.5.3 The tradeoff to exist case

The tradeoff to exist case points out that a future that is worse for a person who does or will exist in that future than another future doesn't always signify a negative contributive value. In cases where one person must be made worse off for at least one person in a group of people that includes that one person to exist at all, we've going to resist the idea that the existence that isn't maximized makes things morally worse. Consider the *tradeoff to exist case* (Figure 4.5.3a).

Figure 4.5.3a: Tradeoff to exist			
	c1	c2	c3
probability →	1	1	1
wellbeing↓	f1	f2	f3
+4		**Ebon**	**David**
+3		**David**	**Ebon**
+0	*David, Ebon*		

Figure 4.5.3a Tradeoff to exist

We can readily accept—per EC—that f1 isn't worse than f2 and f3. What EC doesn't tell us—and what we can't, I think, accept—is that f2 and f3 are worse than f1.

It's true that f2 is worse for the *existing* David and f3 is worse for the *existing* Ebon. But for two reasons we strongly favor the position that f2 and f3 are each at least as good as f1.

First, given the nature of the change between f2 and f3—that it's, we can say, a *merely reversing change*—we think that whatever we say about David in f2 will surely apply to Ebon in f3. Surely moral law doesn't care *who one is*. Surely it's, instead, *impartial, indifferent, neutral* in the context of the merely reversing change as to whether a given tradeoff is made in favor of *one* person or in favor of *another* person. (And surely some credible *principle of anonymity* or another will immediately generate that result.[25])

Of course, f1 avoids the tradeoff—and any morally significant loss—altogether. But here the second thought comes into play. We don't think that moral law *forbids* the tradeoff that is required as a necessary condition for either David or Ebon to exist at all. We don't think that moral law *requires* the nonexistence of *both* David and Ebon. We don't think that f2 and f3 are *worse* than f1. It's just not plausible that moral law insists on nonexistence in every case involving tradeoffs in wellbeing across a given population of people who do or will exist.

In that respect—and again in the context of this one case—we oppose the anti-natalism of David Benatar.[26] We embrace, instead, some form of or another *anti-anti-natalism.*

Now, we'll be looking closely at principles that reflect those two thoughts in connection with the next puzzle, the *anonymity puzzle*, in Chapter 5. As we shall see, *just which* of the aspirant principles that might be labeled "anonymity" or "anti-anti-natalist" we shall actually want to defend turns out to be a quite sensitive matter, so we won't bother to formally introduce any such principle here.

But we can anticipate what those principles will say. We can anticipate, in other words, that *any* plausible account of the tradeoff to exist case will instruct both—per EC—that f1 isn't worse than f2 or f3 and—per the combination of *some* form of anti-anti-natalism and *some* form of anonymity—that f2 and f3 aren't worse than f1. Trichotomy, transitivity, and other conceptual necessities then step in to produce a highly plausible account of tradeoff to exist: f1 is exactly as good as each of f2 and f3.

[25] I will just note now that the anonymity principle we will ultimately accept is *restricted* in nature; see Sections 5.4.1 and 5.4.2.

[26] Benatar 2006.

Those results in hand, we can now assign the relevant contributive values (and here is our backward engineering at work; see Figure 4.5.3 b).

Figure 4.5.3b : Tradeoff to exist with contributive value			
	c1	c2	c3
probability →	1	1	1
wellbeing ↓	f1	f2	f3
+4		**Ebon**	**David**
+3		**David**	**Ebon**
+0	*David, Ebon*		
contrib.value ↓			
+0	*David, Ebon*	**David, Ebon**	**David, Ebon**

Figure 4.5.3b Tradeoff to exist with contributive value

We then check to make sure that we've satisfied the stability requirement. We check, that is, to make sure that no other moral or conceptual principle that we've accepted requires any *distinct* assignment of contributive values. We then apply existence-sensitive addition and obtain the anticipated results—that each of the three futures is exactly as good as each other.

The connection thesis, then, completes our account of the case. Moral law doesn't obligate agents to bring either David or Ebon into existence. But nor does moral law obligate agents to leave them out of existence altogether.

4.6 Wouldn't it be simpler to "minimize aggregate complaints"?

It might seem that there's a simpler way to accommodate the basic existential intuition within the framework of maximizing consequentialism: a way to do that *without* having to work through a collection of moral and conceptual principles to determine, for each and every person who ever exists in any accessible future, what the contributive value is for that person in that future.

We could start with each person *p*'s individual wellbeing level *m* at a given future *x*. If *p* does or will exist in *x*, we might then assign, as the *weight* of *p*'s "complaint" in *x*, the difference between *p*'s wellbeing in *x* and *p*'s wellbeing in any alternate accessible future in which *p*'s wellbeing is maximized. (If such better-for-*p* accessible future exists: if *x itself* is maximizing for *p*, the weight of *p*'s complaint in *x* will be zero; *p*, that is, won't have a complaint in *x*.) We could then add up the weighted complaints that exist in each such future to determine a "complaint-based value" for that future. Finally, we can say that a future *x* is *morally better* than an alternate accessible future *y* if and only if *x*'s complaint-based value is lower than *y*'s complaint-based value.

On its face, such a complaint-based view may not seem an unattractive way of articulating the basic existential intuition. Moreover, its appeal to the addition function should guarantee that it's a view that satisfies the requirements of conceptual necessity (including transitivity and trichotomy).

But it won't work. Consider, again, tradeoff to exist (Figure 4.5.3a). The complaint-based view will immediately instruct that f2 and f3 are morally worse than f1. And we've already agreed—I think—that that result is incorrect. As noted earlier, moral law can't plausibly require that we bring no new people into existence just on the ground that a tradeoff in wellbeing will need to be made across that population of people who do or will exist.[27]

More generally, the complaint-based view—like the raw addition principle—seems to add up the wrong things. The difficulty becomes apparent in the case in which a vast number of people have lives well worth living in one future f1 but nonetheless have a "complaint" in f1 that is assigned some positive weight. We thus

[27] Wlodek Rabinowicz reminded me to go back to *tradeoff to exist*. Again, I am grateful.

can suppose that each such person is a little better off in an alternate accessible future f2 than that person is in f1. And suppose that, in still a third future f3, the members of a non-overlapping and somewhat smaller population, though still a very large population, have lives *far less* than lives worth living. For each such person, since no one who exists in f3 also exists in f1 or f2, there exists the option of never having existed at all. We can surely anticipate that the far more serious complaints of the people who exist in f3 will be assigned much heavier weights than are the weights assigned to the relatively trivial complaints of the people who exist in f1. Nonetheless, depending on the details of the case—depending, that is, on how many more people exist in f1 than in f3—the view that simply adds up the weights of the complaints in each alternate future to determine the complaint-based value of that future and, on the basis of that value, determines the moral value of the particular future, may well insist that f3 is *morally better* than f1. But that result seems clearly false.

5
The anonymity puzzle

5.1 Simple and indefinitely iterated addition and reversal

As we have seen, when principles that work nicely on their own are forced to work together in the odd case—that odd case itself often being a variable population case—some very deep puzzles can arise.

Here, we'll start with a simple case that combines (i) the additional worth-having existence with (ii) a merely reversing change, where both the addition and the reversal may well strike us as completely innocuous. As far as I can see, the simple case, on its own, raises no *obvious* puzzle at all. The puzzle comes when we apply the principles that seem clearly plausible in the context of the simple case to an iterated form of that case. It's at that point—as we shall see—that we realize we have a serious problem.

Thus *simple addition and reversal* (Figure 5.1).[1]

Figure 5.1: Simple addition and reversal			
	c1	c2	c3
probability→	1	1	1
wellbeing↓	f1	f2	f3
+10	**Polly**	**Polly**	**Robbie**
+9	--	**Robbie**	**Polly**
. . .	. . .	. . .	. . .
+0	*Robbie*	--	--

Figure 5.1: Simple addition and reversal

[1] What I here call the *simple addition and reversal* case was outlined by Budolfson in a workshop organized by Dean Spears on Risk and Population, University of Texas at Austin, November 2019. The case that generates the anonymity puzzle—the case, that is, of the *indefinitely iterated addition and reversal*, outlined below—is my own. I am

The Existence Puzzles. M. A. Roberts, Oxford University Press. © Oxford University Press 2024.
DOI: 10.1093/oso/9780197544143.003.0005

It seems—at first glance—clear what we should say about this case. Moreover, it seems clear—again, at first glance—that what we want to say about this case isn't problematic.

We can start with an appeal to the *existence condition* (EC).

> *Existence condition (EC).* Where a future *y* is accessible relative to a future x, *x* is morally worse than *y* (*y* is morally better than *x*), and a choice made in *x* is wrong, *only if* there is a person *p* such that:
>
> (i) *p* does or will exist in *x*, *and*
>
> (ii) *x* is worse for *p* than *y* *or* there is a *third* accessible future *z* such that *x* is worse for *p* than *z*.

According to EC, the fact that Robbie *never exists* in f1 doesn't make f1 *worse* than f2 *or* than f3. f1 is at least as good as f2 and f3. We can then apply the connection thesis to infer that it's perfectly permissible for agents to choose to leave Robbie out of existence altogether.

But what about the other way around? Does EC also instruct that f2 and f3 are *at least as good as* f1?

No. Since f2 is worse for Robbie than f3, EC's necessary condition on f2's being worse than f1 is satisfied. EC is thus completely silent on whether f2 is at least as good as f1. It doesn't, in other words, rule out that f2 is *worse* than f1. Moreover, since f3 is worse for Polly than either f1 or f2, EC's necessary condition on f3's being worse than f1 is also satisfied. EC thus is silent as well on whether f3 is at least as good as f1. It doesn't rule out that f3 is *worse* than f1.

Nor does EC, as a mere *necessary* condition on when one future is worse than another and not a *sufficient* condition, tell us that f2 or f3 is worse than f1.

grateful to Budolfson and Spears for the workshop itself and ensuing discussion which led me to develop the solution to the anonymity puzzle set forth in Section 5.4.

Other principles we've accepted earlier on also fail to produce a complete account of the simple case. Thus the same-people Pareto principle has nothing to say about how f2 or f3 compares against f1. And the Pareto reduction principle remains completely silent on how f2 compares against f1.

Let's, then, approach the open questions via a more roundabout route. Let's—for the moment—set those questions aside and turn instead to what may seem a considerably easier question: that of how f2 compares against f3.

It's true that, as to that question, the principles we've mentioned just above—EC, same-people Pareto, and the Pareto reduction principle—remain silent.

But a principle we haven't yet introduced formally but anticipated in Section 4.5.3 in discussion of the tradeoff to exist case (Figure 4.5.3a) may seem to be immediately helpful in comparing f2 against f3. After all, the *only difference* between f2 and f3 is that the positions of Polly and Robbie have been reversed. The change from f2 to f3 is, in other words, a *merely reversing change*. As noted earlier, moral law surely doesn't care *who one is*. It's, instead, *impartial, indifferent*, or (we said) *neutral* in the context of the merely reversing change as to whether a particular tradeoff is made in favor of one person or in favor of another person.

That very general thought is reflected in the familiar and widely accepted *unrestricted anonymity principle*.

> *Unrestricted anonymity principle.* For any futures *x* and *y* such that *y* is accessible relative to *x*, *if* exactly the same people do or will exist in *x* and *y* and each person in *x* has exactly the same wellbeing level that that same person has in *y* except for a merely reversing change across some of those people, *then x* is exactly as good as *y*.

Where a *merely reversing change* between two futures occurs when the populations and wellbeing positions are identical between two futures but the positions those individuals occupy have simply been swapped around, unrestricted anonymity easily and quickly generates the result that the one future is exactly as good as the other. Since f2 and f3 clearly meet those conditions, we can easily and quickly infer that f2 is exactly as good as f3.

Now, unrestricted anonymity *doesn't* answer the two questions we set aside earlier—the question of how f2 compares against f1 and the question of how f3 compares against f1. But, in a subtle way, it gets us much closer to what we shall want to say in reply to those two questions. For we can now appreciate that, given unrestricted anonymity, a great deal is at stake in how we answer either one of those questions. We can now appreciate that, given unrestricted anonymity, *whatever* we say about how f2 compares against f1, we *must also say* about how f3 compares against f1, and *whatever* we say about how f3 compares against f1, we *must also say* about how f2 compares against f1.

So let's ask: Do we say that *both* f2 and f3 are *worse* than f1—perhaps on the ground that both f2 and f3 include at least one person who both exists and suffers a loss of wellbeing while f1 nicely avoids all such morally significant losses? (Note that if that's what we want to say, we shall need to revisit what we said in the tradeoff to exist case!) Or do we instead say that *both* f2 and f3 are *at least as good as* f1?

To ask the question is practically to answer it. Even if our instincts in respect of how f3 compares against f1 are a little fuzzy, it seems beyond churlish to insist that f2 is worse than f1—to insist that moral law *requires* that Robbie *not* be brought into an existence that is, though not maximized at +10, nonetheless at +9 well worth having.

Of course, the question arises: What principle generates the result that f2 isn't worse than f1? It may seem that the obvious answer to that question is the *mere addition principle*. But that seemingly—*seemingly*—innocuous and unassuming principle is one that we have clearly and on very strong grounds already rejected in Chapter 3.

But the fact that we've rejected the mere addition principle doesn't even begin to show that f2 *is* worse than f1. The claim that f2 *isn't* worse than f1 could easily still be true notwithstanding the fact that we happen to have rejected a principle that generates exactly that claim.

In fact, I think we can say more. Perhaps, given that we've rejected its easy progenitor—that is, the mere addition principle, a principle that, in the context of the three option case, too freely lets agents off the hook for bringing an additional person into existence—we can't credibly claim that the intuition that f2 isn't worse than f1—now limited to the context of simple addition and reversal—is *widely shared*. On the other hand, perhaps it's comparisons like that of f2 against f1 that made the mere addition principle seem credible to begin with. In any case, the intuition that f2 isn't worse than f1 is surely, on reflection, at the very least *deeply held*.

Still, however deeply held and widely shared the intuition might be, we remain in need of an *alternate* principle, an *anti-anti-natalist principle*. We need a principle that generates the right result—that f2 isn't worse than f1—but that is at the same time a principle (unlike the mere addition principle) we shall actually *want* to defend.[2]

Now, I think we can articulate just such a principle—though we'll obviously need to see it written out in black and white before we can test it. Given, however, the analytical pitfalls that we are just about to encounter in connection with the *iterated* form of simple addition and reversal in the very next section, let's defer that black-and-white formulation of the alternate principle until we have a better understanding of the complications that we face.[3]

But let's sum up what we have so far. EC tells us that f1 is at least as good as f2 and f3. Unrestricted anonymity tells us that f2 is exactly as

[2] If *anti-natalism* is a position that generally prefers nonexistence over existence and that specifically declares both f2 and f3 worse than f1, then we can call the position that declares f2 and f3 at *least as good as* f1 *anti-anti-natalist*. Moreover, if *pro-natalism* generally prefers existence across the board and specifically declares f1 worse than both f2 and f3, then we can call the position that f2 and f3 are each, though at least as good as f1, *not better than* f1 *anti-pro-natalism*. Take your pick!

[3] See Section 5.4 (solution to anonymity puzzle).

good as f3. And we anticipate that still another principle—to come—will secure the result that f2 isn't worse than f1—that is, that f2 is at least as good as f1. Those results in hand, conceptually necessary principles then tell us more: that f3, just like f2, is at least as good as f1 and—for the record—that f2 and f3 are each exactly as good as f1.

We now have a complete account of simple addition and reversal. But, as noted earlier, what we don't yet have is any obvious *problem*. As far as I can see, there's nothing puzzling—nothing, that is, *obviously* puzzling—in the account we've just given of the simple case.

5.2 The case of indefinitely iterated addition and reversal; the puzzle

But things change quickly when we turn to the case of *indefinitely iterated addition and reversal* (Figure 5.2).[4]

Figure 5.2: Indefinitely iterated addition and reversal

choice	c1	c2	c3	c4	c5	...	cn
probability→	1	1	1	1	1	1	1
wellbeing↓	f1*	f2*	f3*	f4*	f5*	...	fn*
+10	**Polly**	**Polly**	**Robbie**	**Robbie**	**Sam**	...	**Tia**
+9	--	**Robbie**	**Polly**	**Polly**	**Robbie**	...	...
+8	--	--	--	**Sam**	**Polly**	...	...
...	...	...	...	...	...	...	...
+.00003	--	--	--	--	--	--	**Polly**
+.00002	--	--	--	--	--	--	**Robbie**
+.00001	--	--	--	--	--	--	**Sam**
+0	*Robbie, Sam ... Tia*	*Sam ... Tia*	*Sam ... Tia*	*...Tia*	*...Tia*	--	--

Figure 5.2: Indefinitely iterated addition and reversal

[4] See Chapter 5 note 1 (credit Budolfson and Spears). For my first publication on the indefinitely iterated case, see Roberts 2021.

This case does no more than indefinitely iterate the fact pattern we see in simple addition and reversal. We then repeat as well the account of the simple case that we gave just above as many times as necessary to obtain a result that we think just *can't* be correct: that fn* is at least as good as f1*.[5]

That result seems every bit as repugnant as the result—and here we go back to Parfit's original repugnant conclusion case—that the future *A* that includes a very large number of people enjoying lives well worth living isn't *better* than—and may even be *worse* than—an alternate future *Z* that includes all those same people and many more besides all of whom have lives that are only barely worth living.

In tradeoff to exist, we justified consigning one or the other of David and Ebon to a less than maximized existence on the ground that some such tradeoff was unavoidable if either David or Ebon were ever to exist at all. But can we also justify consigning Robbie, Polly, Sam, Tia, and many, many others to an existence *just barely worth having*, not so that at least some of them can exist, but rather so that many, many others can exist *on top of them*?

That the iterated line of reasoning generates a conclusion that is indeed repugnant becomes especially clear if we think of each of Polly, Robbie, Sam, Tia, etc. not as single person but as cohorts each consisting of billions or trillions of people, all of whom have lives that are themselves only *barely worth living*.

Now, it's true that there's a distinction to be drawn between Parfit's repugnant conclusion case and indefinitely iterated addition and reversal. In the latter, the existences just barely worth having come with still other existences that are well worth having. But that

[5] For reasons laid out in Section 3.5 having to do with the independence of irrelevant alternatives, the "f1" that appears in the simple case and the "f1*" that appears in the indefinitely iterated case are, notwithstanding the fact that they contain the same people at the same wellbeing levels, *two distinct futures*. The same point holds of "f2" and "f2*" as well as "f3" and "f3*." The future with respect to which fn, for example, *isn't* accessible and the future with respect to which fn *is* accessible are, in other words, two distinct futures.

detail doesn't credibly sanitize the result that fn* is at least as good as f1*. Surely the entirely avoidable suffering of billions or trillions of people can't be made perfectly all right by the fact that that suffering has made it possible for billions or trillions more people to come into existence.

And now we *do* have a puzzle: the *anonymity puzzle*. We produced an account of the simple case that seemed perfectly plausible, an account that looked to be perfectly straightforward and not puzzling at all. We noted that the principles that generated that account seemed to apply seamlessly[6] to the indefinitely iterated case. In doing so, we generated a result that seems clearly false.

Something in what seemed to be a perfectly plausible original account of the simple case seems clearly to have gone wrong. But what?

5.3 When the cures are worse than the disease

5.3.1 Accept repugnant conclusions across the board

Budolfson and Spears argue that many population theories face some version or another of Parfit's repugnant conclusion and thus that whether a theory generates such a conclusion (in, e.g., Parfit's original case, that *Z* is at least as good as *A*, or, by extension, in indefinitely iterated addition and reversal, that fn* is at least as good as f1*) can't be counted against that theory.[7] Thus an advantage of the average view over the total view is widely considered to be that

[6] Some philosophers, aiming to disassociate the simple case and the indefinitely iterated case, will dispute that that's so. Such disassociation may well be based either on (i) Temkin's strategy of rejecting transitivity, a strategy that, as noted earlier, seems conceptually difficult to maintain (see Section 3.3.1), or (ii) a critical level approach, an approach that seems felled by Arrhenius's sadistic conclusion argument (see Chapter 4 note 18).

[7] Spears and Budolfson 2021. The position they describe is consistent with the view that the repugnant conclusion that *Z* is better than *A* really is repugnant. Their point, rather, is that if every credible theory generates a similarly repugnant conclusion, then we can't consider the fact that a theory generates that conclusion objectionable. Still

the average view avoids the repugnant conclusion. Budolfson and Spears, however, argue that even the average view comes with its own version of the repugnant conclusion. Once we see that the average view, just like the total view, generates repugnant results, the average view loses what seemed to be a significant advantage over the total view.

More generally, their position is that *all* population theories—at least, all *reasonably well-established* population theories, whether they include just the axioms that define the traditional total view (totalism) or not—generate *some* version or another of the repugnant conclusion. Unless we want to reject them all—and surely we don't—we can't reasonably reject any one on those grounds.

Such a position demands that we accept the result that fn* is at least as good as f1* even as we acknowledge its repugnance. All roads take us to the repugnant conclusion. We can decline to go down any road at all.[8] Or we can accept that any *correct* population theory will come saddled with some version or another of the repugnant conclusion.

But there is a problem with the Budolfson-Spears strategy. Its credibility relies on the position that *all* population theories—at least, all reasonably well-established population theories—generate some version or another of the repugnant conclusion. But that position isn't one that Budolfson and Spears purport—or that anyone else purports—to have shown. *Perhaps* all population theories that start with a *certain set of axioms* will indeed generate a version of the repugnant conclusion. But that's a reason to question that set of axioms. It's not a reason to accept it.[9]

other theorists have argued that the repugnant conclusion—whether as an objection to the total view or any other view—isn't, on closer inspection, truly "repugnant" at all (see Huemer 2008; Tännsjö 2009).

[8] Rabinowicz, and perhaps Temkin, suggest that way out. See Sections 1.6, 3.3.2, and 3.3.3 (plurality of values, incommensurability).

[9] *Perhaps* all population theories *based on the raw addition principle* (e.g., the traditional total view, i.e., totalism) generate some version of the repugnant conclusion. Indeed, that's why we, in Chapter 4, questioned the raw addition principle. We didn't just

Consider an analogy. Imagine a world in which most reasonably well-established theories of arithmetic instruct that 2 + 2 = 5. We don't then say that the fact that our theory implies that 2 + 2 = 5 can't be counted against our theory. We don't say, "Oh well, let's just set intuition aside." Nor do we try to browbeat ourselves into believing that 2 + 2 = 5. We instead *move on to the next theory.*

The point can be put another way. As far as any of us at this point *know*, not *all* roads *do* take us to some version or another of the repugnant conclusion. It's thus premature to abandon—to *try* to abandon, to *say* we have abandoned—the deeply held, widely shared intuition that we have regarding Parfit's original repugnant conclusion case: that *Z* truly is worse than *A*. Ditto our intuition regarding the indefinitely iterated case: that fn* truly is worse than f1*.

Deeply held, widely shared intuitions will be up-ended from time to time. But before abandoning an intuition of that sort—before, more precisely, *trying* to abandon an intuition of that sort—we need to have in hand a *new platform of deeply held, widely shared intuition*; one that loosens the hold the original intuition has on us; one that enables us to understand exactly where the original intuition has gone wrong; one that renders what we once thought was an *intuition* into something that no longer stands up well to intuition at all.

Which is just what physicists try to do when they work hard to make us understand the evidence in favor of the view that the entire universe exploded out of something so small that it could fit inside a single hydrogen atom. They try to provide us with some *understanding* of the evidence in favor of things having unfolded in that remarkable way.

Can we really be as confident that *Z* is worse than *A* or that fn* is worse than f1* as we are that 2 and 2 don't add up to 5? Well,

say "oh well that's intuition for you," or try to browbeat ourselves into giving up the intuition that *Z* is worse than *A*.

are we as confident that it's wrong to torture the cat for no reason whatsoever—that the future in which the cat is tortured is morally worse, other things equal, than the future in which the cat is left to sleep in the sun—as we are that 2 and 2 *don't* make 5? I think that we are—and that the leap from the claim that the future in which the cat is tortured *really is worse* to the claim that *Z* and fn* alike *really are worse* isn't a very impressive one.

5.3.2 Accept anti-natalism

We earlier brushed aside as churlish the position that f2 and f3 are both worse than f1. That wasn't a very well-articulated objection against anti-natalism. But to do any better job, we must first understand just *why* someone might accept that account.

An argument in favor of anti-natalism that at one time seemed to me to have some initial plausibility is this.[10] Let's take for granted that fn* is worse than f1* in indefinitely iterated addition and reversal. And let's then just note that it's plausible to think that the moral analysis that tells us that fn* is worse than f1* will also tell us that f3 is worse than f1.

What analysis might that be? What analysis would confirm for us that f3 is worse than f1?

In our discussion of the miserable child half of the asymmetry in Chapter 2, we appealed to the Pareto reduction principle to establish that the future in which the miserable Maija exists was morally worse than the future in which she never exists at all. Let's now just note that that principle has application in the context of simple addition and reversal as well. The Pareto reduction principles doesn't, in other words, *require* that the person for whom the less populated

[10] Benatar is widely known as an advocate of anti-natalism (see Benatar 2006). This is not to suggest, however, that, faced with simple addition and reversal he would necessarily argue that f2 and f3 are both worse than f1. As far as I know, the case isn't one he's specifically considered.

future is better has to be the *same person* as the person who is left out of existence altogether. It's also triggered—assuming its other requirements are met—in the case where leaving one person out of existence makes things better for another person.

Let's then just restate that principle here.

> *Pareto reduction principle.* Where a future *y* is accessible relative to a future *x* and each person who does or will exist in *y* also does or will exist in *x*, *x* is morally worse than *y* (*y* is morally better than *x*) *if*
>
> (i) *x* is worse than *y* for at least one person who does or will exist in *x*, *and*
>
> (ii) *x* is better than *y* for *no* person who does or will exist in *y*.

In the simple case, since f3 (which here goes in for *x*) is worse for Polly than f1 (which goes in for *y*) and Polly exists in f1, and since f3 isn't better for anyone—for example, Robbie—who does or will exist in f3, Pareto reduction immediately implies that f3 is worse than f1.

That claim established, the unrestricted anonymity principle combined with various conceptual principles completes the account. Since f3 is worse than f1 and f3 is exactly as good as f2, f2, as well, is worse than f1. The connection thesis then tells us more: whether the choice is made at f2 or at f3, it's wrong to bring Robbie into existence.

I can think of no more persuasive argument in favor of the anti-natalist account of simple addition and reversal than the one I've just laid out.

It seems a plus that the anti-natalist account immediately extends to the indefinitely iterated case. For the same reason—Pareto reduction—that f3 is worse than f1 in the simple case, f3* is worse than f1* in the indefinitely iterated case. Which is exactly the same reason fn* is worse than f1* in that same case. For the same reason—unrestricted anonymity—that f2 is worse than f1 in the simple case *given* that f3 is worse than f1, so is f2* worse than f1* in the indefinitely iterated case *given* that f3* is worse than f1*.[11]

But the anti-natalist account faces an insurmountable obstacle. We've now carefully worked through the most persuasive argument that we—that I—can think of to the conclusion for the simple case that f2 and f3 are *both* worse than f1. But that work hasn't—it seems to me—loosened the hold that the deeply held and at least potentially widely shared intuition that, *whatever* we want to say about f3, f2 really *can't* be worse than f1 has on us. That work hasn't presented us with a new platform of deeply held, widely shared intuition that helps us to understand how it might be that f2 really is, contrary to our original intuition, worse than f1—understand, that is, exactly where our original intuition has gone wrong. "Churlish" still seems exactly the right word for the idea that f2 is morally worse than f1: the idea that moral law *proscribes* Robbie's coming into existence.

But that means that the anti-natalist account of the indefinitely iterated case doesn't actually solve the puzzle at all but rather simply tosses out one of the puzzle pieces. We aren't going to have a solution to the puzzle until we have an account of the case that doesn't leave us intensely suspicious that it's not the intuition, but rather the argument against that intuition, that has gone wrong.

5.4 Identity-sensitive solution to the anonymity puzzle

5.4.1 Strategy

I take for granted that, if we can figure out where our initial account of simple addition and reversal—the account outlined in Section

[11] Again, the "f1," "f2," and "f3" in the simple case and the "f1*," "f2*," and "f3*" in the indefinitely iterated case are not identical. See Section 3.5 and Chapter 5 note 5 (independence principle).

5.1—went wrong and then produce an account that avoids that mistake without abandoning either of our two basic intuitions and while satisfying our formal requirements—consistency, cogency, and conceptual necessity—then the principles that make up that account can be extended seamlessly to the indefinitely iterated case. Thus we start with the simple case.

The account of the simple case that I now want to propose combines three ideas: that (contrary to the initial account) f3 is in fact worse than f1; that we can, in inductive fashion, build on the result that f3 is worse than f1 to show that f2 is at least as good as f1; and that the position that f3 is worse than f1 doesn't commit us to the position that f2 is worse than f1.

I'll call it the *identity-sensitive solution* since it turns on the idea—not that Robbie's moral status is any lower than Polly's, not by even the smallest bit[12]—but rather that it really does make a difference, in certain highly restricted circumstances, *who* it is—whether it is one person rather than another—that we are in a position to make things better for.

I'll outline the strategy in this Section 5.4.1 and then put it to work in Section 5.4.2.

Our initial account of the simple case—the account outlined in Section 5.1—included the claim that f2 isn't worse than f1. It then applied unrestricted anonymity to determine that f3, just like f2, isn't worse than f1.

But now, given our confidence that fn* is worse than f1* in the indefinitely iterated case, we surely find the claim that f3 isn't worse than f1 in the simple case at least questionable. Indeed in the end we'll want to say it's *false*. Of course, we'll need to secure that result—and as we shall see in the next section the Pareto reduction principle will be helpful in that effort. But for now the important point is this: if we insist that f3 *isn't* worse than f1, then it's very hard

[12] I maintain throughout that the varying forms of moral actualism all fail; see Section 2.3.2.

to see how we can credibly also insist that fn* *is* worse than f1*.[13] Moreover, if we *can* secure the result that f3 is worse than f1, then we can easily secure the result that fn* is worse than f1* as well.

We'll thus accept that f3 is worse than f1.

What I think we *can't* accept—given that Robbie *can't* exist without someone or another sustaining a morally significant loss of wellbeing and that, if Robbie is to exist at all, his existence will be well worth having—is that f2 is worse than f1.

Those two points together—that f3 is worse than f1 and that f2 isn't worse that f1—mean that we need to take a closer look at the unrestricted anonymity principle.

Unrestricted anonymity regards f2 and f3 as two peas in a pod. How f2 compares against f1 dictates how f3 compares against f1 and vice versa. But that way of looking at f2 and f3 ignores some of the case's most morally critical details: details regarding just *who Polly and Robbie are*, and, specifically, details regarding how they fare in the various alternate accessible futures that constitute the case. And in doing so unrestricted anonymity—as we shall see—compels us to reject *any and all* of the principles that *do* take those details into account.

The two claims—that f2 is worse than f1 and that f3 is worse than f1—are obviously logically independent. That means that, released from the constraints of unrestricted anonymity, we are free to consider whether we can articulate a clear basis for the position that f2 *isn't* worse than f1 even as we accept that f3 *is* worse than f1.

And that we can do. But by what analysis? Given that f3 is worse than f1, let's now just note that, while f3 is perfectly *accessible*, the fact that f3 is worse than f1 places f3, as it were, *morally* out of bounds. The only options that we then have left—the only options that are both accessible *and* not yet eliminated as morally out of bounds—are f1 and f2. Since f2 is better for Robbie than f1 and f2

[13] See Chapter 5 note 6 (transitivity, critical level theory).

is exactly as good for Polly as f1, we should have no problem at all declaring f2 at least as good as f1.

That's the strategy. We now put that strategy to work.

5.4.2 Implementation

Implementation of the identity-sensitive solution comes in three parts, (a), (b), and (c). As noted earlier, it's enough here to focus on the simple case. We, in other words, take it for granted that the intuitive account we outline for the simple case will apply seamlessly to the indefinitely iterated case.

(a) *Pareto reduction principle*. The principle we can put to work to secure the result that f3 is worse than f1 is just the Pareto reduction principle.

As noted in Section 5.3.2, that principle immediately implies that f3 is worse than f1. That's so, since f1 makes things better for Polly than f3 without making things worse for anyone else in f1—that is, for anyone who *does or will exist* in f1.

Now, in Section 5.3.2, we appealed to that principle for the limited purpose of constructing the most persuasive argument that we—that I—could think of for the anti-natalist conclusion that f2 is worse than f1. We then *rejected* that result.

But that we reject the *result* doesn't mean that we reject *every component* of the analysis that produced that result. And that analysis explicitly relied, not just on Pareto reduction, but also on unrestricted anonymity. We thus remain free—at this juncture—to *accept* Pareto reduction but to *reject* unrestricted anonymity.

At the same time, we should also just note that the fact that the Pareto reduction principle helped us to construct a highly intuitive account of the miserable child half of the asymmetry doesn't prove that we must accept that principle in its original and unrestricted form. In the miserable child case, the person the one future makes things better for is the *same person* as the person left out of existence altogether. We could easily amend the Pareto reduction principle and restrict it to that sort of case. And we could then just note that that restricted principle has no application at all to the simple case.

So, do we accept Pareto reduction *as it stands*? Or do we feel that it goes too far and that we need to restrict it?

Let's step back to get a better look at Pareto reduction in its original and unrestricted form, a look that places it in the context of one of the main efforts of this book: to reconcile the basic maximizing intuition against the basic existential intuition, to show that preserving one of those two intuitions *doesn't* require that we reject—that is, that we *try* to reject—the other.

In that context, Pareto reduction seems close to axiomatic. *Assuming*, of course, that we find the basic existential intuition itself compelling. *Assuming* that we really do think that existence is *just different*. *Assuming* that *one* child's suffering a terrible disease in a case in which that child's disease can accessibly be cured is just on a *completely different moral plane* from *another* child's never existing at all.

Thus, EC tells us that the worth having existence doesn't, other things equal, make things morally better: that it's perfectly permissible, other things equal, for agents *not* to bring additional people into existence. Pareto reduction—as it now applies in the context of how f3 compares against f1 in the simple case—takes things just one short step further. If, per EC, a person's *not* existing at all *doesn't*, other things equal, make things worse and if, as we can all surely agree, a person's *existing and suffering* can *easily* make things worse, then when we have the choice whether to impose the one sort of loss on the one person or the other sort of loss on the other person, we'd best go with the one sort of loss rather than the other.

Now, it would be a serious problem for the current strategy if Pareto reduction *also* instructed that f2 is worse than f1. But it doesn't. Since f2 isn't worse than f1 for anyone who does or will exist in f2, Pareto reduction remains perfectly silent on whether f2 is worse than f1 or not.

(b) *Induction on prior results.* So far, so good. f3 *is* worse than f1. But a complete anti-anti-natalist account of the simple case must also include the result that f2 *isn't* worse than f1. To that end, it isn't enough just to reject the claim that f2 is worse than f1. Instead, we need to secure the result that f2 *isn't* worse than f1—that f2 is at least as good as f1.

One way of securing that result involves an approach that we haven't yet had any need for in this book: that of allowing a given account of a given case to build on itself, not in a way that is circular or question-begging, but in a way that uses *already established* results to reason *inductively* to *further* results.[14]

Let's back up. Throughout this book, it's been accepted that futures that aren't *accessible*—futures that lay outside of the agents' abilities, power, resources—are irrelevant to determining whether a given future *x* is worse than a given future *y*.

Here's an example. In discussion of the Pareto puzzle, we introduced the *two option case* (Figure 3.5) in which Charlotte either never exists at all or exists with a wellbeing level of +5. It doesn't work to try to make sense of that case by denying that there's a *logically possible* future in which Charlotte exists with a wellbeing level of +10 and is thus better off than she is in the future in which she exists with a wellbeing level of +5. Of course there's such a better-for-Charlotte logically possible future! But that fact isn't enough to compel the conclusion—in the two option case—that the future in

[14] The inductive strategy we put to work here (a strategy that recognizes that some outcomes dominate, from a moral point of view, others, rendering those others irrelevant to the moral analysis) isn't inductive in the sense that it will use probabilistic or statistical reasoning to generate conclusions that are at best probably true. It's instead inductive in the sense that it articulates principles that don't generate, in standard deductive fashion, *all* the results we're interested in in one fell swoop but rather allows the prior results generated by those principles to generate, by further application of those same principles, further results. Just to note: the new results generated follow by means of *deductively valid* reasoning—assuming that the premises are true, so, we can be sure, are the conclusions. (The terminology is old and potentially confusing—but I won't try to improve it here!)

which Charlotte exists at +5 is worse than the future in which she never exists at all. We remain confident in the claim that the future in which Charlotte is at +5 *isn't* worse than the future in which she never exists at all in view of the fact that the merely *logically possible* future—the future in which she exists at +10—*wasn't* a future that agents (acting as individuals or together, whether collaboratively or not) had *any hope* of bringing about at all.[15]

The mere *logical possibility* of additional futures, however amazingly awesome they might be, wasn't, in other words, enough to *silence* EC in the two option case. Instead, EC quickly generated the result in the two option case that the future in which Charlotte exists at +5 is exactly as good as the future in which she never exists at all.

The proposal now is that we say exactly the same thing about futures that have *already been established as morally out of bounds.* Futures, in other words, that are *inaccessible* and futures that have already been determined to be *morally out of bounds* can be seen as playing the same sorts of roles in the moral analysis—or, to put the point another way, as, once so designated, not playing any role at all in the moral analysis. That means that futures that have already been determined to be morally worse than still other futures are thus not enough to silence the operation of—for example—EC.

Some such morally out of bound futures may well make things better for a person who does or will exist in a given future. But if those futures have already been determined to be worse than an alternate accessible future—determined, that is, to be morally out

[15] That concept—and the role it plays in EC—was critical to our solution to the Pareto puzzle. Thus in the *three* option case we said—appealing to EC—that f3 is exactly as good as f1 but that, f3 being accessible relative to f2 in that case, f2 is *worse* than f1. But in the *two* option case we said—again appealing to EC—that, f3 *not* being accessible relative to f2*, f2* is exactly as good as f1*. The accessibility, then, of the third future, the future that makes things *still better* for Charlotte, made all the difference in the accounts we gave of the two cases.

of bounds—then EC (i.e., a properly *strengthened* EC) may well still have something to say.

Let's now apply the inductive strategy in the context of simple addition and reversal. The fact that f3 makes things better for Robbie should not be enough to silence EC in the case where f3 has already been *ruled morally out of bounds as morally worse* than an alternate accessible future. And it has: we have already established, by application of the Pareto reduction principle, that f3, though perfectly *accessible* (i.e., within the bounds of agents' ability, power, and resources), is *worse* than f1. That places f3 *morally out of bounds.*

The only futures that are then left—the only futures that are both accessible *and not yet already eliminated as morally out of bounds*—are just f1 and f2. Since f2 is better for Robbie than f1 and f2 is exactly as good for Polly as f1, we should have no problem at all articulating a principle that generates just the result that we want: that f2 is, after all, at least as good as f1.

I find it hard to see how anyone could reject that application of the inductive strategy. But we still need to formalize it. And we can easily do that by simply strengthening EC. (Which is not to say that there's anything amiss with the original EC. It's fine. The new principle is simply stronger: it adds some new results to the collection of results generated by the original principle.)

> *Existence condition with induction* (EC+I): Where *x* and *y* are possible futures and *y* is accessible relative to *x*, *x* is morally worse than *y*, and a choice *c* made at *x* is wrong, only if there is a person *p* and an alternate accessible future *z* such that:
>
> (i) *p* does or will exist in *x*,
>
> (ii) *x* is worse for *p* than *y* *or* there is a *third* accessible future *z* such that *x* is worse for *p* than *z*, *and*
>
> (iii) *z* isn't ruled out (by prior application of a sufficient condition on moral worseness, e.g., Pareto reduction) as morally worse than any alternate future that is also accessible relative to *x*.

We can easily see that EC+I generates just the result that we want. Both people who do or will exist in f2 having been made as well off as (in the case of Polly) she accessibly can be made or as (in the case of Robbie) moral law itself allows, EC+I quickly instructs that f2 is at least as good as f1.

Thus a corrected and complete account of simple addition and reversal.

And, as anticipated earlier, the principles involved in that account can now seamlessly be applied to the indefinitely iterated case. We now have a principled basis for the claim that fn* is worse than f1* *and* a principled basis for the claim that f2* is at least as good as f1*.

In dealing with simple existence and reversal, the principle that gave us a starting point for the inductive analysis was Pareto reduction. (Once we secured the result under Pareto reduction that f3 is worse than f1, we could then move on to say that f2 is at least as good as f1.) But there's no reason to think that in other cases other principles—principles that we might introduce as we work toward a more complete statement of person-based consequentialism—might serve as the starting point.

Thus in other cases our starting point might be a *priority principle* (a principle that I won't aim to articulate in this book), one that we find highly intuitive, that we accept, and that we have carefully tested. Suppose such a principle implies that a given future *x*, given the avoidably appalling state that *x* assigns to a person *p*, is worse than a given accessible future *y*. Then, the existence condition in its inductive form—EC+I—by virtue of the fact that the priority principle has *already ruled x morally out of bounds* may then have something to say that will enable us to complete our account of the case.

Or it might be a principle that ensures that the *numbers count*—that, like the same people Pareto principle, establishes that it makes things better, other things equal, for ten people to enjoy wellbeing gains than for five people to enjoy wellbeing gains. Again, it needs to be a principle we find highly intuitive, that we accept, and that we have carefully tested. Given that that principle has already ruled morally out of bounds one or more alternate accessible futures, EC+I may again generate useful results.

(c) *Reject unrestricted anonymity in favor of restricted anonymity.* As anticipated, the identity-sensitive account rejects unrestricted anonymity. Given that f2, but not f3, is as least as good as f1, unrestricted anonymity must go.

When existence *isn't* on the table—when *all* of the accessible futures in the particular case contain exactly the same people—anonymity works perfectly well. When existence *is* on the table—as it is in the simple and indefinitely iterated cases, even though the two futures to be compared, f2 and f3, contain exactly the same people—anonymity, if not carefully restricted, can sometimes fail.

When anonymity is properly restricted, it's a great principle. It comports perfectly with the idea that moral law generally doesn't care *who* you are—that moral law is, other things equal, indifferent or impartial between a given tradeoff being made in favor of the one person or the other. But we can accept those points while also insisting that the fact of a *merely reversing change* in certain variable population cases may not tell us all that we need to know about how the futures that constitute those cases are to be compared.

As noted, one properly restricted form of anonymity would limit application to cases in which exactly the same people do or will exist in every accessible future.

But another properly restricted form of anonymity is more flexible—and of more interest here since our cases typically include at least one person whose existence is at stake. It's that more flexible principle that can help us to complete the account of the tradeoff to exist case (Figure 4.6.3a) that we deferred earlier on.

> *Restricted anonymity principle.* For any futures *x*, *y*, and z such that *y* and *z* are accessible relative to *x*, *if* exactly the same people

> do or will exist in *x* and *y*, and *if* each such person has exactly the same wellbeing level in *x* that that same person has in *y* except for a merely reversing change across a subset of those people consisting of p and q, *and if* each person who does or will exist in *x* and *y* has as much wellbeing in *x* and *y* as that person has in *z*, then, if either one of *p* and *q* has at least as much wellbeing in *x* as that person has in any further accessible future, then *y* is at least as good as *z*.

If, in other words, *one* of p's or q's wellbeing levels is maximized in *x* (and each other condition is met), we may infer that *y* is at least as good as *z*. By implication: since the difference between f2 and f3 in tradeoff to exist is limited to a merely reversing change and f2 is maximizing for David, and since (in contrast to simple addition and reversal) the conditions are otherwise met, we may infer (by running the principle twice) that f2 and f3 are each at least as good as f1.

EC tells us more: that f1 isn't worse than f2 or f3. Conceptual principles then complete the picture. Since f1 isn't worse than f2 or f3, and since f2 and f3 aren't worse than f1, f2 and f3 are both exactly as good as f1.

The connection thesis completes the account. Moral law doesn't obligate agents to bring either David or Ebon into existence. But nor does moral law obligate agents to leave them out of existence altogether.

Let's now go back to the case of simple addition and reversal. The underlying deficiency of the unrestricted anonymity principle is that it fails to take into account—that it whitewashes over—the distinction between *what happens to Polly in f2 and what happens to Robbie in f3*, a distinction that can be made if and only if our principle finds a way to take into account what happens to Polly and to Robbie *in f1* as well. It's that distinction that the identity-sensitive solution turns on.

Specifically, among the *accessible* futures that *haven't already* been ruled morally out of bounds are *two* futures that make things better for Polly. EC+I's necessary condition (as well as EC's; take your pick) on f3 being worse than f1 is thus easily satisfied. We can thus consistently take the position—thanks to Pareto reduction—that f3 is worse than f1. But things are very different for Robbie in f2: among the futures that are accessible and haven't already been ruled morally out of bounds, *none* makes things better for Robbie than f2. The condition is thus failed and we infer—thanks to EC+I—that f2 isn't worse than f1.

The *identity-sensitive* solution thus takes the position that, on occasion, just *who one is* bears on the moral analysis—that, notwithstanding the fact that the populations and the wellbeing positions are identical in f2 and f3, making things worse for Polly in f3 is morally distinct from making things worse for Robbie in f2.

It's not *who you are* in the "who's your daddy" sense of that phrase that matters. But *who you are* in a given future in the sense of what is going on with you in alternate accessible futures can be critical. And we thus reject unrestricted anonymity.

The identity-sensitive solution to the anonymity puzzle we've sketched here rejects anonymity in its unrestricted form. But we haven't simply rejected unrestricted anonymity by fiat, by waving our hands. We haven't simply pointed out the obvious—that rejecting unrestricted anonymity opens the door to one way of saving the intuition that fn* is worse than f1*. Rather, we have articulated just *why* unrestricted anonymity fails: it fails in virtue of the fact that it whitewashes a distinction that, on analysis, we recognize as morally critical.

Once we wash off the whitewash, we find ourselves, I think, with a new platform of shared intuition, one that helps us to understand just how unrestricted anonymity—though widely accepted—can, on occasion, go wrong. And thus we solve the puzzle without throwing out any of the puzzle pieces.

5.5 Objections and replies

5.5.1 Wouldn't the mere addition principle provide a simpler way to avoid anti-natalism?

It might seem that a simpler way to secure the result that f2 is at least as good as f1—to secure, that is, the anti-anti-natalist thrust of the identity-sensitive account—would be to resurrect the mere addition principle. We could then avoid the (minimal) trouble of invoking the inductive approach.

According to the mere addition principle, all we need to see, to infer that f2 is at least as good as f1, is that Robbie's existence in f2 is a *mere* addition: it's an existence worth having, and one that makes things worse for no one in f1 at all. How could such an addition make things *worse*?

But let's not waste our time. We've already rejected the mere addition principle in Chapter 3. We just really don't need *any* principle that, like the mere addition principle, begs the very questions we are now working so hard now to settle.

Now, if we had no other principle that would do the work of securing the result in the simple case that f2 isn't worse than f1, we'd *arguably* have a basis for resurrecting the mere addition principle (or taking some other very dramatic action). But we do have another principle: a better principle.

5.5.2 Doesn't the identity-sensitive solution imply moral actualism?

In drawing the distinction between Polly's situation in f2 and Robbie's situation in f3, it might seem that we are assigning a certain moral status to one class of people we deny to others. Specifically, it might seem that we are assigning a moral status to Polly on the ground that Polly *exists* in *all three futures* and assigning no moral status to Robbie at all on the ground that Robbie *doesn't* exist in *all three futures*. We are holding it against Robbie that Robbie's existence is—we might say—merely *contingent* and counting it in favor of Polly that Polly exists—we might say—*necessarily*. We are saying that Robbie's loss in f2 *doesn't* matter morally while Polly's loss in f3 *does* matter morally.

But making a person's *moral* status a function of that person's *existential* status—however that is specifically accomplished, by way of moral *actualism* or specifically by way of moral *necessitarianism*—would seem to be a mistake. Or so we explicitly determined in Section 2.3.

In fact, however, the identity-sensitive solution *doesn't* rely on the idea that some people do matter morally and others don't. If we revised simple addition and reversal to include a *fourth* future, one in which neither Polly nor Robbie ever exists at all, we would obtain exactly the same results we've already registered: that f3 is worse than f1, and that f2 is at least as good as f1. Nor have we even noted, in either presenting or analyzing the case, *which* future happens to be actual; nor do we try to relativize our betterness rankings to particular subclasses of people (e.g., those who exist in f2 and f3 but not in f1). We are safe, in other words, from charges of moral actualism.

5.5.3 Isn't unrestricted anonymity itself a critical piece of the puzzle?

Certainly, theorists for whom unrestricted anonymity is ingrained—who feel *certain* that f2 is exactly as good as f3 in simple addition and reversal—will think that that principle is a critical piece of the puzzle. But those same theorists are accustomed to a framework in which the comparison of one future against a second can be accomplished without a glance at any third future. Which is just to say—per the accessibility axiom—that they are accustomed to a framework in which certain details of the one future or the other future—including the details that distinguish Polly's situation in f3 from Robbie's situation in f2—are screened out of the analysis. Once we appreciate that those details aren't incidental and are rather critical to the analysis of the case, we can also appreciate that unrestricted anonymity, though generally exactly right, can in the odd case get things exactly wrong.

Now, theorists for whom unrestricted anonymity is ingrained often happen to be theorists for whom the repugnant conclusion in any of its various instantiations is also no big deal. (Either the conclusion isn't repugnant at all, or it's repugnant but, since it's supposedly an implication of all viable moral theories, it's a conclusion we are forced to hold our noses and accept.)

What I just want to underline here is that theorists who fall into that camp have an off ramp: for them, the anonymity puzzle is no puzzle at all.

But the rest of us—for whom the results that fn* is at least as good as f1* and that *Z* is at least as good as *A really are* repugnant; for theorists for whom the intuitions that fn* really is worse than f1*and that *Z* really is worse than A are deeply held—there *is* a puzzle.

And any proposed solution to that puzzle that simply denies the intuition that fn* isn't at least as good as f1* *isn't within the method of this book.* Such a proposal doesn't even begin to solve the puzzle. Instead, it just throws out one of the puzzle pieces.

6
The better chance puzzle

6.1 Probability and moral evaluation

6.1.1 The better chance case

It is plausible that choices that, at the moment just prior to performance, look to be choices that will produce less than amazingly wonderful futures but are such that each and every alternate choice stands only a very small chance of producing a better future and a very great chance of producing a much worse future are often permissible.

That thought is nicely demonstrated in ordinary same people cases. When you are sick, we think that it's morally—and legally—permissible for your doctor to prescribe a pill that has a 90% chance of curing 90% of what ails you and a 10% chance of leaving you just as you are *if* the doctor's *only other available choice* is to prescribe another pill that has a 10% chance of completely curing you and a 90% chance of killing you. It's perfectly fine, in other words, for your doctor—based on information available just prior to choice—to make a choice that has a probability of 0.9 of leaving you in good health and a probability of 0.1 of leaving you just as you are when your doctor's *only other choice*—again, based on information available prior to choice—has a probability of 0.1 of leaving you in excellent health but a probability of 0.9 of killing you.

That same thought also applies in certain variable population cases. Where a choice increases the chances that an additional person will come into existence, we might well forgive the fact

The Existence Puzzles. M. A. Roberts, Oxford University Press. © Oxford University Press 2024.
DOI: 10.1093/oso/9780197544143.003.0006

that that choice perhaps doesn't *quite* maximize wellbeing for that person.

Consider, for example, the *better chance case* (Figure 6.1). There, the agent—a woman—must choose between undergoing a fairly effective and relatively safe treatment for an infertility issue and declining that treatment.

Figure 6.1: Better chance case						
	c1: agent *doesn't* choose fertility treatment			c2: agent *does* choose fertility treatment		
probability→	0.000001	0.999999		0.001	0.999	
wellbeing ↓	f1	f2	*other futures*	f3	f4	*other futures*
+10	**Yanni**	--	**[child other than Yanni]**	--	--	--
+9	--	--		**Yanni**	--	**[child other than Yanni]**
...	...	...	...	...	...	...
+0		*Yanni; other children*	*Yanni; other children less the one who exists*		*Yanni; other children*	*Yanni; other childrenless the onewho exists*

Figure 6.1 Better chance case

If the agent chooses not to undergo treatment—if she chooses c1—a particular child, Yanni, will very probably never exist at all. (Indeed, it's very probable that, without treatment, the agent will not have any child at all.) If, against all odds, Yanni *does* come into existence under c1, he will have a wellbeing level of +10, a life well worth living. In contrast, if the agent chooses treatment—if she chooses c2—Yanni's chances of coming into existence will be much better. Now, even under c2, Yanni's coming into existence will remain highly improbable. The fertility treatment may well not work or, if it does work, it may well happen that some other child, a child *nonidentical* to Yanni, will come into existence instead of Yanni. Still, c2 increases Yanni's chances of coming into existence by a few orders of magnitude.

The downside is that the fertility treatment comes with mildly adverse side effects for *any* child who is then produced. At +9, Yanni's existence in f3 would still be well worth having. But c2 effectively *caps* his wellbeing level at +9. Under c1 and c1 alone is there *any* chance that Yanni's wellbeing will be *maximized* at +10. Downside notwithstanding, we all surely agree that c2 is *perfectly permissible.*

Let's stipulate—for ease of discussion and not because it will have any bearing on our moral analysis—that the agent thinks so, too, and that she accordingly chooses c2, that f3 in fact unfolds, and that Yanni in fact comes into existence.[1] We may think it's too bad Yanni sustains a small loss of wellbeing in f3—and a morally significant loss of wellbeing at that since Yanni exists in f3.[2] But we recognize that, just *prior* to choice, the then-not-yet-existing Yanni faced an across-the-board, grave existential risk: while neither c1 nor c2 comes close to *assuring* Yanni's future existence, c2 makes Yanni's coming into existence *far more likely* than c1: a (relatively) robust 1 in 1000 versus a miniscule 1 in 1,000,000.

This is a case, then, in which the *better chance* that c2 creates for Yanni of his ever coming into existence at all functions to make c2 at f3 a permissible choice *notwithstanding* the fact that c1 at f1 makes things better for Yanni—creates more wellbeing for Yanni—than c2 at f3.

The fact that Yanni's existence at +9 under c2 in f3 is well worth having—that it's clearly *better for him* than never existing at all—is important. But our work in connection with the Pareto puzzle in Chapter 3 shows that the fact that, even when other things are equal, the additional existence is worth having *isn't sufficient* to make a choice permissible. What converts c2 from a choice that would otherwise be considered wrong into a choice that we all surely consider perfectly permissible seems clearly to be the *better chance* that Yanni will ever come into existence at all that comes with c2.

[1] On the view of this book, this stipulation has *no bearing* at all on the moral analysis. It does, however, mean that we can more easily talk about Yanni's situation.

[2] See Section 3.4.1 and Appendix B (loss distinction thesis).

As we shall shortly see, that phenomenon leads us directly into the *better chance puzzle*. But it also immediately raises some interesting questions. The most critical among those questions is just this: What is the *underlying mechanism*—the formula—responsible for making that conversion happen?

It might seem that the question of mechanism is easy enough to answer. Given that c2 at f3 doesn't maximize wellbeing for Yanni, it might seem obvious that what converts c2 at f3 from the wrong choice that it would otherwise be into a permissible choice is the fact that c2 maximizes what is called *expected value* for Yanni. Calculations of expected value—as we shall see—take into account both a given choice's *accessible results* and the *probability*, for each such result, that that result will unfold under that choice.[3] As we shall also see, however, expected value theory is problematic. Accordingly, in what follows, we'll need to take up still another question: Can we find *a better way* of taking probabilities into account? I think that we can.

But let's start with the puzzle.

6.1.2 The puzzle

The *better chance puzzle* arises when we try to say how we happen to know—and we do intuitively think we know—that, while Yanni's better chance of existence under c2 in the better chance case comes with enough moral sizzle to drown out the fact that f3 is worse for Yanni than f1 and render c2 permissible, that moral sizzle isn't enough to make c2 not just permissible but also *obligatory*.

[3] A further question is *just how far* we should take the claim that c2 in f3 is permissible due to Yanni's better chance of coming into existence under c2. Do we want, for example, to say that that same better chance helps to determine, not just c2's *permissibility*, but also how f3 compares against f1, f2, and f4 in respect of *moral betterness*? I think not. But we'll come back to that question in Section 6.2.2.

A slightly revised case raises the question more plainly. In the revised case, the chances of existence for Yanni are exactly as they are in the original case *but* the *possible wellbeing levels* under each of the two choices are identical—are, say, not +10 and +9 but rather +10 and +10. If Yanni's better chance of existence under c2 comes with enough moral oomph to make c2 permissible in the original case, then why is it that in the revised case that moral oomph doesn't function to convert c2 from a choice we'd otherwise consider *merely permissible* into a choice that we are compelled to say is *obligatory*?

And why is it that, while *any* person's—Yanni's in the original and revised cases or anyone else's in another case—better chance of existence can (depending, we assume, on the details of the case) function to convert a choice we'd otherwise consider wrong into a choice we all surely consider permissible, the *fact* of that same person's existence doesn't seem to function in that way at all? Why is it that—in, for example, the asymmetry case (Figure 2.1)—the fact (the *certainty*) that the happy Haaken will exist under c4 *doesn't do a thing* to make us think that c4 itself is anything more than *merely permissible*?

Back to the better chance case in its original form. We want to say that, while it's *permissible* for the agent in the better chance case to choose to undergo treatment, it's also *permissible* for her to *decline* treatment.[4] We want to say that c2 isn't obligatory and that c1 isn't wrong.

But can we have it both ways? The one way is inspired by a highly plausible take on the *basic maximizing intuition* itself. The better chance of a worth-having existence that Yanni has under c2, given

[4] It's important to note that that intuition has *nothing* to do with the agent's autonomy or our respect for autonomy but rather squarely concerns what it is *morally permissible* for her to do. Respect for autonomy may be relevant when an agent wants to make a choice that places *the agent* at risk. But when the agent's choice puts others (including the agent's own progeny) at risk, and when the fact of risk really isn't up for debate (it's not a matter of, e.g., allowing a child to read a book that others find offensive; it's a matter, rather, of letting a child die whom any competent medical practitioner could save), any *credible* "respect for autonomy" principle will remain silent.

what it does *for Yanni*, has a very definite and highly salutary moral function. Without that better chance, c2 would clearly be wrong. The other hails directly out of the *basic existential intuition*. Thus the existence condition (EC) insists that c2 isn't to be considered morally preferable to c1: that, other things equal, we're *not obligated* to confer either existence itself or the better chance of existence on additional possible people. c1 and c2 are both perfectly permissible choices.

Some theorists may take the position that the moral significance of the probabilities at stake in cases like the better chance case proves that the basic existential intuition—along with EC, along with the Pareto reduction principle, along with still other components of person-based consequentialism we've introduced in earlier chapters—is just false.

But all that has up to this point actually been *proved* is that our basic intuitions are again on a collision course. The goal of this chapter is to reconcile those intuitions against each other—to solve the puzzle, not by way of throwing out any of the puzzle pieces, but by coming to see how the pieces fit together.

Of course, intuitions can go awry. But if the proposal that *purports* to solve the better chance puzzle simply tosses out a deeply held, widely shared intuition without putting forward a new platform of deeply held, widely shared intuition—one that loosens the hold the original intuition has on us—then that proposal will not have actually solved the puzzle but will only have set it aside.

6.2 Expected value: The wrong way to make a wrong a right

6.2.1 The concept of expected value; extending the existence condition to take probability into account

How can it be that the *better chance of existence* can convert a choice that would otherwise be considered wrong into a choice that is perfectly permissible when the *actual fact of existence* seems not to have any moral impact at all?

Let's start by trying to identify the *underlying mechanism* that explains just how it is that Yanni's better chance of existence under c2 in the better chance case makes c2 permissible.

It may have seemed to many theorists (and at one time seemed to me[5]) that it's the fact that c2 maximizes *expected wellbeing*—that is, *expected value* (EV)—for Yanni that makes c2, whether performed in f3 or in f4, permissible.[6]

> The *expected value* of a given choice *c* for a person *p* at a future *x* (EV(*c*, *p*, *x*)) = the summation of: the wellbeing level *p* has under *c* at *x* and the wellbeing level *p* has under *c* at each future accessible relative to *x*, multiplied, for each such future, by the probability that future will obtain given *c*.[7]

We then calculate as follows:

> EV(c1, Yanni, f1) = $10 \times 0.000001 + 0 \times 0.999999 = 0.00001$; and
> EV(c2, Yanni, f3) = $9 \times 0.001 + 0 \times 0.999 = 0.009$.

[5] For reasons I lay out in Section 6.2.3, that idea now seems hopelessly flawed. For earlier versions of my argument questioning the expected value approach, see 2019c, 2022a, and 2022b.

[6] If, under an expected value approach, c2 is permissible at f3, c2 is also permissible at f4. Thus the expected value of a given choice is the same regardless of the future in which that choice is made. For reasons that shall become clear, however, we'll routinely talk about the expected value of a choice for a person *at a future*. For a clear introduction to expected value theory, see Feldman 2006. In that paper, Feldman argues against expected value theory on grounds of impracticality—grounds other than those I describe in this chapter.

[7] To say that a person has a certain wellbeing level under a given choice at a given future means, among other things, that that choice is in fact performed at that future. One other note: expected value theories are typically formulated not in terms of *accessible* futures, but rather *possible* futures. For purposes here, however, that's a distinction without a difference since the probability of a possible future unfolding that isn't itself accessible is zero.

We obtain the same value for EV(c1, Yanni, f2) as for EV(c1, Yanni, f1), and the same value for EV(c2, Yanni, f4) as for EV(c2, Yanni, f3).[8]

Since the expected value of c2 for Yanni, wherever performed, is greater than the expected value of c1 for Yanni, wherever performed, c2 is the choice that maximizes expected value for Yanni.

We might then propose that, when no one else's wellbeing or existence is at stake, a choice that *maximizes expected value* for a person is permissible.

Such a sufficient condition on permissibility—on its face—seems plausible. That's especially so—and we'll come back to this point in Section 6.2.2—*if* we take care at this juncture *not* to aggressively overreach. If we take care not to *assume* that the maximization of expected value is the *uniquely salient feature* in the evaluation of choice. We want to retain the result that, other things equal, the choice that, like c2, maximizes expected value is permissible. We don't want—inadvertently or not—also to take a position that forces us to say that c2—having maximized expected value—is *obligatory*.

What we need is a principle that makes the point we want to make regarding Yanni's better chance of existence under c2 *without* jettisoning the work that we've already done in articulating the basic existential intuition—including, most prominently, EC itself.

And we can come up with just such a principle by simply adding to the part of EC that governs the evaluation of choice a further necessary condition—a *probability-based* condition—on when a given choice is wrong.

Moreover, in light of the fact that the better chance puzzle arises in the context of how *choices* are to be evaluated and not how *futures*

[8] See Chapter 6 note 6 (on the expected value of a choice independent of where performed).

are to be compared in respect of their moral betterness, we can also make things simpler.[9] We can, for present purposes, cull out the parts of EC that rank futures—*without* rejecting those parts—and focus only on the parts of EC that evaluate choice. Thus the following extension of EC—an extension that is, again, perfectly consistent with EC in its original form.

> *Existence condition for choice with expected value* (ECC+EV).
> A choice c made at a future x is wrong *only if* there is a person p and an alternate available choice c' made at an alternate possible future y accessible relative to x such that:
> (i) p does or will exist in x,
> (ii) x is worse for p than y, *and*
> (iii) $EV(c, p, x) < EV(c', p, y)$.

Where a choice c is performed in a future x, ECC+EV implies that that choice *isn't* wrong—is *perfectly permissible*—*if*, for each person who *does or will exist* in x, *either* that person's *wellbeing* is maximized in x *or* that person's *expected value* under c in x is maximized.

Since c2 maximizes expected value for Yanni, ECC+EV implies that c2 (whether performed in f3 or in f4) is permissible. And it does so without jettisoning the idea that the choice that makes things worse for *no one at all*—no existing or future person—is also permissible. Thus ECC+EV also implies that c1 at f1, where Yanni's wellbeing is maximized, isn't wrong *and* that c1 at f2, where Yanni never exists at all, isn't wrong, either. Ditto c2 at f4.

Thus, a highly intuitive account of the better chance case: an account that reflects our maximizing values when it recognizes the critical role probability-based facts play in our moral analysis but

[9] For discussion of how probabilities affect not the evaluation of choice, but rather the comparison of futures in respect of their moral betterness, see Section 6.2.2. There, I take the position that they don't.

one that does so without forcing us—*trying* to force us—to jettison our existential values.

6.2.2 Avoiding overreach

ECC+EV thus produces a highly plausible account of the better chance case.

We haven't, though, quite solved the better chance puzzle. But before we say why that's so, I want to underline two respects in which ECC+EV limits the impact of Yanni's better chance to exist under c2 and why transgressing those limits—why overreach in this context—is a mistake. We'll take the time to do that now, despite the fact that we'll shortly reject ECC+EV on other grounds, since we'll want to preserve those features of ECC+EV going forward.

(a) *Probabilities relevant to the evaluation of choice but not the comparison of futures.* As noted, ECC+EV is restricted to how probabilities bear on the evaluation of *choice and choice alone.* It thus doesn't require any revision in any of our earlier work on how *futures* are to be compared in respect of their moral betterness. That work includes the part of EC that provides a necessary condition on which one future is worse than another as well as the same people Pareto principle.[10] Those two principles together, in combination with conceptual principles that we've already accepted, tell us that f1 is better than f3 and that f2 and f4 are exactly as good as f1.

Does that restriction to choice keep expected value theory from living up to its full potential? Is it a mistake *not* to extend expected value theory to the ranking of *futures*?

I have no doubt that the divergent probabilities in the better chance case—or in any case—are woven into the details of the

[10] It also includes the Pareto reduction principle and the existence condition with induction (EC+I), though those principles have no application to the cases we consider in this chapter.

distinct futures that constitute that case. Thus whatever it is that makes Yanni's existence more likely under c2 than under c1 has *much* to do with the details of the futures that accessibly unfold under those choices. It's c1 *in combination with* the laws of physics that obtain in f1 and f2 and the history those futures happen to share (a history that can't accessibly be undone) that together make Yanni's coming into existence *less* likely under c1, and it's c2 *in combination with* all those same laws and that same history that make Yanni's coming into existence *more* likely under c2.

That means that we perhaps could, if we chose to do so, find a way to take probabilities into account in ranking futures.

But it doesn't follow that that's the theoretically correct thing to do. If making things morally better is a matter of making things better for people—and surely it is—then what matters for people would seem to have little to do with the silent probabilities that happen to be embedded in a given future in which that person does or will exist. We may well appreciate that no wrongs have been committed against us. But that fact on its own (apart from the positive emotion that comes with that appreciation) *doesn't* make things *better for* us. The physician who truthfully informs you on your deathbed that he or she made the right expected value calculation in treating you *doesn't* make things *better for you*. It may be nice to hear (or it may just be annoying). But that probabilistic detail doesn't seem to move either your wellbeing level or the moral betterness of the future in which you find yourself.

It thus is not obvious at all that expected value theory should have any say at all in determining how f1 compares against f3 or how f2 and f4 compare against f1. Our earlier work on those comparisons—according to which f1 is better than f3, and f2 and f4 are exactly as good as f1—in view of the fact that it's *moral betterness* that we are aiming to compare and not something else entirely—perfectly reflects both the basic *existential* intuition and the basic *maximizing* intuition.

Failing, then, to keep the *separate tasks*—the evaluation of choice and the ranking of futures—*separate* won't advance our understanding of how moral law works at all. Instead, it would function only to tie our hands when it comes to actually solving, rather than just setting aside, our puzzle.[11]

(b) *Probability-related facts not the uniquely salient feature in evaluating choice.* At least some theorists stand behind a more aggressive use of expected value theory. They favor an approach that insists, not just that c2 is *permissible*, but also that c2 is *obligatory*—*and* that c1 is *wrong*.

A more aggressive approach includes, most prominently, the idea that expected value is a choice's *uniquely salient feature* for purposes of determining permissibility. It's true that any such more aggressive approach—just like the less aggressive approach captured in ECC+EV—comes with a plus: it generates the highly intuitive result that the otherwise wrong c2 in the better chance case itself is indeed permissible. It accepts that particular piece of the puzzle.

But the *minus* of the more aggressive approach is that it throws out the rest of our puzzle pieces. Thus it implies that the highly intuitive claim that c1 is *perfectly permissible* is just false. It would try to have us say, instead, that it's *morally wrong* for the agent in the better chance case to decline the fertility treatment altogether—to fail to do her part to create the better chance that some additional child or another will make its way into existence. And—having gone that far—it would try to have us say as well that it's *morally wrong* in

[11] If—*if*—(i) we could bring ourselves to accept the position that f3 is better than f1 (which seems preposterous) and the position that f4 is better than f2 (which also seems preposterous) and (ii) we, at the same time, found that the basic existential intuition applied to *choice* still had a strong hold on us, then we would need to reject the connection thesis: the thesis that the tasks of evaluating *choices* and ranking futures are closely, if not *perfectly*, connected. And what then? Then we would need to open up all over again a question we thought we had put to bed in Section 1.8.2: *What are we doing* when we are purporting to compare *futures* in respect of their moral betterness *if* that task is not closely connected with the evaluation of *choice*? And that question, for the reasons stated in that earlier chapter, seems to me to be closed.

the context of the asymmetry (Figure 2.1) to fail to bring the happy child into existence.[12]

But I think that's a mistake. The better thing to say is just this: if the agent in the happy child case isn't obligated to confer existence on the happy Haaken—and, per the basic existential intuition, the agent isn't—then the agent in the better chance case isn't obligated to confer a better chance of existence on Yanni.

Of course, any theorist is free to *deem* correct—to *try* to accept—the position that the agent in the better chance case is *obligated* to create a better chance of existence for Yanni. But to do that *without* providing us with any new platform of deeply held, widely shared intuition that would serve to loosen the hold the contrary position has on us—and, beyond that, to loosen the hold the basic existential intuition itself has on us—doesn't even begin to help us solve the better chance puzzle. Instead, it simply asks us to ignore it.

What should at least make us question the more aggressive approach at a more theoretical level is the fact that we have *already shown* that a plausible account of the better chance case can be given using just the resources that have so far been put on the table, including the more modest ECC+EV. Whence, then, the need for the more aggressive approach? What, exactly, is the argument?

As noted earlier, we'll end up rejecting ECC+EV on other grounds in what follows. But what we won't do is put a more aggressive approach in its place.

12 And it would *try* to have us say in the context of Jaime versus Harry (Figure 1.2) that it's perfectly permissible to leave Jaime to suffer his terrible disease and bring Harry into existence. The more aggressive approach is one that many theorists, including Bostrom (see Preface note 21 and accompanying text), seem to favor. But I think that they've made a mistake. The intuition that it's OK *not* to bring the happy child into existence remains firmly rooted in our moral consciousness. So does the intuition that bringing Harry into existence doesn't even begin to make up for failing to step in to cure Jaime of his terrible disease. There's nothing in our discussion—or any reasoned discussion—of just how important probability-based facts are or the plusses and minuses of expected value theory that even *begins* to dislodge either of those two deeply held, widely shared intuitions.

6.2.3 The case of the all-but-known disaster

ECC+EV produces an intuitively plausible account of the better chance case. The case of the *all-but-known disaster* (Figure 6.2.3), however, shows that it's not a complete success.

Figure 6.2.3: All-but-known disaster 1M = 1,000,000				
	c1: agent doesn't choose risky life-extending treatment for her child		c2: agent chooses risky life-extending treatment for her child	
probability→	0.9999	0.0001	0.9999	0.0001
wellbeing↓	f1	f2	f3	f4
+1M	--	--	--	**Elnora**
+8	**Elnora**	**Elnora**	--	--
+0	--	--	--	--
−10	--	--	**Elnora**	--

Figure 6.2.3: All-but-known disaster

We can give some color to this case. Let's suppose that the agent, a mother, must make a certain sensitive medical decision on behalf of her child Elnora, a child who does or will exist no matter what choice the agent makes. The agent must choose whether to decline or accept a certain risky life-extending treatment on behalf of Elnora. The treatment will, if successful, produce an enormous benefit for Elnora. It will extend Elnora's already reasonably good life for *thousands and thousands* of years. But if the treatment fails, disaster will strike: Elnora's wellbeing level will plunge well into the negative range where it will stay for the remainder of Elnora's life.

What makes the potentially life-extending treatment *risky*—*really* risky—are the probabilities at play: the probability is very low—only 0.0001—that the treatment, if chosen, will succeed, and very high—0.9999—that the treatment, if chosen, will fail.

Thus the agent *all but knows* that, if she chooses c2, Elnora will be left with a life substantially *less* than a life worth living. The agent *all but knows* that c2 will be a complete disaster for her child.

What happens to Elnora if the agent *declines* the risky life-extending treatment on behalf of Elnora? The agent can then be certain that Elnora will have, at +8, a reasonably good life. Let's stipulate that, at +8, she will have a wellbeing level that is just about the same as both the agent's own wellbeing level and the wellbeing levels of others in the agent's own and in Elnora's generational cohorts.

Two features of this case should be highlighted. First, in contrast to the better chance case, Elnora in all-but-known disaster faces *no* existential risk. Whether the mother, the agent, chooses c1 or c2, Elnora's existence, or Elnora's coming into existence, is a certainty. (Perhaps Elnora already exists—or perhaps she will exist whether the agent chooses c1 or c2.)

Second, c2 is a single, *one-off, high risk/high reward,* choice. Specifically: the option for the agent to pursue a *long-term* strategy that allows for the choice of c2 *in the context of a sequence of choices* that includes not just c2 but also successive c2-like choices—choices that *repeat* the risk-and-reward pattern that we see under c2, choices that will sometimes lead to horrific results for Elnora but sometimes lead to enormous gains for Elnora—is *not* available to the agent.

The wellbeing levels thus displayed under c2 at f3 and f4 represent not peaks and valleys along the trajectory of Elnora's life in f3 but rather Elnora's *overall, lifetime* wellbeing levels at f3 and at f4.

Elnora may thus end up as the *single-trial non-beneficiary* of the high risk/high reward c2.

Is the agent's choice of c2 wrong?

No, according to ECC+EV. We could easily, unobstructedly, say that c2 at f3 is wrong *but for* the *tiny* probability that a *very great* benefit will accrue to Elnora under c2. But balancing that tiny probability against that very great benefit in the manner prescribed by ECC+EV changes everything.

We calculate as follows:

EV(c1, Elnora, f1) = 8 × .9999 + 8 × .0001 = 7.9992 + .0008 = 8; and
EV(c2, Elnora, f3) = −10 × .9999 + 1M × .0001 = −9.999 + 100 = 90.001.

c2 thus maximizes expected value on behalf of Elnora—whether performed in f3 or in f4. Thus c2—whether performed in f3 or in f4—is, under ECC+EV, *perfectly permissible.*

But can that result be correct? Do we think that the fact that Elnora might—*might, against all odds,* the chances of things turning out well for Elnora under c2 being a scant 1 in 10,000—obtain an enormous benefit converts what would otherwise be her clearly *wrong* choice at f3 into a *permissible* choice?

I don't think that we do. The concept of expected value helped to make sense of our intuitions in the better chance case—and in a slew of other cases as well. But it doesn't help us make sense of all-but-known disaster. Though c2 maximizes *expected value* for the one existing or future person Elnora who might possibly be affected by how the choice is made, we can surely agree—we surely have a strongly held, widely shared intuition—that c2 at f3 is *wrong.*

To test that intuition further—to make the case more vivid, *not* to change any details of the case that we've already stipulated and *not* because it will, or should, make any difference under any *correct* moral analysis—let's now add one final stipulation: that the agent *actually does* choose c2, and the entirely predictable f3 *actually does* obtain.

We now see in our mind's eye at the actual future the miserable child, the wrongful life, the hapless mother. It now seems clearer than ever that c2 at f3 is wrong.

Of course, in *another case altogether*—call it *long-run risk reduction*—we may well say that a c2-*like* choice is permissible. In that case, the agent has the option of completing a *sequence* of high risk/high reward choices, commencing with a c2-like choice and continuing with (perhaps very many) successive c2-like choices, choices that repeat the risks and rewards for Elnora that come with c2 itself. *Provided* that the available sequence is sufficiently long *and* that the agent *in fact* plays out the long-run strategy, plausibly the *first member* of that sequence *made in the context of a future in which the long-term strategy is carried out* plausibly *is* permissible. After all, *at some point* (we may well think) Elnora will *surely* luck out and accrue the enormous benefit—which, in turn, means that the risk that comes with the first member of that sequence—*in the context of a future in which the long-term strategy is played out*—is not really much of a risk at all.

To put the point another way, long-run risk reduction has us imagine peaks and valleys along the trajectory of Elnora's lifetime wellbeing level. It has us imagine Elnora as losing now, and now, and now, and then, finally, against the odds, gaining, and then again losing now, and now (part of the long-term strategy should surely be to quit at the very first gain).

But all-but-known disaster is *not* that sort of case. In all-but-known disaster, the first roll of the dice is for keeps. The accessible futures that include the choice of c2 are limited to just f3 and f4. And in each of those futures it's stipulated that c2 exists as just a *single, lonely, one-off* choice—and not as the beginning of a risk-reducing sequence of further c2-like choices.[13]

[13] In general, it's a mistake to think that what we say about the permissibility of a choice made (an act performed) in one future in one case must always be what we say about the permissibility of that same choice made in another future in another case. Thus the fact that c2 is permissible relative to (when chosen in) certain accessible futures in long-run risk reduction gives us *no reason at all* to say that c2 isn't wrong relative to (when chosen in) f3 in all-but-known disaster.

At least, that this would be a mistake is an essential tenet of any consequentialist approach. As Feldman points out, the same medicine might either save or kill a patient depending on whether or not it's followed up by a second medicine, and we can consistently take the position that giving the one medicine is permissible relative to (when made in) the future in which it's followed up by the second but impermissible relative to the future in which it's not (Feldman 1986).

Now, some theorists might deploy the concept of *risk aversion* to try to defend the expected value approach and explain away the intuition that c2 at f3 is wrong (or perhaps to say that, relative to the risk averse agent, c2 is wrong, but relative to the risk neutral agent, c2 is permissible). And perhaps inquiries into risk aversion may help to fill out a plausible account of long-run risk reduction. (Such considerations might—*might*; I'm unsure they actually *do*—help us defend, for example, the idea that, even when a sequence of c2-like choices would dramatically reduce the chance of a bad outcome for Elnora, it might still be rational for the agent to decline to commence the sequence.)

But in all-but-known disaster it seems *highly implausible* that, even from the perspective of the evaluator *neutral* in respect of risk, c2 at f3 is permissible. More plausibly, even from that perspective c2 at f3 remains wrong given that the agent *all but knows* c2 will end in disaster for her child.

Thus the appeal to expected value is problematic. That should not come as a surprise to us. Expected value theory has faced problems before. Theorists still enthralled with expected value theory may continue to insist that the rational and right thing to do in the context of the well-known two-envelope problem is to switch the envelopes (and then to switch back, etc.). But outside that camp that response has seemed wildly inadequate. Yes, it's been a challenge to say exactly where the theory goes wrong when applied to that case. But that *at least in its application* in the two-envelope problem the theory has somehow gone awry seems very clear.[14]

At the same time, we obviously can't let go of the idea that probabilities play a critical role in moral evaluation. In the better chance case itself, for example, it seems obvious that it's the

[14] My own view on that riveting problem is that it shows that expected value theory must at least be applied with caution: it fails in cases in which we, in effect, know more than we are supposed to know to ensure a correct application of the expected value calculation (Roberts 2009a). I thank Edmund Gettier for his work in helping me understand the gravity of the two-envelope problem.

balancing of Yanni's better chance of existence under c2 against his less-than-maximized existence in f3 that converts the otherwise wrong c2 into a choice that is perfectly permissible. The question we face now is whether there exists any alternate mechanism of bringing probabilities into the picture that is itself more plausible.

6.3 Probable value: A better way to make a wrong a right

6.3.1 A closer look at expected value

Totalism takes an aggregative approach.[15] It moves directly to determine whether one future is better than another, once it's given the respective summations for each such future of *raw* wellbeing levels.

Now, as Chapter 4 ("The addition puzzle") argues, the problem with totalism isn't necessarily that it *aggregates*—that it loves *addition*. It's, rather, that it *prematurely* aggregates. It aggregates wellbeing levels that haven't yet been adjusted in a way that would take our existential values into account. It aggregates without first attending to—and often without ever attending to—all of a given case's morally critical details. (Which means it ends up adding up the wrong things.)

To go back to the case of Jaime versus Harry: the summation of individual wellbeing levels at f1 is exactly the same as the summation at f2. Totalism, accordingly, immediately instructs that f1 is exactly as good as f2. But that result is insensitive to the fact that in

[15] Ditto a traditional form of *averagism*, which determines whether one future is better than another by taking those same summations and then dividing each by the number of people who do or will exist in the particular future.

Just a reminder: *totalism* for purposes here is just the traditional total form of consequentialism—totalism as defined by the raw addition principle. It works by adding up units of raw wellbeing, *unadjusted* to reflect the values of equality, fairness, priority, justice, and desert—and *unadjusted* as well to reflect our *existential* values.

the one future Harry's wellbeing level is low because he *never exists* while Jaime's wellbeing level is low because he *exists and suffers*. Can the one future really be *exactly as morally good as* the other? No. But to get any more accurate result, we need to be able to say more about what is going on in the two futures than that the individual wellbeing levels—10 and 0 in the one future and 10 and 0 in the other—add up to the same amount. We need to be able to distinguish between the zero wellbeing level that Jaime faces and the zero wellbeing level that Harry faces.

Moreover, there's nothing in the basic maximizing intuition itself or in maximizing consequentialism per se that forbids our attending to the existential details of a given case instead of whitewashing over them.

Thus the moral principles introduced *and accepted* in earlier chapters—the principles that help to define person-based consequentialism—*do* attend to those existential details. And they do so by taking a more *granulated* approach—by *disentangling* elements of our cases that it seems that we need to keep separate and not treat as morally indistinct. Thus in comparing one future against another, we—prior to aggregating, if we ever aggregate at all—consider *each* plight of *each and every person in each future one at a time*—and, beyond just that, for each such person relative to each such future, what is going on with that person *and* each other person in each accessible alternate future. Thus each *existing* person's plight, each *future* person's plight, each *merely possible* person's plight—these are all potentially critical moral details that no plausible moral theory will ignore.

Now, the totalist would note, correctly, that the summation of individual wellbeing levels for a given future actually does reflect the wellbeing level of *each and every person* who does or will exist in that future. What the totalist leaves out are the moral details relating to the plights themselves: that one person's wellbeing level is zero because that person *never exists at all* in the particular future and that another person's wellbeing level is zero because that person *exists and suffers*; that one person's wellbeing level is, at, say, +5, maximized for that person; that another person's wellbeing level at +5 could accessibly have been raised at no cost to anyone else at all.

We may, as Chapter 4 suggests, in the end determine that aggregation is critical. We still need to avoid *premature* aggregation: that is, adding up the wrong things. If we are to produce a theory that we might actually want to defend, then, before we aggregate, we must put quantifiers to work and examine and address *separately* the plights of each and every person in each accessible future.

The expected value calculation—just like totalism—is aggregative in nature. In fact, it takes aggregation a step further. It first multiplies distinct sorts of values (probabilities and results) together and then takes the relevant summation for each distinct future that might unfold under a given choice to produce a single value: the expected value of a given choice for a given person at a given future.

Now, any correct theory designed to take probabilities into account in evaluating choices can't proceed as though outliers don't exist. In, for example, all-but-known-disaster, a correct theory can't just *screen out* the fact that Elnora exists under c2 in f4 and is fabulously well off there. But nor, it seems, can it screen out the fact that the outlier (f4 under c2) in that one-off case has skewed our expected value calculation in a way that—if we accepted it—compels us to say that c2 at f3 is *perfectly permissible*: to say, more generally, that choices that *both* seem clearly wrong just prior to choice *and* that in fact turn out to be absolute disasters are in fact *perfectly permissible*.

And what is at the root of that unfortunate skewing is the theory itself—the theory that, at a critical juncture in its evaluation of a given case, simply whitewashes over the distinction between the product we arrive at when we multiply the minuscule chance by the spectacular result and the product we arrive at when we multiply the solid chance by the very good result.[16]

[16] Similarly, switching out talk about how probabilities and results are to be combined for purposes of the expected value calculation for talk about how *prospects* are to be

To get to a more accurate result in such a case, we'll instead need to disentangle the separate components that go into producing the identical products: the risk on the one hand and the result on the other; the probability, at a given future, that a choice will end in that future and the probability, at another future, that the same choice will end in the other future. We need a more *granulated* approach.

6.3.2 The concept of probable value

A concept that assigns a critical role to probability but does so in a way that helps to disentangle certain morally critical details of the choice under scrutiny, including details of the futures that might unfold under each of those choices, is the concept of *probable value (PV)*.

Let's start with how that concept applies in all-but-known disaster. We'll then turn back to the better chance case itself.

The underlying idea is that what makes c2 at f3 wrong in all-but-known disaster—the case in which c2 is performed and, entirely predictably, results in f3, which is itself a complete disaster for Elnora—can be located in a substantially narrower set of facts than what expected value theory contemplates. Thus expected value theory forced us to say that the tiny chance of f4 unfolding under c2 makes c2 at f4 *and* at f3 permissible. The test that makes use of the probable value calculation—as we shall see—doesn't make that tiny chance or that possible benefit for Elnora—that outlier—*irrelevant* to the test. But it also doesn't allow that chance or that result unduly to distort the moral evaluation. Moreover, it achieves that balance without compelling us to say, in the better chance case, that the choice that creates the better chance of existence for Yanni but

evaluated mashes together components that we need to disentangle from each other and examine and address separately.

doesn't maximize Yanni's wellbeing—that is, c2 in f3 in the better chance case—is somehow wrong.

Under the probable value approach, the tiny chance of f4 unfolding given c2 is relevant to the mechanics of bringing probabilities to bear in the context of moral evaluation *only* in virtue of the fact that it, being so tiny, means that there is a very great chance that f3 will unfold under c2 instead—a very great chance, that is, that c2 will end in disaster for Elnora. Under a probable value approach, the probability-significant feature of c2 at f3—what will determine, that is, whether the necessary condition on c2's being wrong is *satisfied* or (in contrast, as the expected value approach provides) or is *failed*—is just the very high probability, calculated just prior to choice, that f3 will obtain under c2. The very high probability that f3 will obtain given c2—more precisely, that the *wellbeing result r* (the *negative* wellbeing result *r*; the result for Elnora of −10 that c2 produces for Elnora at f3) will obtain—is the probability-significant feature that is critical for evaluating c2 at f3.[17]

It's that number that we should multiply by the wellbeing result *r* for Elnora at f3 to produce the *probable value of c2 for Elnora at f3* (PV(c2, Elnora, f3)).

[17] Here, we focus on the probability not that a given *future*, but rather that a given *wellbeing result for a given person* will obtain. We do that in virtue of the fact that such a *wellbeing result* can be shared across any number of futures. Thus a choice very unlikely to produce a particular *future* may at the same time be very likely to produce a particular *result*. The *expected* value calculation automatically takes into account all those distinct futures. The *probable* value calculation doesn't do that—and thus must incorporate some alternate means of taking into account the case in which *many tiny* chances of producing futures that have in common a particular result for a particular person add up to a *significant* chance of producing that result. To put the point another way: where we aim to evaluate one choice and see that an alternate choice, once we add up those many tiny chances, creates a significant chance of a better *result* for the individual (though not for any one future in which that result obtains), we want to leave the door open for the result that the one choice is wrong. I am grateful to Tomi Francis for a case that demonstrates the need to revise an earlier definition I proposed of probable value, one that defined probable value by reference to the probability that specific *futures*, not specific *results*, would unfold under the relevant choice (Nonidentity Workshop, Institute for Future Studies, Stockholm, February 8–9, 2020).

The definition of *probable value*, then, is just this:

> Where a choice c performed at a future x creates a probability n of the wellbeing result r a person p in fact has in x, the *probable value* of c for p at x ($PV(c, p, x)) = n(r)$.

And ECC+EV amended to include a necessary condition relating to *probable value* in place of a necessary condition on *expected* value is then:

> *Existence condition for choice with probable value* (ECC+PV). A choice c made at a future x is wrong *only if* there is a person p and an alternate available choice c' made at an alternative possible future y accessible relative to x such that:
> (i) p does or will exist in x,
> (ii) x is worse for p than y, *and*
> (iii) $PV(c, p, x) < PV(c', p, y)$.

In analyzing all-but-known disaster, we can start by calculating PV(c2, Elnora, f3). That will be just the very low wellbeing result Elnora has at f3 under c2 multiplied by the probability, given c2, that that result will obtain. Thus PV(c2, Elnora, f3) = −10 × 0.9999 = −9.999.

In contrast, PV(c1, Elnora, f1) is the wellbeing result for Elnora at f1 under c1 multiplied by the probability, given c1, that that result will obtain. Thus, even though the probability that *f1* will unfold under c1 is (only!) 0.9999, the probability of the *wellbeing result* that c1 in fact produces for Elnora at f1 is exactly 1 since, however the future unfolds under c1, Elnora's wellbeing level will be +8. Thus PV(c1, Elnora, f1) = 8 × 1 = 8, and ditto PV(c1, Elnora, f2).

Since Elnora exists in f1 and f2, *and* has more wellbeing in f1 and f2 than she has in f3 *and* PV(c1, f1, Elnora) is greater than PV(c2, f3, Elnora), the conditions that ECC+PV provides on c2 at f3 being wrong are all satisfied. ECC+PV is thus itself silent on whether c2 at f3 is permissible. That fact, in turn, opens the door to the conclusion that c2 at f3 is *wrong*.

And that's a significant advantage for ECC+PV over ECC+EV: we aren't *compelled* by ECC+PV—as we are by ECC+EV—to say that c2 at f3 is *permissible*.

Now, ECC+PV will evaluate c2 performed at f4 quite differently. Since f4 maximizes wellbeing for Elnora—Elnora is better off in f4 than in any alternate accessible future—and one of the necessary conditions ECC+PV provides is thus failed, ECC+PV implies that c2 at f4 is permissible.

Is that a problem for ECC+PV—more generally, for the strategy of simply adding another necessary condition to the necessary conditions EC itself provides? Is it a problem that a choice that *looked* to be wrong starting out has, against all odds, turned out to be permissible? If it is, then it's also a problem for ECC+EV, where we also simply added the condition without renouncing EC. But I think it isn't. Moral agents who have moral character will certainly stay away from choices that, prior to choice, look to be as problematic as c2 looks to be. But if things, against all odds, turn out well, it's not clear and indeed highly controversial whether the choice itself, that feature of the outer and not the inner world, is morally wrong. Thus, consistent with the original EC, ECC+PV, and for that matter ECC+EV as well take it that *wrongness* at a given future requires that things in fact, at the end of the day, be made *worse for* a person who does or will exist in the future than they are in at least one alternate accessible future. "No harm, no foul."

6.3.3 Missing results?

So far, so good. But we may want more. For we also think that c1, wherever performed, in all-but-known disaster is perfectly permissible. Yet ECC+PV's necessary conditions for when c1 is wrong are all satisfied: Elnora exists in both f1 and f2; the alternate accessible future f4 is better for Elnora than f1 or f2; and an alternate available choice c2 at an alternate accessible future f4 creates more probable value (at 1M × 0.0001; that is, 100) for Elnora than does c1 in f1 or f2 (at 8). (PV(c1, Elnora, f1) < PV(c2, Elnora, f4), and PV(c1, Elnora, f2) < PV(c2, Elnora, f4)).

ECC+PV thus fails to establish that c1 at f1 or at f2 is permissible. Now, it remains a huge plus for ECC+PV that—in contrast to ECC+EV—it avoids the surely false implication that c2 at f3 is permissible. And another significant plus: since ECC+PV establishes only a handful of *necessary* conditions (and no *sufficient* conditions) on when a choice is wrong, we'll never obtain from that principle the highly implausible result that c1 at f1 or c1 at f2 is *wrong*. (Whew.)

It would be nice to have a principle that would tell us that c1 at f1 and c1 at f2 are *permissible*. But what's critical, for the moment, is just to point out that ECC+PV leaves the door open for that result: that is, that it *avoids* the result that c1, wherever performed, is wrong.

6.3.4 The probable value solution to the better chance puzzle

Let's now apply ECC+PV to the better chance case. And let's start with c1 at f1, where the woman's choice not to undergo fertility treatment, against the odds, ends in existence for Yanni—and an existence that, as it happens, maximizes wellbeing for Yanni. ECC+PV, which retains the original intuition that wrongdoing requires worseness for a person who does or will exist at the relevant future, easily instructs that c1 at f1 is permissible. That's so, since Yanni's wellbeing is maximized in f1.

Then: c1 at f2, where the woman's choice not to undergo fertility treatment, perfectly predictably, ends in Yanni's never existing at all. According to ECC+PV—which, again, retains the original intuition that wrongdoing requires worseness for a person who does or will exist at the relevant future—c1 at f2 is permissible. That's so, since Yanni never exists in f2.

Then: c2 at f3. It's here that the concept of probable value becomes relevant. PV(c2, Yanni, f3) = 9 × 0.001 = 0.009, while PV(c1, Yanni, f1) = 10 × 0.000001 = 0.00001 and PV(c1, Yanni, f2) = 0 × 0.999999 = 0. There being no alternate choice performed at any alternate accessible future that creates more PV for Yanni than c2 at f3 does, the necessary condition on wrongdoing that ECC+PV provides is failed—and c2 at f3 is permissible.

6.3.5 Summing up

ECC+PV provides a complete evaluation of better chance case: all choices at all futures are permissible (yay!). Moreover, in contrast to ECC+EV, ECC+PV avoids the clearly false result in all-but-known disaster: that is, the result that c2 at f3 is permissible. That, in itself, is progress.

Finally, and also in all-but-known disaster, ECC+PV generates the result that c2 at f4 is permissible. A choice that looked to be wrong starting out under ECC+PV (as well as under EC) has turned out, against all odds, to be morally permissible. Agents of good moral character won't make such a bad moral bet. But agents of bad moral character may well make such a bet and yet *occasionally*, according to ECC+PV, end up doing the right—i.e., a *permissible*—thing. That result seems at least plausible provided that we keep our focus not on the agent's *character*, but on the *choice* the agent in fact makes within the context of a future that in fact unfolds.

6.4 Objections and replies

6.4.1 The nonidentity problem

One of Parfit's own formulations of what has been called the *person-affecting intuition* is just this: for a choice to be "bad"—that is, morally *wrong*—that choice must make things "bad for"—that is, *worse for*—a person who does or will exist.[18] What he then called the *nonidentity problem* attempted to show that that intuition is false.

That attempt has been widely considered—including by Parfit himself—as successful. And it's true that many of the principles that have been put forward that aim to articulate that intuition clearly *are* false.[19]

ECC+PV avoids any number of pitfalls. Nonetheless, the most potent versions of the nonidentity problem—the *probabilistic* versions, an instance of which we turn to just below[20]—at first

[18] Parfit 1987, 363. For this formulation of the underlying intuition to work as a principle we might actually want to defend, it's important to understand the "bad for" condition as requiring the far-reaching inquiry that EC itself requires—and to keep in mind that it provides only a necessary and not a sufficient condition on when a choice is "bad." Cf. Parfit's formulation in Parfit 2017.

[19] For a list of such clearly false principles, see Chapter 1 note 8 (list of failed attempts).

[20] *Probabilistic* versions of the nonidentity problem include Parfit's depletion and risky policy cases, Kavka's pleasure pill and slave child cases, and cases of climate change and historical injustice (see Parfit 1987, 351–379; Kavka 1981; Broome 1992; Sher 2005; Herstein 2008). As I argue in this chapter, analyses of these critical cases often come to their conclusions of "no harm done"—their conclusions that the person who comes into existence after the clearly wrong choice has been performed aren't made worse off but are if anything benefited as a consequence of that choice—on the back of a very deep confusion—indeed, a fallacy—as to how the probabilities in these critical cases in fact function. I've made the same argument elsewhere (see Roberts 1998, 2007, 2009a).

Another form of the nonidentity problem is raised by cases in which agents have the option to bring a particular child into a better existence and instead bring that very same child into a lesser existence. The structure of those cases is exactly the structure of the three option case (see Chapter 3). A variation on that version of the problem stipulates that, had agents not chosen to bring the child into the lesser existence, they *would* have failed to bring that child into existence at all. On that basis, some theorists—incorrectly, I think—conclude that the child is not harmed and not made worse off when the child is brought into the lesser existence (see, e.g., Boonin 2014). Any such counterfactual account, however, of when a person is worse off in a given future or is harmed in that future is obviously problematic. I am made worse off in the actual future, and thereby harmed, when you shoot me in the shoulder even though, had you not shot me in the shoulder,

glance may seem nicely to counterexample that principle. *And* to counterexample ECC+EV *and* to counterexample Parfit's own formulation of the underlying intuition.

The idea behind the nonidentity problem is that the choice that is made at a given time and place and that seems clearly wrong to us in view of what it does to people who come into existence *after* that choice is made is often also a choice that gives those very same people a *better chance* of ever coming into existence at all. The idea, in other words, is that, had any *alternate* available choice been substituted in for the choice that seems clearly wrong to us, those *particular* people very probably would never have existed at all. Avoiding the clearly *wrong* choice may well bring a *nonidentical*, if better off, person into existence in place of any one of those people. But it very probably would not have made *any one person* any better off at all.

Thus the apparent counterexample, indeed a multitude of apparent counterexamples,[21] against ECC+PV *and* ECC+EV *and* Parfit's own formulation of the underlying intuition.

And thus the argument in favor of an *impersonal* moral theory in place of any *person based* theory, including ECC+PV: a theory capable of finding a choice at a given future wrong *even when*, for each and every person who does or will exist in that future, that choice

you *would* have shot me in the heart (assuming, of course, that the further alternative choice of your just standing there was a choice that was available to you in a future that was accessible to you). For further discussion, see Roberts 2019b.

Still another form of the nonidentity problem is raised by cases in which the child whose existence is at stake is *certain* to have an existence worth having under a certain choice. Moreover, the future that unfolds under that choice is maximizing for that child. Thus no other accessible future is better for the child than the future that in fact unfolds, and nothing more can accessibly be done for the particular child than what has been done. Even in the case in which agents have the option of bringing a better off "nonidentical" child—a higher-wellbeing child—in place of the one, I continue to find it hard to see that agents have done anything wrong—other things equal—in bringing the one child into existence (rather than the other child) or that the future in which the one child (as opposed to the other child) exists is morally worse. I find the obligation of *procreative perfectionism*, in other words, hard to swallow. (And so does EC.) For further discussion, see, e.g., Roberts and Wasserman 2017.

[21] See Chapter 6 note 20.

maximizes both wellbeing *and* probable value (*and*, for that matter, expected value) for that person.

Thus Parfit asks: How many of us would have existed at all had motor cars never been invented?[22] Just *who* shall exist in the future is, as Kavka put it, *highly precarious*.[23] No moral theory can fail to take the phenomenon of the precariousness of existence into account—can deem all such identity-shifting choices permissible—and still be considered remotely plausible. Yes, choices help to determine just *who* shall exist in the future. But plausible moral theories don't allow that fact on its own to let the moral agent off the moral hook.

For purposes here, given the similarities in the most potent versions of the nonidentity problem—the probabilistic versions—it's enough to consider a very simple case. Kavka has us

> [envision] a pill that, when taken just before sexual relations, has two effects. It heightens the pilltaker's sexual pleasure a tiny bit and insures that any child conceived would be mildly handicapped. As *pausing to take the pill* would change who is conceived, and as existence with a mild handicap is not bad on the whole, no one would be rendered worse off if a prospective parent not using contraceptive devices were to take the pill before sex. But, surely, taking it would be wrong.[24]

Kavka concedes—in a note—that the choice *might* not actually "change who is conceived." What in fact happens, he writes, is that any *alternate* choice—in particular, the choice to substitute in any alternate choice that we agree is *permissible* for the choice that we agree is clearly *wrong*—would make it "enormously improbable"

[22] Parfit 1987, 361.
[23] Kavka 1982, 93.
[24] Kavka 1982, 98 (emphasis added).

that that one child, the "mildly handicapped" child, would ever exist at all.[25]

Why? Why is the coming into existence of any particular person so highly precarious? Let's assume (for purposes here) that *any* shift in the sperm and egg cells involved in the conception of a particular person will change the identity of the person then conceived. What Kavka points out is that any change in the "timing or manner" of conception will result in—more precisely, will *very, very probably* result in—*exactly* such a shift.

And why is that? The explanation lies in the fact of there being *so many spermatozoa* in the human ejaculate. Any little shift in the timing and manner of conception—very, very probably—mean a shift in exactly *who* is conceived.

Let's call the child who eventually comes into existence and is burdened by the agent's choice to take the pleasure pill "Zooey." Since the chances of Zooey's existence would surely have been "enormously improbable" had the agent—the "prospective parent"—made *any* other clearly permissible choice—paused, for example, to take an aspirin, or a sip of water, or a deep breath—the *probable value* of any such alternate choice for Zooey will be very low. In contrast, the probable value of the choice that we agree is wrong will be relatively high. If, say, the chance Zooey will exist under the alternate, *permissible* choice is a mere 0.000001—exactly the same as the probability of Yanni's coming into existence under the agent's choice not to undergo treatment in the better chance case—then the chance Zooey will exist under the choice we agree is wrong is a whopping—well, what, exactly? All that *seems* very

[25] Thus Kavka's note (made specifically in connection with his slave child contract case, which itself is still another version of the nonidentity problem):

> It is enormously improbable that the couple, if they turned down the slaveholder, could succeed in producing the same child they would have produced had they accepted, even if they tried. For it is unlikely that they could arrange conditions of conception similar enough to "what would have been" to ensure that the very same sperm would fertilize the same egg.

Kavka 1981, 100 note 15.

clear—at least until we look at the case more closely (and we will)—is that it's surely *far greater* than a mere 0.000001. And so, accordingly, is the probable value that the choice to take the pleasure pill creates for Zooey.

And that, in turn, means that ECC+PV's necessary condition on a choice being wrong is failed: there being *no alternate choice* that creates more probable value for the child than the choice to take the pleasure pill, that choice must be permissible.

Yet we know that it's not.[26]

Figure 6.4.1a sums up the case *as we've just described it.* (I label this depiction of the case "confused." Looking ahead, we'll question it.)

Figure 6.4.1a: Pleasure pill case/confused						
	c1: agent *doesn't* take pleasure pill (takes aspirin instead)			c2: agent *does* take pleasure pill		
probability →	0.000001	0.999999		0.001	0.999	
wellbeing ↓	f1	f2	*other futures*	f3	f4	*other futures*
+10	**Zooey**	--	**[child other than Zooey]**	--	--	--
+9	--	--		**Zooey**	--	**[child other than Zooey]**
+0	--	*Zooey; other children*	*Zooey; other children less the one who exists*	--	*Zooey; other children*	*Zooey; other children less the one who exists*

Figure 6.4.1a Pleasure pill case/confused

Now, we can simply note that the details of the pleasure pill case precisely track the details of the better chance case itself.

And that, in effect, is the crux of Parfit's argument: taking the pleasure pill and undergoing fertility treatment are, from the perspective of any future burdened child—Yanni in f3 in the better

[26] Boonin, inexplicably to me, argues that it's permissible, as are the choices of depletion, risky policy, slave child, etc. (Boonin 2014).

chance case, Zooey in f3 in the pleasure pill case—one and the same thing from a moral point of view.

Of course, had we *not* extended EC to include a probability-related necessary condition (as we did in creating both ECC+EV and ECC+PV), the counterexample would have failed. For EC itself easily avoids the problem result. It's clear, after all, that there exists *some* alternate accessible future (*some* accessible future in which, e.g., the agent takes the aspirin rather than the pleasure pill) in which Zooey exists but *isn't* burdened with the "mild handicap" that is an effect of the pleasure pill. It's thus not that Zooey *can't* exist and be better off—there's nothing blocking that result; nothing in logic, in metaphysics, in the laws of physics or even biology. Rather, it's just that that better existence for Zooey would have been rendered—in Kavka's words—"enormously improbable" had the agent done anything other than what the agent in fact did.[27]

Yet the condition that takes probability into account was critical in solving the better chance puzzle itself. It was that condition that enabled us to generate the plausible result that the choice to undergo fertility treatment in the better chance case was permissible. But now that same condition seems to force us to accept a conclusion that we know is false: that the agent's choice to take the pleasure pill is *also* permissible.

Reply. I have elsewhere argued that a clear understanding of the probabilities at stake in the pleasure pill case and in other versions of the probabilistic form of the nonidentity problem show that this problem doesn't—contrary to the widely accepted view—even begin to prove that ECC+EV is false.[28] The same clear understanding now shows that it doesn't prove that ECC+PV is false, either.

[27] See Chapter 6 note 25 (Kavka quote).

[28] For further discussion, see Roberts 1998, 2007, and 2009a, and Roberts and Wasserman 2017.

In a way that I am confident was not intended by their authors, nonidentity cases that share the probabilistic structure of the pleasure pill case exploit our widely recognized tendencies to misconstrue matters relating to probability. Thus the pleasure pill case tries hard to make us think that the agent's pausing to take the pleasure pill serves somehow to *increase* the chances of the particular child's coming into existence as compared against the chances of that same child's coming into existence under *any alternate, clearly permissible choice.*[29] It, in effect, tries to make us think that taking the *pleasure* pill works in the same way that taking the *fertility* pill works in the better chance case. But to think about the case in that particular way is to fall into what I've elsewhere called the *nonidentity fallacy.*[30]

And fallacy it is. For the pleasure pill isn't a fertility pill. Whatever the agent does—just as in the better chance case—the particular child's coming into existence is improbable. But—unlike in the better chance case, the pleasure pill *not* being a fertility pill—the probability of the child's coming into existence under the choice to pause to take the pleasure pill is *no greater than* the probability of the child's coming into existence under the choice to pause to take the aspirin.

It's not, after all, as though the choice to take the pleasure pill then dictates—determines with any significant degree of probability—just how the agent will proceed, step by step, moment by moment, to take the pleasure pill and how the couple will then proceed, step by step, moment by moment, to conceive a child; there are a million, a trillion, a quadrillion ways the couple could then proceed. Ditto the choice to take the aspirin: on that side, too, there are a million, a trillion, a quadrillion ways the agent and then the couple could proceed.

[29] And here we must include not just the choice that the agent *would* have made instead, but also any choice that the agent accessibly *could* have made instead. For why that's so, see Chapter 6 note 20 (counterfactual account, Boonin).

[30] See Roberts 1998, 2007, and 2009a, and Roberts and Wasserman 2017.

And, given the *better result* for the child if the child comes into existence under the choice to take the aspirin, we find the third condition of ECC+PV satisfied alongside the first two—and the door thus open for the conclusion that the choice is *not permissible* at all but is instead *clearly wrong.*

Thus Figure 6.4.1b presents a correct picture of the pleasure pill case.

Figure 6.4.1b: Pleasure pill case/correct						
	c1: agent *doesn't* take pleasure pill (takes aspirin instead)			c2: agent *does* take pleasure pill		
probability→	0.000001	0.999999		0.000001	0.999999	
wellbeing ↓	f1	f2	*other futures*	f3	f4	*other futures*
+10	**Zooey**	--	**[child other than Zooey]**	--	--	--
+9	--	--		**Zooey**	--	**[child other than Zooey]**
...	...	...	...	...	...	...
+0	--	*Zooey; other children*	*Zooey; other children less the one who exists*	--	*Zooey; other children*	*Zooey; other children less the one who exists*

Figure 6.4.1b Pleasure pill case/correct

The concept of probable value—in combination with a clearer understanding of the pleasure pill case, and specifically, the probabilities at stake—thus positions us to provide a plausible account of that case and other probabilistic forms of the nonidentity problem just as nicely as the concept of expected value does—which is to say, quite nicely.

And what of non-human animals? The swine? The equine? Factory farming and other mistreatment of non-human animals is forgiven by some theorists on the ground that, but for such mistreatment, the animals would—could? *probably* would?—never have existed at all and that their lives are worth living, if only barely so. Such theorists invite us to fall into the same nonidentity fallacy outlined above. Contrary to that way of thinking about things, we can easily imagine alternate available choices that would have created the *same very low* probability of coming into existence for any particular animal burdened by factory farming as continuing the practice of factory farming does: take the cow, collect the semen and breed on about the same schedule as the factory farmer anticipates breeding under current practice. But treat the resulting calf very differently from, and very much better than, the way he or she would be treated on the factory farm.

Now, a *still more confused* understanding of the probabilities at stake in the pleasure pill case has it that Zooey's coming into existence is *certain*, given the choice to take the pleasure pill. Why might someone understand the case in that way? It's true that, in many versions of the case, it's *stipulated* that that's in fact what happens. But to think that that stipulation changes the underlying facts about the *probabilities* at stake in the case is simply confused. Probability, in the sense relevant to the evaluation of choice, is to be calculated as of the moment *just prior to choice*. That I have in fact drawn four aces on a given occasion doesn't mean that, prior to my choosing to bet everything I own playing some ridiculous game, it was *certain* that I would draw four aces. It's just another fallacy to think that what in fact unfolds under a given choice was, prior to that choice, a foregone conclusion. Calculated prior to choice, Zooey's coming into existence was exactly as probable under the choice to pause to take the pleasure pill as it was under the choice to pause to take the aspirin.

6.4.2 The case of the all-but-known success

In all-but-known disaster, we considered a choice that, just prior to performance, *looked to be* a choice that would produce disaster for at least one future person and, as the future in fact unfolded, *did* produce disaster for that person.

We now turn to a case in which a choice that, just prior to performance, *looks to be* a choice that will produce a very good future for a particular person—a clear *success*—but instead *against all odds* produces a truly horrible future for that same person. This is the case of the *all-but-known success* (Figure 6.4.2).

Figure 6.4.2: All-but-known success				
	c1: mom undertakes mission		c2: mom doesn't undertake mission	
probability →	0.9999	0.0001	0.9999	0.0001
wellbeing ↓	f1	f2	f3	f4
+10	**Teddy**	--	--	--
. . .	. . .	. . .	. . .	. . .
+1	--	--	**Teddy**	**Teddy**
. . .	. . .	. . .	. . .	. . .
. . .	. . .	. . .	. . .	. . .
. . .	. . .	. . .	. . .	. . .
. . .	. . .	. . .	. . .	. . .
. . .	. . .	. . .	. . .	. . .
−1000	--	**Teddy**	--	--

Figure 6.4.2 All-but-known success

Again we can add color to this case. It's another mother-and-child scenario—and another one-off case. Here, the mother—the agent—must choose whether to undertake a mission to rescue her only child Teddy from space aliens who have confined him in a cage allowing him only the minimal conveniences of life (nutrition, hydration, and occasional ablution) or to do nothing and leave him to live out a life only *barely* worth living. If the woman's mission succeeds, Teddy will be restored to a wellbeing level of approximately what the woman herself will have and what others in her own and Teddy's generational cohorts will have. Because of the woman's overall proficiency and vast experience in previous extremely dangerous search-and-rescue efforts, the chances that her mission will succeed are extremely high. But if her mission fails, the space aliens are sure to become aware of her efforts (her transport vehicle leaving a signature trace in the alien atmosphere, easily recorded by their sophisticated and highly sensitive monitoring devices) and they will (certainly) respond by torturing Teddy in horrible ways for the remainder of his very long natural life, leaving Teddy with an existence *far* less than one worth having.

Let's stipulate that the agent in fact chooses to proceed with the mission—that is, that she chooses c1.

And let's further stipulate that the mission, against all odds, in fact fails, that f2 unfolds instead of f1 and that Teddy is left to suffer in the horrible ways we have just described.

This is the sort of case that reminds us that to *all but know* something is not to *know* something.

ECC+PV tells us that c1 at f1 is permissible. Teddy's wellbeing is maximized in f1 under c1, and so is the probable value of c1 for Teddy at f1.

But what we need to focus on here is the evaluation of c1 at f2. In choosing c1, has the agent made a *permissible* choice—just one that, against all odds, has ended in *disaster* for her child?

I think that it's not at all obvious what we should say about c1 at f2.

But let's—for the moment; we'll come back to this point shortly—*tentatively* assume that c1 at f2 *is* permissible. If that's so, then let's just note that that's a result that ECC+PV *doesn't* generate. Thus Teddy exists in f2, alternate accessible futures are better for Teddy than f2, and alternate choices performed in at least at some of those alternate accessible futures create more probable value for Teddy than does c1 at f2 does. With all three of its conditions satisfied, ECC+PV remains silent on the question of the permissibility of c1 at f2. But nor does ECC+PV imply that c1 at f2 is *wrong*. As a mere necessary, and not a sufficient, condition on wrongdoing, ECC+PV isn't capable of generating the result that c1 at f2 (or any other choice) is wrong. The position that c1 at f2 *is* permissible is thus entirely consistent with ECC+PV.

So ECC+PV itself remains neutral. Let's then move on.

We understand that, if c1 at f2 is in fact permissible, then it's the *probabilities* at stake in the case that make that so. If c1 at f2 is permissible, it's because it's overwhelmingly likely, given c1, that Teddy will end up with a far better result than he'd have under any alternate choice.

To put the point another way, if c1 at f2 is permissible, it may well be that c1 at f2 is permissible *in virtue of the fact that* c1 at f1 is permissible. The thought there would be that, once a choice is deemed permissible at one future, we are bound to say that that same choice is also permissible in each alternate accessible future in which it's performed.

But—as applied to all-but-known success—can we really be sure that that position is correct? Can we be *confident* that c1 at f2 is really permissible? Isn't the truth instead that we may well be missing something important about the probabilities that are at stake in all-but-known success? If so, then we are also missing something important about the probabilities that are at stake in other cases as well. That recognition isn't enough to *refute* ECC+PV. But it may be enough to *weaken* our confidence in ECC+PV: to force us to demur on ECC+PV.

Reply. The objection just stated makes the point that ECC+PV implies that c1 at f1 is permissible but doesn't tell us whether c1 at f2 is permissible or not. It then makes the point that it's a mystery what we would need to say—beyond ECC+PV—to explain a result that it, for purposes of discussion, we have *tentatively* assumed correct: that c1 at f2 is permissible as well.[31]

But we need to avoid rushing to the conclusion that any such explanation is in order. The better view on reflection seems to be that,

[31] To accept that c1 is permissible at both f1 and f2 might seem to cry out for a return to the necessary condition based on the concept of *expected* value that we considered earlier—the condition we rejected in favor of the condition based on the concept of *probable* value. But that would be a mistake. It's interesting that a necessary condition on expected value would generate the result in this case that c1 at f2—just like c1 at f1—is permissible. But we can't escape the problem result that that same necessary condition generates in all-but-known disaster.

though c1 at f1 is perfectly permissible and the mom herself, the agent, beyond reproach, c1 at f2 is nonetheless *wrong*.

To take the position that c1 at f1 is permissible but that c1 at f2 is wrong would mean that agents *don't* in every case have complete control, prior to choice, on whether the choice they make will turn out to be permissible or not. Which is not to say that they don't have a permissible option; they do—c1 at f1. They just don't have complete control over whether, should they happen to choose c1, it will be f1 or f2 that will then unfold. And thus they don't have complete control over whether c1 is permissible or not.

Just as the choice that *looks to be* wrong in all-but-known disaster may *turn out to be* permissible, so might the choice that *looks to be* permissible in all-but-known success *turn out to be* wrong.

The picture then would be as follows. In all-but-known success, the agent, in choosing c1, faces a tiny risk of doing the wrong thing. That risk eventuates (it's stipulated, we said, that f2 unfolds from c1 rather than f1). But c1 at f2 is wrong. What has happened? A choice that *looked to be* perfectly permissible prior to choice—c1—has *turned out to be* a choice that is performed at f2 rather than f1. And c1 at f2 is wrong.

On that view, moral law doesn't offer a guarantee that it will, prior to choice, certainly and consistently point us toward the permissible choice—that moral *law* can't be counted on to entirely obviate moral *risk*. Sometimes, despite our best efforts and most careful calculations, we end up doing the wrong thing. (Sometimes we end up gouging out our own eyes.)

Let's just note that this view of c1 at f2 *isn't* a roundabout way of lending any support to the position that—in a case like all-but-known success—the agent is obligated to make the "conservative" choice of c2 rather than the choice of the riskier c1—obligated, that is, to *avoid* the moral risk. Just the reverse. Nothing in what we've said so far supports the position that the agent, by simply choosing c2 over c1, can make *sure* that the choice she makes will turn out to be permissible.

Thus, if c2 *is* permissible, that won't be a result that we obtain from ECC+PV. Moreover, it's not at all clear that c2 *is* permissible. It's not at all clear that the agent's obligation *isn't* to take on the moral risk and do all that she can to secure f1 for Teddy rather than leaving him to live out his life in f3 or f4 at the very low wellbeing level of exactly 1.

What makes it at least plausible that c2 is wrong is, in part, the fact that this is a one-off case; the agent's alternative to c2 is c1 and c1 alone. It's not part of the case that the agent's alternative to c2 would commence a *sequence* of c1-like choices that, over an extended period of time, is virtually certain to assign to Teddy the horrific wellbeing level he has in f2.

The upshot is that, if c1 at f2 is wrong, and if c2, wherever performed, is also wrong, then an implication of moral law is that we must on occasion bear a certain degree of moral risk.[32] While we'd all *like* to have perfect advance knowledge of whether the choice we are about to make is permissible or not, that fact in itself is hardly a credible argument for the position that c1 at f2, just like c1 at f1, is permissible. The better view seems to be that c1 at f2 is wrong.

32 To say this is not to deny the principle of normative invariance, which, as I understand it, requires the moral evaluation of choice not to be affected by whether the agent *actually* makes that choice or not: the fact that we actually make a choice can't, that is, convert what would otherwise be a permissible choice into a choice that is wrong. The claim here is rather that the permissibility of a choice (whether that choice and that future are actual or not) may depend in part on whether that choice is made within the context of one future (and thus brings about the results contained within that future) or another future (in which case that same choice may bring about another set of results).

7

Person-based consequentialism: A new way of doing the best we can

The traditional total view—*totalism*—is often, and not unfairly, criticized—and often for reasons that have no surface connection with any of the several puzzles we've examined in this book.[1] According to totalism, doing the best we can is a matter of bringing about the most wellbeing in the aggregate that we can. Various repugnant conclusions and egregious inequalities in wellbeing are not just tolerated but *made obligatory* by totalism whenever those repugnancies and inequalities serve to maximize aggregate wellbeing—and often *permitted* when we could just as easily avoid them.

And now the existence puzzles—each one of which can be reformulated as an argument that indirectly favors the position that totalism is *required* by the basic maximizing intuition by purporting to prove that the basic existential intuition is false.

But do we really think that there's *no difference* between, on the one hand, making things so bad for the existing or future child that that child's wellbeing level is reduced to zero and, on the other, declining to bring another child into existence to begin with?

Consider, one last time, the case of Jaime versus Harry (Figure 1.2). Do we really think that Jaime's *ordinary* loss in f2 is

[1] Again a reminder: the traditional total view (totalism) for purposes here determines the value of a given future by adding up the raw wellbeing levels of the people who do or will exist in that future—the wellbeing levels *unadjusted* to reflect the values of equality, fairness, priority, justice, and desert and, most critically here, *unadjusted* as well to reflect our *existential* values.

The Existence Puzzles. M. A. Roberts, Oxford University Press. © Oxford University Press 2024.
DOI: 10.1093/oso/9780197544143.003.0007

morally indistinct from Harry's *existential* loss in f1? I don't think that we do. And—let's just note—we now have all the principles that we need to provide a complete account of that case. The existence condition (EC) tells us that f1 is at least as good as f2 and that c1 is permissible. And the Pareto reduction principle tells us more: that f1 is better than f2, given that leaving Harry out of existence altogether makes things better for Jaime. The connection thesis then completes the picture: c1 is permissible, indeed, obligatory, and that c2 is wrong. If we still love addition, we can apply inversive existence-sensitive addition and say still more: the contributive value of Jaime's existence in f1 is just zero, as is the contributive value of Harry's existence in f2. Since, however, the contributive value of Jaime's existence in f2 is negative, we obtain just the same result we obtained before we added things up: f2 is worse than f1.

Let's change questions. Do we really think that it's *obligatory* to bring an additional person into existence when that can be done at no cost to anyone else—or even perhaps at some *considerable* cost to someone else (e.g., a parent or an already-existing or future sibling)? Again, I don't think that we do. EC itself, along with the connection thesis, has already provided us with a complete account of the happy child case (Figure 2.1). f1 is exactly as good as f2, and c1 and c2 are both permissible. As to the cases that lie on the gradient—where one person's worth-having existence is to be achieved at some minor or some considerable choice to someone else, and where the wellbeing level of the additional person more than offsets the wellbeing loss to anyone else—the Pareto reduction principle can then step in to say that that's just not how the moral calculus that underlies the basic maximizing intuition can plausibly be thought to work. Reducing, say, a potential mom's wellbeing level from 100 to 10 so that her possible child can make their way into existence and there have a wellbeing level of 100 *isn't* a morally better outcome—and it *isn't* the kind of result we're morally obligated to bring about.

Thus our *maximizing* values tell us to do the best we can for people (where, as always here, the term "person" is understood to include not just many human beings, but also many non-human animals). They tell us to create the *most* good, the *most* wellbeing, for people that we can. Our *existential* values tell us not to take that idea too far. There's a constraint: making things better for people by way of bringing them into a worth-having existence isn't, on its own, a way to make things morally *better*.

In this book, a more *granulated* approach has helped us to disentangle the *wellbeing* details of our cases from their *existential* details and thus to articulate a collection of principles—together, *person-based consequentialism*—that itself works to reconcile our two basic intuitions, the basic maximizing intuition and the basic existential intuition, against each other. Thus rather than focusing on creating the most good—the most *wellbeing*—for people in the aggregate, we have throughout used quantifiers to talk about *each* person's plight one at a time at *each* accessible future (whether that person does or will exist in that future or not) *without* making the mistake of saying that some people have a moral status that other people lack. (Thus each person, existing, future, or mere possible, matters morally and in exactly the same way as each other person.[2]) We have then been able to consider the options for making things better *for that particular person* and to consider as well how those options may affect still *other particular people one at a time*. Having done that—and only, I think, in virtue of the fact that we *have* done that—we can make the distinction between making things better for a person by way of bringing that person into existence to begin with and making things better for a person by way of making the existence that person does or will have in a given future better.

[2] Thus we've rejected moral actualism in all of its forms. Just as, other things equal, you are *not* obligated to bring another child into existence, your parents were not obligated to bring you into existence (nor mine me). Just as, other things equal, your bringing another child into existence doesn't make for a morally better future, your parents bringing you into existence didn't, on its own, make for a morally better future.

Thus arguments denouncing the asymmetry have been put forward as reasons to at least favor, if not wholeheartedly embrace, totalism. Since it's *wrong* to bring the miserable child into existence, it *must be obligatory* to bring the happy child into existence. And what theory more cleanly secures that particular result other than totalism? But, as we have seen, the argument itself just isn't valid. We can consistently and cogently take the highly intuitive position that it makes things morally worse, and is wrong, to bring the miserable child into existence but that it doesn't make things morally worse, and is perfectly permissible, *not* to bring the happy child into existence.

The Pareto puzzle starts with the idea that making things better for one person without making things worse for anyone at all makes things morally better and then takes it for granted that we're not so mean-spirited as to want to say that bringing a perfectly happy child into existence, other things equal, can ever make things worse. But is it really mean-spirited to insist that, when agents have the option of bringing that same happy child into a still *better* existence, it does, after all, make things worse to bring that child into the *lesser* existence? I think it's not mean-spirited at all: it's, rather, that little fillip that reconciles our basic maximizing intuition—that, other things equal, we ought to make things better rather than worse for that child—against our basic existential intuition—that it doesn't make things worse, and would have been perfectly permissible, not to bring that child into existence to begin with.

The addition puzzle questions whether any theory that is not, at base, additive in nature can demonstrably abide by the demands of cogency, consistency, and conceptual necessity. For that purpose, addition may well seem important. And, if we start with the idea that what we are to add up are units of wellbeing—that is, units of *raw, unadjusted* wellbeing—then we end up with totalism. But we can start elsewhere: with the idea that what we are to add up is something other than wellbeing and something—*contributive value*—that allows us to make the distinction between the additional wellbeing that is created by way of bringing an additional person into existence and the additional wellbeing that is created by way of making things better for a person who does or will exist in still another future. If we further understand contributive value to be determined by appeal to a certain *value inversion*—one that on occasion assigns a negative contributive value to a positive wellbeing level—we can then solve our puzzle. We can explain just how it can be that a given worth-having existence can *both* contribute to the moral value of a given future as compared against one future *and not* contribute to the moral value of that same future as compared against another future.

An *unrestricted* principle of anonymity may unintentionally serve as a means of pushing us sideways in the direction of totalism—and in the direction of a version of the repugnant conclusion that is totalism's constant and unpleasant companion. And thus the anonymity puzzle. But there, too, we find a gap in the argument. It's a gap some theorists might not pay attention to but at the same time a gap that isn't clearly closed by any principle of logic—or even of fairness or rationality—*given that* more *restricted* principles of anonymity are also available. Again: the argument is invalid. We thus can agree that it makes no moral difference whether it's you or I who has to suffer if one of us has to suffer and no one else has any interest at stake. But that doesn't mean that we have to agree as well that that quintessentially fair principle doesn't become radically unfair when transplanted into a case where it's not just the interests of the two of us that are at stake but the interests of a third person as well, a person whose coming into existence is not a foreordained conclusion.

And, finally, the better chance puzzle, which has its source in a bit of reasoning that may well explain why so many consequentialists, so many population ethicists, so many climate ethicists, so many social choice theorists feel they have no choice but to accept totalism. If the better *chance* of the additional existence can make things morally better—and it clearly can—surely the actual *fact* of that additional existence can make things morally better as well. But there, too, as we have seen, we can agree that the better chance of a child coming into a worth-having existence can indeed make things morally better—it can convert a choice that we'd otherwise consider clearly wrong into a choice that we consider perfectly permissible—and still easily have room to say that it remains perfectly permissible never to bring that child into existence to begin with. I have argued that the concept of *expected value* isn't what we want—that the narrower concept of *probable value* more accurately captures how the probabilities at stake in a given case play into moral evaluation. But whether we stay with an expected value approach or not, it should now be clear that the "hard mathematical logic" of bringing probabilities to bear in the right way in a given case doesn't, after all, march us into the jaws of a version of longtermism that is unsustainable in every meaningful sense of that term.

Is the aggregative approach defined by the traditional total view simpler than the more granulated approach I've outlined in this book? Is totalism easier to state than person-based consequentialism? Certainly. Does it make my life *simpler and easier* if I give you my bank routing information and you transfer all of your immediately available funds to me? Does it make things *simpler and easier* for the parent to deem the child more adept at satisfying the parent's own needs the more deserving and more gifted child? Does it make things *simpler and easier* for God if all God has to worry about is the bottom line—aggregate wellbeing—and *not* how well *each and every one* of God's creatures great and small *one by one* is faring—and yes, faring at each and every accessible alternate future (whether that creature does or will exist in that alternate future or not)? Yes. But why on earth should we think even for a moment that what is *simpler and easier* tells us anything at all about what makes things *morally better*?

Anyway, is person-based consequentialism really that complicated? We're pretty adept at this point at deploying quantifiers.[3] We can now easily talk about *each member* of infinite sets of natural numbers, rational numbers, irrational numbers. And modal logic—the logic of possible worlds—has opened the door wide to all kinds of imaginings regarding the many, many alternate ways in which the future might unfold beyond the way it has so far unfolded and seems set to unfold going forward.

Philosophers have asked the question whether we can meaningfully talk about individuals—e.g., people—who, unlike, for example, natural numbers, which are considered to exist in all possible worlds, will never exist in the actual future but who (we want to say) do or will exist in alternate accessible futures and whose sufferings in those alternate futures moral law must take into account. But there, too, the matter seems to have been settled: we may not agree on just *how* we manage to do it, but it's no longer thought that we *can't* do it; that we *can't*, meaningfully and whether truthfully or not, say things such as "any third child I *might* have produced *would* have created hardships for the two children I have already have or will produce." Maybe that's true! Or maybe it's not. It's still something I can think about—and something that moral law can surely take into account when determining whether an alternate accessible future in which any such third child exists is better or worse than the future in which that same child never exists at all.

Of course it often benefits a parent to have a child, and often to have another child. It often benefits a child to have siblings. And it often benefits one generation to have the next generation coming right along. The theme here isn't that one child is better than two, or that two children are better than three. The theme here is rather

[3] As noted earlier, quantifiers, as ways of describing reality, have surely been there all along in our natural languages if only brought to service a hundred or so years ago by Frege and Russell.

that producing the additional child, other things equal, doesn't, on its own, make things morally better and can *easily*, on occasion, make things morally worse.

Thus in the odd case it may well be that producing just one child *is* better than producing two or that producing two children *is* better than producing three—or, in view of climate change, that a future containing fewer billions of people *is* better than a future containing more billions of people, or that a future in which humanity persists enjoying fulsome levels of wellbeing for hundreds of thousands of years *is* better than a future in which humanity continues indefinitely but at greatly reduced wellbeing levels. Rather than resolve those issues by appeal to the en masse calculation totalism requires, we should adopt principles that take into account the plight of *each* person as an individual one at a time at *each* accessible future whether that person does or will exist at that future or not.

The moral principles that have been considered *and accepted* in this book—the principles that, together with a handful of conceptually necessary principles (principles, that is, that we have no choice but to accept), help to define person-based consequentialism—don't together form a *complete* theory. They don't tell us, for every future x and every future y accessible relative to x, whether x is better than (or worse than or exactly as good as) y, and, for every choice that (with some positive degree of probability) gives rise to x, whether that choice is permissible or not. But we do have the option of adding to the stock of principles we've already accepted: of adding further *sufficient* conditions on when a future is morally worse or when a choice is wrong that are themselves constrained by the *necessary* conditions we've already adopted—including EC—or may adopt going forward and the handful of conceptual principles we seem to have no choice but to accept. My sense is that the additional principles that we'll add to our collection—that we will in the end accept—will reflect both our basic maximizing intuition *and* our basic existential intuition—and that they'll do so by *granulating* rather than *aggregating* across each and every population accessible within the context of the particular case.

The end game would be this. Once those conditions are in place—once that desideratum is realized—the further position that *nothing else* makes things worse and that *nothing else* is wrong would surely seem eminently plausible.

In the meantime, there's much we can condemn based on the principles we already have in place and—just as important—much that we can exonerate as well, including, other things equal, the choice *not* to bring the additional person into existence to begin with. Thus I end with Narveson's much maligned yet still perfectly intuitive (and still quite witty) way of putting things: we are "in favor of *making people happy*" but, other things equal, entirely "neutral about *making happy people*."[4]

[4] Narveson 1976, 73 (emphasis added).

APPENDIX A

Nonexistence comparability

It might be thought that the key to reconciling the basic maximizing intuition and the basic existential intuition—those two *moral* intuitions—against each other lies in metaphysics or perhaps logic. The idea would be that it's not fully cogent to say that the future in which a person has a worth-having existence is *better for that person* than the future in which that person never exists or that the future in which a person never exists is *worse for that person* than the future in which that person has a worth-having existence.[1] In short, the idea is that a basic assumption of this book—that is, *nonexistence comparability*—is just false.

Let's go back to the case of Jaime versus Harry (Figure 1.2). Consider the sentence "f1 is worse for Harry than f2." This, it's thought, is just a predicate with no subject term (along the lines of "____ has zero wellbeing"; "_____ is red"; "_____is human"; "_____ is a reptile"). It's a failed *attempt* to attribute a property to an individual, Harry, in a future in which Harry never exists at all.

We are left with a sentence that can't be either true or false. Predicates with no subjects are simply not the *kinds of things* that can be either true or false.

Thus Feinberg writes that "Since it is necessary to be if one is to be better off, it is a logical contradiction to say that someone could be better [or worse] off though not in existence."[2]

Since no parallel question of cogency arises when it comes to what we want to say about Jaime, who exists in both f1 and f2, the sentence "f1 is better for Jaime than f2" is fully cogent.

We can then just note that f1 is *better for someone* than f2 and that it's not the case that f2 is *better for anyone at all* than f1. Finally, putting the basic existential intuition to work—the idea, in Parfit's words, that what is "bad" must be "bad for someone"—we quickly reach the highly intuitive result that f1 is *morally better* than f2.

I think, however, the question of cogency requires a closer look.

[1] Theorists who have argued in support of that conclusion include Bader 2022; Arrhenius and Rabinowicz 2015, 424–443; Broome 1999, 168; Feinberg 1998; Heyd 1992. Theorists who have found positions identical to or very close to nonexistence comparability perfectly cogent include Feit 2016, Fleurbaey and Voorhoeve 2015, and Roberts 2003.

[2] Feinberg 1988, 158.

When the case was first introduced in Chapter 1, it was stipulated that f1 is better for Jaime than f2 and that f2 is better for Harry than f1. And it was further stipulated that Harry never exists in f1. On that basis, it was then claimed that Harry has a *zero wellbeing level* in f1.

The case as described at that time seemed to represent at least a conceptual possibility. We seemed able to conceive of the case arising at some possible future or another. Moreover, the claim, based on Harry's nonexistence in f1, that Harry has a *zero wellbeing level* in f1 seemed highly plausible. It's a claim rooted in the thought that the futures—the worlds—in which we never exist are futures that offer us no happiness, no misery, no capability, no disability, no benefits, no burdens. *Whatever* wellbeing consists in, it's going to add up to *no wellbeing at all* (i.e., to a *zero* wellbeing level) in any future in which we never exist at all.[3]

If that much is so, and given the further stipulation that Harry's wellbeing level in f2 is +10, Harry clearly seems to have *more wellbeing* in f2 than in f1. f2 is thus *better for* Harry than f1.

The problem with the challenge—whether it's from metaphysics or from logic—is that it's not at all clear that its take on the sentences that the assumption of nonexistence comparability considers cogent is correct.

We can accept that the person *we analysts*, aiming to give an account of a particular case, want to make a claim about—want to attribute a property to—must exist in *some future or another*. But *as analysts* we don't focus on any one future; we, instead, look at the bigger picture. We secure reference to a particular person by virtue of the fact that that person *does or will exist in at least one of the futures* in the *array of futures* that the particular case takes to be *accessible*. But we needn't *confine* our talk about that person to talk about that person *in that future*. We can instead *start* with a person in a future in which that person does or will exist—for example, Harry in f2—and move on from there to say, for example, that Harry *doesn't exist* in f1. If we can cogently say that much, then we can also cogently say that Harry *has zero wellbeing* in f1—and thus that f1 is worse for Harry than f2. The purportedly missing subject term turns out not to be missing at all.

Now, it's true that the denizens of *f1* will be unable to secure a *direct* reference to Harry. They can't, after all, pick Harry out of the f1 crowd since there

[3] Tedeschi 1966. This is not to say that the claimed equivalence between "having no F" and "having zero F" does not sometimes fail. For example, it's questionable whether we can say that, since the number 4 has no height, its height is zero inches. The former is true; the latter is either false or highly misleading. But sometimes the claimed equivalence works. To say there's no sugar in the pantry is *just to say* that there's zero sugar in the pantry. To say that my grandmother, who doesn't live in China, has no money in China is *just to say* she has zero money in China. Ditto wellbeing: to say I have no wellbeing in any of those many futures in which I never exist is just to say I have zero wellbeing in each of those futures.

is, and can be, *for those speakers* no official naming operation (such as "I dub thee 'Harold'") between the name "Harry" and the person *Harry*. But *those* speakers aren't *us*; *we who are analyzing the case* aren't subject to the same domain of referents that limit the speakers' ability in f1 to attribute properties directly to *Harry* and to *Harry* alone.

Which is not to say that those same speakers can't say anything about Harry at all. They can't *name* him "Harry" or *directly* attribute properties to him and to him alone. But they can make statements that come with implications for Harry.

We can do the same here at the actual world. Consider the claim that "If Obama had had a third child, that child would have been a senator but could have been an astronaut." Such a statement is both cogent and plausibly true, and it's true even though *no such child* does or will exist in the actual world and even though—now looking out from our perch at the actual world at the full array of accessible worlds—we can't identify any *one* child who fits the description "Obama's third child." The fact is that there are many such possible children. But there's nothing in that reality that undermines the cogency or plausibility of the assertion that "If Obama had had a third child, that child would have been a senator but could have been an astronaut."

Any *plausible* form, in other words, of the metaphysical position called *modal actualism*—the position that only individuals who exist *at the actual world* exist at all—must find a way to make sense of the claims that we seem cogently and plausibly able to make about merely possible people.[4] If it can't, then cases like that of Obama's third child ground an argument favoring some form or another of the competing position—that is, *modal possibilism*.

A second point, too, challenges the metaphysical hypothesis. If we can't cogently say that f2 is better for Harry than f1—that Harry's wellbeing level in f2 is greater than in f1—then it's hard to see how we can cogently claim that the existence you happen to have, or the existence I happen to have, in the *actual* world is *better for us* than our never having existed at all. But surely it is. My existence in the actual world, and I trust yours as well, has come with benefits that far exceed its burdens. Whatever wellbeing consists in, my wellbeing level, and I trust yours as well, in the actual world falls in the positive range. It's not that never existing at all would have been a terrible, torturous thing for you or me; nonexistence wouldn't have meant a wellbeing level *below* the zero level. It would have instead meant no wellbeing at all for us—no happiness, no misery, no benefits, no burdens; a zero wellbeing level.

Similarly, if *we can't* cogently claim that f2 is *better for* Harry than f1, then it's hard to see how we can cogently claim that existence can sometimes be *worse for* people than never having existed at all. Now, in the actual world, such cases

[4] See McMichael (1983). See also Stalnaker 2012; Sider 2002; and Rosen 1990.

may be rare (given the availability of pain medications and euthanasia). We can nonetheless imagine cases of children suffering tortuous, unrelenting, unavoidable misery (due to a genetic abnormality, we can imagine, of the sort nothing can be done about), cases in which existence seems far less than an existence worth having; cases in which it seems correct to say that it would have been better for the child had that child never have existed at all. The fact is that any of us could have had—or could have been made to have by careless or malevolent agents or by forces of nature—an existence far less than an existence worth having. The idea that we can't cogently *say* that that's so—that metaphysics or logic disables us from making the claim we thought we'd just made—seems implausible.

Is the statement that Harry has zero wellbeing in f1—or that you or I have zero wellbeing in any future where we never exist—*inherently* self-contradictory? Does it, by attributing a property to Harry in f1, of necessity imply that Harry *exists* in f1, the very future in which he never exists at all? I don't see that it does. We don't say that Harry in f1 is in fact *a concrete instantiation* in f1 of the property of having zero wellbeing. Again, as analysts, we are looking at the bigger picture. We are talking about *Harry*, who *does* exist in f2, and making the claim about Harry in f2 that Harry has no wellbeing—which is just to say *zero* wellbeing in f1—at all. And surely—in virtue of the fact that Harry never exists in f1—he doesn't.[5]

[5] Roberts 2003a. Fleurbaey and Voorhoeve (2015) agree that there's no absurdity in the claim that existence can be better—or worse—for a person than nonexistence. I have argued in this book that we can accept that claim—accept, that is, what I call *nonexistence comparability*—and consistently also accept the existence condition (EC). Thus we can take the position that the fact that a future in which I have a worth-having existence is better for me than any future in which I never exist doesn't imply (even other things equal) that my existence makes the world a *morally better* place or that bringing me into existence was a *moral obligation* on the part of my parents or my other forebears or anyone else. In contrast, Fleurbaey and Voorhoeve move (I think too quickly) from nonexistence comparability to a theory that implies the mere addition principle. That principle is, of course, inconsistent with EC and is rejected in Sections 3.4.1 and 3.4.2.

APPENDIX B

The loss distinction thesis

The shorthand terminology of *losses* (or *harms*) and *gains* (or *benefits*) provides an alternative way of conveying what the existence condition (EC), the same-people Pareto principle, the Pareto reduction principle, and each of the other principles that this book stands behind—together, *person-based consequentialism*—are all about.

In this book, we are working within the context of a consequentialist approach. The relevant terms, accordingly, must be understood in ways that comport with that approach. Thus we here accept a widely comparative, *modal* account of loss, and say that a person sustains a *loss* in one future as compared against another future *if and only if* the one future is *worse for* that person than the other—*if and only if*, that is, that person has *less wellbeing* in the one future than in the other. Losses, then, can be triggered either by actions or omissions and either by the choices that agents make or by natural forces.

To my ears, using the term "loss" in that way doesn't sound artificial or merely stipulative at all. Though it's admittedly broad: my *choice not to* give you $100 imposes a *loss* on you just as my *choice to* steal $100 from your wallet does. But "loss" in that broad sense is just a metaphysical concept: it's just a matter of a person's having less wellbeing in one future than in another. It's when we take the analysis further and try to make the moral or legal distinction between losses that are wrongly imposed and losses that aren't that we can be more discerning. In a given case, we might thus say that my not giving you $100 isn't wrong—though it many cases surely it *is* wrong!—and, in another case, that my stealing $100 from your wallet is wrong—though we can certainly imagine cases in which it's *not* a wrong at all!

That concept of *loss* in mind, we can describe person-based consequentialism as—in effect, though it's explicitly articulated without any appeal to the shorthand terminology—distinguishing not (as moral actualism and the other failed approaches outlined in Section 2.3 of the main text would have it) *people* according to whether they *matter morally* or not, but rather *losses* according to whether they have *moral significance* or not.

Specifically, we can assert the *loss distinction thesis*.

> *Loss distinction thesis.* Any loss sustained by any person in any future has *moral significance*—counts, that is, *against* the future in which it's sustained (making that future, potentially, *worse* than other futures), or

> *in favor of* any alternate accessible future (making that alternate future, potentially, *at least as good* as or *better than* the one)—*if and only if* the person who sustains that loss *does or will exist* in the one future.

Just like EC, the loss distinction thesis provides only a necessary, not a sufficient, condition on when a given future is morally worse or a choice morally wrong. The loss can make a future in which it is sustained *morally worse* than another future only if the person who sustains the loss *does or will exist* in that future. While *ordinary* losses have full, cross-future, moral significance, *existential* losses, we can say, have none at all.

The loss distinction thesis imposes still other necessary conditions on when a loss has moral significance as well. Consistent with EC—but now shifting to the terminology of "loss"—the loss distinction thesis requires that there *be* a loss (in the widely comparative, modal sense of "loss" defined above). If a person's wellbeing has been *maximized* in one future as compared against all other possible futures, then there's no *loss*.

Moreover, for a person's loss in one future to have moral significance, at least one alternate future that makes things better for that person must be not just *logically possible*, but also *accessible* relative to the one future. It must be a future that agents, whether working as individuals or together (and whether in collaboration or not), have the ability, the power, the resources to bring about (however improbable that future might have remained under any of the agents' choices). Thus the loss I sustain in the *actual* world as compared against the *logically possible* world in which I exist forever and have a high level of wellbeing throughout is a *loss*. (It's after all true that I have less wellbeing in the one future as compared against the other.) But it's *not* a *morally significant* loss.

Application to the asymmetry. What does the loss distinction thesis tell us about the asymmetry? Since Maija exists in f2, the loss distinction thesis instructs that the fact that f2 is worse for her than f1 has full moral significance. Roughly put, that means that her *loss* in f2 counts against f2 and against c2. The thesis further instructs that, since Maija never exists in f1, there's nothing there of any moral significance to count against f1 or against c1.

What about Haaken? Though f3 is worse for Haaken than f4—though he sustains a *loss* in f3—according to the loss distinction thesis that fact has no moral significance at all. For Haaken never exists in the future in which he sustains the loss. That loss thus doesn't count against f3 or against c3.

Haaken is in a different position in f4. There, Haaken's wellbeing is maximized relative to each other future that happens to be accessible in the particular case relative to f4. He sustains no loss—and thus there's nothing of moral significance there, either, that might count against f4 or against c4.

Those results are just the results we obtained earlier from EC, the Pareto reduction principle, and the various conceptual principles we seem to have no choice but to accept. Application of the connection thesis only underlines their intuitive force: it's wrong to bring the miserable Maija into existence but not wrong to decline to bring the happy Haaken into existence.

Good consequentialists that we are, we want to avoid the position that only *losses* can potentially have moral significance but that somehow *gains* don't. For the consequentialist, just as *x is worse than y for p* and *y is better than x for p* are just two sides of the same coin, so are *losses* and *gains*.

But we can't via any mindless mechanical means extract from the loss distinction thesis any plausible view on when *gains* have moral significance. We can't just substitute the term "gain" for "loss" in the loss distinction thesis and come up with a plausible principle—or even a principle that generates results that are consistent with those we've already obtained from the loss distinction thesis itself. Given that losses and gains are just two sides of the same coin, it won't work to say that Haaken's *loss* in f3 doesn't matter morally but that his *gain* in f4—since he exists in f4—*does* matter morally.

To remain consistent with the loss distinction thesis, what we then instead need to say is this: for any *gain* accrued by any person in any future to have *moral significance*, that gain must itself make things better for a person than things are in an alternate accessible future in which that person does or will exist. The *morally significant gain*, in other words, is just a gain that reverses a loss that itself, under the loss distinction thesis, has moral significance.

We thus can provide a plausible and consistent set of results for the asymmetry whether we want to talk in terms of losses or in terms of gains. Whichever way we go, whether we talk about losses and gains or in terms of the more precise principles formulated in Section 2.4 of the main text, we have solved the puzzle *without* throwing out any of the puzzle pieces.

The irrationality objection against EC taken up in connection with the asymmetry in Section 2.5.2 can also be stated—and actually extended—using the language of *losses* and *gains*. That objection goes as follows. If we accept the loss distinction thesis and the idea that existence is necessary for *losses* to have moral significance, why, *on pain of irrationality*, aren't we forced also to accept a parallel condition for *gains*? How can Maija's *gain* in f1 have moral significance if she *doesn't exist* there? And, on the other side, if existence is *sufficient* to imbue *losses* with moral significance, why isn't existence also *sufficient* to do the same for *gains*? Why doesn't Haaken's existence in f4 imbue his *gain* in f4 with moral significance?

Just as in Section 2.5.2, however, we can reply to that objection. Here, it may be helpful to start out with a certain clarification. Any thought that the loss distinction thesis—notwithstanding its title—supposes that losses *but not gains* have moral significance is a misunderstanding of that account. To say that Haaken has a *loss* in f3 relative to f4 is to say he has a *gain* in f4 relative to f3. Similarly: to say Maija has a *loss* in f2 relative to f1 is to say she has a *gain* in f1 relative to f2.

When, accordingly, the loss distinction account asserts that there's a moral distinction to be drawn between different sorts of losses, it's simultaneously asserting that there's a moral distinction to be drawn between different sorts of gains. Thus: Haaken's *loss* in f3 has no moral significance; neither does his *gain* in f4; Maija's *loss* in f2 has full moral significance; so does her *gain* in f1. Thus as noted earlier: the morally significant gain is just the gain that *reverses* what is, under the loss distinction thesis, a morally significant loss.

That clarification in mind, let's return to the irrationality objection itself. We are called on to explain why, if the existence of a given person in a future in which the loss is sustained imbues that person's *loss* with moral significance, the existence of a given person in a future doesn't imbue that person's *gain* in that future with moral significance.

The best answer to that question is that *it just does*: that's just the theory. If one wants a theory that explains the asymmetry, then the loss distinction thesis will be of interest. If one wants a theory that rejects the asymmetry—and, on top of that, contradicts itself—then the theory that insists that existence at a future imbues both losses *and* gains at that future equally with moral significance is for them.

More generally, it's hard to see why the fact that a theory *makes a distinction* is a basis for rejecting that theory. We don't, after all, think that a theory that implies that 7 is prime but 9 isn't must be rejected on the ground that it makes a distinction between 7 and 9. Rather, we understand that the theory of prime numbers tells us exactly why 7 is a prime and 9 isn't.

The loss distinction account, similarly, tells us exactly why a given loss has moral significance when the gain that doesn't merely reverse a morally significant loss (when the gain instead accrues by virtue of a person's being brought into a worth-having existence) doesn't. One might reject the account. But the argument that it's irrational (or arbitrary or ad hoc) fails.

The Pareto puzzle. The results generated by the Pareto minus solution to the Pareto puzzle also comport perfectly with the results we can obtain from the loss distinction thesis. According to that thesis, the only future in which Charlotte or anyone else sustains a *morally significant loss* is f2. That's so since she doesn't exist at all in f1, her wellbeing is maximized in f3, and, finally, she exists in f2 *and* f2 is worse for her than f3.

Now, the loss distinction thesis doesn't generate the sorts of betterness comparisons or permissibility results that the Pareto minus solution—laid out in Section 3.4 of the main text—itself generates. But the picture it paints clearly supports those results. The morally significant loss Charlotte sustains in f2 counts against f2 whether it is f1 or f3 we are comparing f2 against. That fact *doesn't go away* when we shift our attention from how f2 compares against f3 to how f2 compares against f1. In contrast, we see no such morally significant loss in f1 or in f3 (no *morally significant* loss for f1; no *loss at all* for f3). Plausibly, then, as we've already said f1 is exactly as good as f3, and f2 is worse than both.

All of that is, again, highly intuitive—especially when we bring the connection thesis into the picture. Other things equal, we can permissibly bring an additional child into existence or not. But not just *any* existence will do: it would be wrong, other things equal, to bring that child into existence and make things *worse* for that child when we could have made things *better*.

APPENDIX C

Broome on the neutrality intuition

Broome's account of the three option case. Broome believes—and so do I—that the three option case, along with some principles that we, it seems, have no choice but to accept, nicely demonstrates that the neutrality intuition is false.[1] On his view, the correct thing to say about the three option case—the case that gives rise to it—is that yes, f3 is better than f2 but (contra the neutrality intuition) f3 is also better than f1. That, even as Broome himself notes that he is among those "many people" who find the underlying intuition (the intuition that, while we are obligated to *make people happy*, we *aren't* also obligated to *make happy people*) "strongly attractive."[2]

Of course, given that the argument to inconsistency itself relies on principles *beyond* the neutrality intuition, and given that the neutrality intuition itself *combines* the existence condition (EC) and the mere addition principle, it's clear from the start that we have other ways of avoiding the inconsistency without rejecting EC. Why, then, does Broome think that rejecting EC—that rejecting *that* component of the neutrality intuition rather than the mere addition principle or any of the other principles the argument to inconsistency relies on—is the correct way to avoid the inconsistency?

His reasoning, as I understand it, is as follows. Just suppose we try to retain the idea that Charlotte's existence in f3 is morally neutral: that it makes f3 neither better nor worse than f1, that f1 is exactly as good as f3. We then try to

[1] Specifically, Broome argues against what he calls the *principle of equal existence*, itself a combination of the existence condition (EC) *and* the mere addition principle and which he associates roughly with what he calls the *person-affecting view* (Broome 2004, 145–146). Where, other things equal, EC implies that an additional worth-having existence doesn't make things *better*, and mere addition implies that such an existence doesn't make things *worse*, the principle of equal existence implies that such an existence is simply *neutral* (making the future that excludes that existence exactly as good as [i.e., neither better nor worse than] the future that includes it; see Broome 2004, 143–146). For reasons that shall become obvious, for purposes here we will disaggregate the two intuitions.

[2] Broome 2004, 143. Broome, more precisely, finds the intuition that "adding a new person to the world is very often ethically neutral," making things neither better nor worse. It's plausible, however, that Broome's main target is the component of that intuition that says that the addition of the worth-having existence doesn't make things *better*—that is, that he, like many others, doesn't mean particularly to question the claim that the addition of the worth-having existence doesn't make things *worse*. The former idea is articulated by EC, the latter by the mere addition principle.

provide a plausible account of that idea and (of course) at the same time avoid inconsistency. Finding that we can't, we reject EC.

The first step in reconstructing his argument is just to ask *what it is* that makes Charlotte's existence in f3 neutral relative to f1. Is it that (i) there's *exactly one* wellbeing level—say, +10, the wellbeing level that Charlotte herself happens to have in f3—for all people and all cases, such that existence at that wellbeing level and that wellbeing level *alone*—at that single "sharp boundary"[3]—is neutral? Or it is that (ii) there's a "neutral range" of wellbeing levels such that existence at any wellbeing level that falls within that range, whoever the person and whatever the case, doesn't make things better or worse?[4]

Let's consider these two options one at a time. (i) The *sharp boundary* construction avoids the inconsistency. For, if Charlotte's existence at +10 in f3 falls *exactly* at that "sharp boundary," Charlotte's existence at +5 in f2 *must fall below that boundary*. We then easily avoid the result that f2 is *exactly as good as* f3 and thus the inconsistency with the (surely correct) result that f3 is *better than* f2.

The problem, Broome argues, is that the sharp boundary construction seems highly implausible. That construction itself runs "counter to strong intuitions."[5] After all, there are a *lot* of cases out there, and existences that are better for people in those cases will come with a *lot* of different wellbeing levels—perhaps even an infinite number of wellbeing levels. The sharp boundary construction would mean that most of those existences won't be neutral at all since most of them won't end up at *exactly* +10. It's true that Charlotte's existence in f3, having ended up at +10, would be neutral. But the existences of Charlotte's *actual or possible* siblings, many of whom have more or less wellbeing than she does, would make things either *better* or *worse*. We'd be forced to conclude that, other things equal, Charlotte's parents have no obligation to bring Charlotte into existence but that—contra the basic existential intuition, contra whatever seems *right* about EC—they *do* have the obligation to bring some of Charlotte's siblings into existence and the obligation *not* to bring some of Charlotte's *other* siblings into existence. The sharp boundary construction thus simultaneously manages both to defy intuition *and* produce a set of highly arbitrary results—results that seem barely rational if rational at all.

Broome has also put the problem with the sharp boundary construction in another way. Suppose we assume that the neutral existence falls at a single sharp boundary. *What are the chances* that Charlotte's existence at +10 in f3 in the three option case falls *at exactly that* boundary? *What are the chances* that intuition in that case produces the result that we want out of that intuition—that f3 isn't better than f1? Ridiculously small—since, as we've already noted,

[3] Broome 2004, 142.
[4] Broome 2004, 144–146.
[5] Broome 2004, 142.

worth-having existences can potentially fall at a *lot*, perhaps even an *infinite number*, of different wellbeing levels.

(ii) Broome thus moves on to the *neutral range* construction of the intuition. But that construction is even more disastrous. If Charlotte's existence in f3 at + 10 simply falls within a range of wellbeing levels such that existence at any one of those multiple levels is neutral, then, *even if* her existence in f2 falls below that range, we can reproduce the argument to inconsistency by simply revising our case to ooch up Charlotte's wellbeing level in f2 just enough that her existence in f2 in the revised case does fall within the neutral range. We then very quickly can reason to inconsistency.

The upshot, Broome thinks, is that, rather than try to save the underlying intuition—the intuition that f3 isn't better or worse than f1—the better approach is to reject the principle that generates it—the *neutrality intuition*—from the start.

But as we've already noted the neutrality intuition itself combines EC *and* the mere addition principle. *Which component* of the neutrality intuition is it that we are we to reject? EC, which implies that f3 isn't *better than* f1 and that f2 isn't *better than* f1, or the mere addition principle, which implies that f3 isn't *worse than* f1 and that f2 isn't *worse than* f1?

Broome doesn't explicitly say. At certain points, he writes as though they come together as a single unanalyzable whole.[6] However, given that his aim in producing the argument to inconsistency to begin with is to explore the intuition that we are generally obligated to *make people happy* but not to *make happy people*, it's not implausible to think that it's EC he thinks we must reject: the component that implies that Charlotte's existence in f3 doesn't make f3 *better than* f1, while leaving intact the component that implies that Charlotte's existence in f3 doesn't make f3 *worse than* f1.

* * *

A problem with Broome's argument against the sharp boundary construction. In Section 3.3.1, I argued that Broome's strategy for avoiding inconsistency doesn't actually solve the Pareto puzzle. (Not that he intends it to do that work; his immediate interest seems instead to be in avoiding the inconsistency.)

In this Appendix, I focus instead on Broome's argument against the sharp boundary construction of the idea that Charlotte's existence in f3 makes f3 neither better nor worse than f1—that her existence in f3 is *morally neutral*. I agree that the neutral *range* construction fails. But I think the *sharp boundary* construction is worth another look.

Specifically, I question how Broome is understanding what it is to say that Charlotte's wellbeing level of +10 in f3 in the three option case falls *exactly* at

[6] Broome 2004, 143.

the single neutral level. For it seems that we can say that but, at the same, time *deny* that +10 marks a single neutral wellbeing level for *all* people in *all* cases.

It's true that, to preserve EC, we shall need to say that Charlotte's existence at +10 in f3 doesn't make f3 better than f1. But why should we think that that means that there can't be still *other* worth-having existences in still *other* cases that, just like Charlotte's in f3 in the one case, fail to make things morally better?[7] What justifies the universal generalization, from Charlotte's existence in f3 at +10 being morally neutral, to the result that everyone's existence in any future at +10 is also morally neutral?

After all, it seems clear that what makes +10 neutral in the three option case is *highly case specific*. The fact that Charlotte's +10 in f3 doesn't make things better—indeed, that it makes things neither better *nor worse*—is a function of two facts: both that anything *less* than +10 (e.g., +5 in f2) means there's an alternate accessible future—f3—that makes things better for Charlotte without making things worse for anyone else *and* that anything *more* than +10 just *isn't there* as an alternate accessible future.

Thus it's no coincidence that Charlotte's existence in f3 falls exactly along the single sharp boundary of +10 in the three option case. There's no implausibility, no mystifying improbability, no disturbing coincidence that we have any need to explain any further.

Consistent with the idea that Charlotte's existence in the three option case makes things neither better nor worse is the idea that, in still other cases, things will be different. Perhaps, for example, in Calvin's case, which, let's say, is just like Charlotte's except that for Calvin there exists a *fourth* accessible future, one in which his wellbeing is increased, at no cost to anyone else, to +12 (thus the *four-option case*). As to that case, we can explain, for the same sorts of reasons we explained why the neutral level for Charlotte in the three option case is +10, that the neutral level for Calvin in this new case is not +10 *but rather* +12.

Still other cases show that there may exist more than a single neutral boundary for a single person *within a given case*. Suppose that in a case involving a *merely reversing change*, the alternative accessible futures for Cali and Cody are just these three: neither Cali nor Cody exist; both have existences worth having, but Cali is better off than Cody; and both have existences worth

[7] Broome himself notes that the "neutral level may depend on context" (Broome 2004, 143). At that point, however, his concern is to note, not that Charlotte's existence at +10 might be neutral in one context but not in another (as in a case in which +10 fails to maximize wellbeing for her), but rather that the value of nonexistence itself might not be assigned any one "constant *numerical* value" (contra the claim of nonexistence comparability). In making that point, he is leaving room for the idea that "which other people exist, and on how their lives go." may help to determine the neutral level (143). The upshot of that idea, in turn, is that what counts as an existence worth having—or an existence *less* than an existence worth having—might itself vary depending on sociological context.

having, but the two individuals now merely *reverse positions*. Here, we'll intuitively want to say that neither Cali's nor Cody's existence in the second future or the third future makes those futures either better or worse than the first. Which is to say that both Cali's existences in *both* the second and the third futures are *neutral*: *one* person, *one* case, yet *two* distinct neutral existences. Ditto for Cody.

To sum up. Within a given case and for a particular person, it may often happen (as in the three option case) that the *neutral existence* forms a *single sharp* boundary. But that that's so doesn't mean that the neutral existence forms that *very same sharp boundary* for every case and for every person. The fact that +10 is neutral for Charlotte in her three option case doesn't imply that +10 is neutral for Calvin in his four option case. Nor does the fact that Cali's existence in the *second* future is neutral in the merely reversing change case mean that his existence in the *third* future *isn't* neutral.

Bibliography

Algander, Per. 2012. "A Defence of the Asymmetry in Population Ethics." *Res Publica* 18(2): 145–157.

Arrhenius, Gustaf. 2000. "An Impossibility Theorem for Welfarist Axiology." *Economics and Philosophy* 16: 247–266.

Arrhenius, Gustaf. 2003a. "Feldman's Desert-Adjusted Utilitarianism and Population Ethics." *Utilitas* 15(2): 225–236.

Arrhenius, Gustaf. 2003b. "The Person Affecting Restriction, Comparativism, and the Moral Status of Potential People." *Ethical Perspectives* 3–4: 185–195.

Arrhenius, Gustaf. 2009. "Can the Person Affecting Restriction Solve the Problems of Population Ethics?" In Melinda A. Roberts and David T. Wasserman, eds., *Harming Future Persons*, 289–314. Springer.

Arrhenius, Gustaf. forthcoming. *Population Ethics*. Oxford University Press.

Arrhenius, Gustaf, and Wlodek Rabinowicz. 2015. "The Value of Existence." In Iwao Hirose and Jonas Olson, eds., *The Oxford Handbook of Value Theory*, 424–443. Oxford University Press.

Bader, Ralf. 2022. "Person-Affecting Utilitarianism." In Gustaf Arrhenius, Krister Bykvist, Tim Campbell and Elizabeth Finneron-Burns, eds., *Oxford Handbook of Population Ethics*, 251–270. Oxford University Press.

Benatar, David. 2006. *Better Never to Have Been*. Oxford University Press.

Bentham, Jeremy. 1996. *An Introduction to the Principles of Morals and Legislation*. In H.L.A. Hart and J.H. Burns, eds., *The Collected Works of Jeremy Bentham*. Clarendon (first published 1789).

Boonin, David. 2014. *The Non-Identity Problem and the Ethics of Future People*. Oxford University Press.

Bostrom, Nick. 2013. "Existential Risk Prevention as Global Priority." *Global Policy* 4(1): 15–31.

Broome, John. 1992. *Counting the Costs of Global Warming*. White Horse Press.

Broome, John. 1999. *Ethics out of Economics*. Cambridge University Press.

Broome, John. 2004. *Weighing Lives*. Oxford University Press.

Broome, John. 2015. "General and Personal Good: Harsanyi's Contribution to the Theory of Value." In Iwao Hirose and Jonas Olson, eds., *The Oxford Handbook of Value Theory*, 249–266. Oxford University Press.

Budolfson, Mark, and Dean Spears. 2021. *Social Choice and Welfare*: 1–22.

Carlson, Erik. 1995. *Consequentialism Reconsidered*. Kluwer.

Chang, Ruth. 2022. "How to Avoid the Repugnant Conclusion." In Jeff McMahan, Tim Campbell, James Goodrich and Ketan Ramakrishnan, eds., *Ethics and Existence*, 389–429. Oxford University Press.

Dasgupta, Partha. 1993. *An Inquiry into Well-Being and Destitution*. Clarendon.

Dasgupta, Shamik. 2018. "Essentialism and the Nonidentity Problem." *Philosophy and Phenomenological Research* 96(3): 540–570.

Ehrlich, Paul. 1968. *The Population Bomb*. Sierra Club/Ballantine Books.

Feinberg, Joel. 1988. "Wrongful Life and the Counterfactual Element in Harming." *Social Philosophy and Policy* 4(1): 144–178.

Feit, Neil. 2016. "Comparative Harm, Creation and Death." *Utilitas* 28: 136–63.

Feldman, Fred. 1975. "World Utilitarianism." In Keith Lehrer, ed., *Analysis and Metaphysics*. Reidel.

Feldman, Fred. 1986. *Doing the Best We Can: An Essay in Informal Deontic Logic*. Reidel.

Feldman, Fred. 1995a, "Justice, Desert, and the Repugnant Conclusion." *Utilitas* 7: 189–206.

Feldman, Fred. 1995b. "Adjusting Utility for Justice: A Consequentialist Reply to the Objection from Justice." *Philosophy and Phenomenological Research* 55(3): 567–585.

Feldman, Fred. 1997. "World Utilitarianism." In *Utilitarianism, Hedonism, and Desert: Essays in Moral Philosophy* (Cambridge Studies in Philosophy), 17–35. Cambridge University Press.

Feldman, Fred. 2004. *Pleasure and the Good Life*. Clarendon.

Feldman, Fred. 2006. "Actual Utility, the Objection from Impracticality, and the Move to Expected Utility." *Philosophical Studies* 129(1): 49–79.

Feldman, Fred. 2010. *What Is This Thing Called Happiness?* Oxford University Press.

Fleurbaey, Marc, and Alex Voorhoeve. 2015. "On the Social and Personal Value of Existence." In Iwao Hirose and Andrew Reisner eds., *Weighing and Reasoning: Themes from the Philosophy of John Broome*, 95–109. Oxford University Press.

Foot, Phillipa. 1967. "The Problem of Abortion and the Doctrine of the Double Effect." *Oxford Review* 5: 5–15.

Gustafsson, Johan E. 2022. "Money-Pump Arguments." In Martin Peterson, ed., *Elements in Decision Theory and Philosophy*. Cambridge University Press.

Hare, Caspar. 2007. "Voices from Another World: Must We Respect the Interests of People Who Do Not, and Will Never, Exist?" *Ethics* 117: 498–523.

Harsanyi, John. 1977. "Morality and the Theory of Rational Behavior." *Social Research* 44(4): 623–656.

Herstein, Ori. 2008. "Historic Injustice and the Nonidentity Problem: The Limitations of the Subsequent-Wrong Solution and Towards a New Solution." *Law and Philosophy* 27: 505.

Heyd, David. 1992. *Genethics: Moral Issues in the Creation of People.* University of California Press.

Heyd, David. 2009. "The Intractability of the Nonidentity Problem." In Melinda A. Roberts and David T. Wasserman, eds., *Harming Future Persons*, 3–27. Springer.

Holtug, Nils. 2010. *Persons, Interests and Justice.* Oxford University Press.

Holtug, Nils. 2021. "Population and Prioritarianism." In Gustaf Arrhenius, Krister Bykvist, Tim Campbell and Elizabeth Finneron-Burns, eds., *Oxford Handbook of Population Ethics*, 38–62. Oxford University Press.

Huemer, Michael. 2008. "In Defense of Repugnance." *Mind* 117(468): 899–933.

Ishiguro, Kazuo. 2005. *Never Let Me Go.* Faber and Faber.

Kagan, Shelly, and Peter Vallentyne. 1997. "Infinite Value and Finitely Additive Value Theory." *Journal of Philosophy* 94(1): 5–26.

Kavka, Gregory. 1981. "The Paradox of Future Individuals." *Philosophy & Public Affairs* 11: 93–112.

Kripke, Saul A. 1959a. "A Completeness Theorem in Modal Logic." *Journal of Symbolic Logic* 24(1): 1–14.

Kripke, Saul A. 1959b. "Semantical Analysis of Modal Logic" (abstract from the Twenty-Fourth Annual Meeting of the Association for Symbolic Logic). *Journal of Symbolic Logic* 24(4): 323–324.

Lazari-Radek, Katarzyna de, and Peter Singer. 2014. *The Point of View of the Universe.* Oxford University Press.

Lewis, David. 1986. *On the Plurality of Worlds.* Blackwell.

Lewis-Kraus, Gideon. 2022. "Sam Bankman-Fried, Effective Altruism, and the Question of Complicity." *The New Yorker* (Dec. 1). https://www.newyorker.com/news/annals-of-inquiry/sam-bankman-fried-effective-altruism-and-the-question-of-complicity

MacAskill, William. 2022. *What We Owe the Future.* Basic Books.

McMahan, Jeff. 1981. "Problems of Population Choice." *Ethics* 92(1): 96–127.

McMahan, Jeff. 2009. "Asymmetries in the Morality of Causing People to Exist." In Melinda A. Roberts and David T. Wasserman, eds., *Harming Future Persons*, 49–68. Springer.

McMichael, Alan. 1983. "A Problem for Actualism About Possible Worlds." *Philosophical Review* 92(1): 49–66.

Mill, John Stuart. 2002. *Utilitarianism.* Ed. George Sher. Hackett (first published 1861).

Moore, G. E. 1912. *Ethics.* William and Norgate.

Mulgan, Tim. 2006. *Future People: A Moderate Consequentialist Account of Our Obligations to Future Generations.* Oxford University Press.

Narveson, Jan. 1967. "Utilitarianism and New Generations." *Mind* 76: 62–72.

Narveson, Jan. 1976. "Moral Problems of Population." In Michael D. Bayles (ed.), *Ethics and Population*, 59–80. Schenkman.

Nebel, Jake. 2017. "Priority, Not Equality, for Possible People." *Ethics* 127: 896–911.

Ng, Yew-Kwang. 1986. "Social Criteria for Evaluating Population Change: An Alternative to the Blackorby-Donaldson Criterion." *Journal of Public Economics* 29: 375–81.

Ng, Yew-Kwang. 1989. "What Should We Do About Future Generations?" *Economics and Philosophy* 5: 235–253.

Ng, Yew-Kwang. 1990. "Welfarism and Utilitarianism: A Rehabilitation." *Utilitas* 2(2): 171–193.

Otsuka, Michael. 2018. "How It Makes a Moral Difference that One Is Worse Off than One Could Have Been." *Politics, Philosophy & Economics* 17: 192–215.

Otsuka, Michael. 2021. "Prioritarianism, Population Ethics and Competing Claims." In Jeff McMahan, Tim Campbell, James Goodrich, and Ketan Ramakrishnan, eds., *Ethics and Existence*, 527–556. Oxford University Press.

Ord, Toby. 2020. *The Precipice: Existential Risk and the Future of Humanity.* Hachette.

Parfit, Derek. 1976. "On Doing the Best for Our Children." In Michael D. Bayles, ed., *Ethics and Population*, 100–115. Schenkman.

Parfit, Derek. 1987. *Reasons and Persons.* Oxford University Press (originally published 1984).

Parfit, Derek. 2002. "Equality or Priority?" In Matthew Clayton and Andrew Williams, eds., *The Ideal of Equality*, 81–125. Palgrave Macmillan.

Parfit, Derek. 2011. *On What Matters: Volume Two.* Oxford University Press.

Parfit, Derek. 2017. "Future People, the Non-Identity Problem, and Person-Affecting Principles." *Philosophy & Public Affairs* 45(2): 118–157.

Parsons, Josh. 2002. "Axiological Actualism." *Australasian Journal of Philosophy* 80(2): 135–147.

Persson, Ingmar. 2017. *Inclusive Ethics.* Oxford University Press.

Rabinowicz, Wlodek. 2009. "Broome and the Intuition of Neutrality." *Philosophical Issues* 11: 389–411.

Rabinowicz, Wlodek, and Gustaf Arrhenius. 2015. "The Value of Existence." In Iwao Hirose and Jonas Olson, eds., *The Oxford Handbook of Value Theory*, 424–442. Oxford University Press.

Roberts, Melinda A. 1998. *Child Versus Childmaker: Future Persons and Present Duties in Ethics and the Law.* Rowman & Littlefield.

Roberts, Melinda A. 2002. "A New Way of Doing the Best That We Can: Person-Based Consequentialism and the Equality Problem." *Ethics* 112(2): 315–350.

Roberts, Melinda A. 2003a. "Can It Ever Have Been Better Never to Have Existed at All? Person-Based Consequentialism and a New Repugnant Conclusion." *Journal of Applied Philosophy* 20(2): 159–185.

Roberts, Melinda A. 2003b. "Is the Person-Affecting Intuition Paradoxical?" *Theory and Decision* 55(1): 1–44.

Roberts, Melinda A. 2007. "The Nonidentity Fallacy: Harm, Probability and Another Look at Parfit's Depletion Example." *Utilitas* 19: 267–311.

Roberts, Melinda A. 2009a. "The Nonidentity Problem and the Two Envelope Problem." In Melinda A. Roberts and D. Wasserman, eds., *Harming Future Persons*, 201–228. Springer.

Roberts, Melinda A. 2009b. "What Is the Wrong of Wrongful Disability? From Chance to Choice to Harm to Persons." *Law and Philosophy* 28(1): 1–57.

Roberts, Melinda A. 2010. *Abortion and the Moral Significance of Merely Possible Persons: Finding Middle Ground in Hard Cases.* Springer.

Roberts, Melinda A. 2011a. "The Asymmetry: A Solution." *Theoria* 77: 333–367.

Roberts, Melinda A. 2011b. "An Asymmetry in the Ethics of Procreation." *Philosophy Compass* 6(11): 765–776.

Roberts, Melinda A. 2018. "Does the Worth-Having Existence Make Things Better?" Climate Ethics Kick Off Conference. Institute for Futures Studies, Stockholm.

Roberts, Melinda A. 2019a. "Does the Additional Worth-Having Existence Make Things Better?" In Paul Bowman and Katharina Berndt Rasmussen, eds., *Studies on Climate Ethics and Future Generations* (vol. I, 27–39). Institute for Futures Studies.

Roberts, Melinda A. 2019b. "Why Wear Blinders? Boonin and the Narrow Approach to the Nonidentity Problem." Book symposium, David Boonin, *The Non-Identity Problem and the Ethics of Future People in Law.* In Erik Magnusson, ed., *Ethics and Philosophy*, 7: 102–126.

Roberts, Melinda A. 2019c. "The Better Chance Puzzle and the Value of Existence." Parfit Memorial Conference (organized by Jeff McMahan). Oxford University.

Roberts, Melinda A. 2020. "Parfit, Population Ethics and Pareto Plus." In A. Sauchelli, ed., *Derek Parfit's Reasons and Persons: An Introduction and Critical Inquiry.* Routledge.

Roberts, Melinda A. 2021. "Anonymity and Indefinitely Iterated Addition and Reversal." In Joe Roussos and Paul Bowman, eds., *Studies on Climate Ethics and Future Generations* (vol. IV, 221–237). Institute for Futures Studies.

Roberts, Melinda A. 2022a. "Nonidentity, Better Chance and the Value of Existence: A Defense of Person Based Consequentialism." In Gustaf Arrhenius, Krister Bykvist, Tim Campbell and Elizabeth Finnerson-Burns, eds., *The Oxford Handbook of Population Ethics*, 226–250. Oxford University Press.

Roberts, Melinda A. 2022b. "The Value and Probabilities of Existence." In Jeff McMahan, Tim Campbell, James Goodrich and Ketan Ramakrishnan, eds., *Ethics and Existence*, 38–60. Oxford University Press.

Roberts, Melinda A. 2022c. "Population, Existence and Incommensurability." Incommensurability Conference, Center for Population Level Bioethics, Rutgers University.

Roberts, Melinda A., and David T. Wasserman. 2017. "Dividing and Conquering the Nonidentity Problem." In Matthew Liao and Collin O'Neil, eds., *Current Controversies in Bioethics*, eds., 81–98. Routledge.

Rosen, Gideon. 1990. "Modal Fictionalism." *Mind* 99(395): 327–354.

Rosen, Gideon. 1995. "Modal Fictionalism Fixed." *Analysis* 55(2): 67–73.

Ross, Jacob. 2015. "Rethinking the Person-Affecting Principle." *Journal of Moral Philosophy* 12: 428–461.

Salt, Henry. 1892. *Animals' Rights: Considered in Relation to Human Progress*. George Bell & Sons.

Scanlon, Thomas. 1998. *What We Owe to Each Other*. Harvard University Press.

Sen, Amartya. 1995. *Inequality Reexamined*. Harvard University Press.

Sen, Amartya. 2005. "Human Rights and Capabilities." *Journal of Human Development*, 6(2): 151–166.

Sher, George. 2005. "Transgenerational Compensation." *Philosophy and Public Affairs* 33: 181–200.

Sider, Ted. 2002. "The Ersatz Pluriverse." *Journal of Philosophy* 99(6): 279–315.

Sidgwick, Henry. 2006. *The Methods of Ethics*. Elibron Classics (first published 1874).

Singer, Peter. 1972a. "Is Act-Utilitarianism Self-Defeating?" *Philosophical Review* 81: 94–104.

Singer, Peter. 1972b. "Famine, Affluence and Morality." *Philosophy and Public Affairs* 1: 229–243.

Singer, Peter. 1973. "Animal Liberation." *New York Review of Books*. April 5.

Singer, Peter. 1974. "All Animals Are Equal." *Philosophical Exchange* 1: 103–116.

Singer, Peter. 1975. *Animal Liberation: A New Ethics for our Treatment of Animals*. New York Review/Random House. (Later editions published 1976–2009).

Singer, Peter. 1976. "A Utilitarian Population Principle." In Michael Bayles, ed., *Ethics and Population*, 81–99. Schenkman.

Singer, Peter. 2010. *The Life You Can Save*. Random House.

Singer, Peter. 2011. *Practical Ethics* (3rd ed.). Cambridge University Press.

Singer, Peter, and Katarzyna de Lazari-Radek. 2014. *The Point of View of the Universe*. Oxford University Press.

Slote, Michael, and Philip Pettit. 1984. "Satisficing Consequentialism." *Proceedings of the Aristotelian Society*, Suppl 58: 139–176.

Smart, J. C. C. 1956. "Extreme and Restricted Utilitarianism." *Philosophical Quarterly* 6(25): 344–354.

Smart, J. C. C., and Bernard Williams. 1973. *Utilitarianism: For and Against*. Cambridge University Press.

Spears, Dean, and Mark Budolfson. 2021. "Repugnant Conclusions." *Social Choice and Welfare* 57(3): 567–588.

Stalnaker, Robert. 2012. *Mere Possibilities*. Princeton University Press.

Stephen, Leslie. 1896. *Social Rights and Duties* (essays). S. Sonnenschein.

Tännsjö, Torbjörn. 2009. "Why We Ought to Accept the Repugnant Conclusion." *Utilitas* 14(3): 339–359.

Taurek, John. 1977. *Philosophy and Public Affairs* 6(4): 293–316.

Tedeschi, G. 1966. "On Tort Liability for Wrongful Life." *Israel Law Review* 1: 513–538.

Temkin, Larry. 1993. *Inequality*. Oxford University Press.

Temkin, Larry. 2002. "Equality, Priority, and the Levelling Down Objection." In Matthew Clayton and Andrew Williams, eds., *The Ideal of Equality*, 126–161. Palgrave Macmillan.

Temkin, Larry. 2012. *Rethinking the Good: Moral Ideals and the Nature of Practical Reasoning*. Oxford University Press.

Thomson, Judith Jarvis. 1985. "The Trolley Problem." *Yale Law Journal* 94(6): 1395–1415.

Voorhoeve, Alex, and Marc Fleurbaey. 2015. "On the Social and Personal Value of Existence." In Iwao Hirose and Andrew Reisner, eds., *Weighing and Reasoning: Themes from the Philosophy of John Broome*, 95–109. Oxford University Press.

Wasserman, David T., and Melinda A. Roberts. 2017. "Dividing and Conquering the Nonidentity Problem." In Matthew Liao and Collin O'Neil, eds., *Current Controversies in Bioethics*, 81–98. Routledge.

Weinberg, Rivka. 2016. *The Risk of a Lifetime*. Oxford University Press.

Willenken, Tim. 2012. "Deontic Cycling and the Structure of Commonsense Morality." *Ethics* 122: 545–561.

Index

For the benefit of digital users, indexed terms that span two pages (e.g., 52–53) may, on occasion, appear on only one of those pages.